Fourth Edition

COURSE DESIGN

A Guide to Curriculum Development for Teachers

GEORGE J. POSNER
CORNELL UNIVERSITY

ALAN N. RUDNITSKY
SMITH COLLEGE

Longman

Course Design: A Guide to Curriculum Development for Teachers, Fourth Edition

Longman, 10 Bank Street, White Plains, N.Y. 10606

Associated companies:
Longman Group Ltd., London
Longman Cheshire Pty., Melbourne
Longman Paul Pty., Auckland
Copp Clark Pitman, Toronto

Senior acquisitions editor: Laura McKenna
Production editor: Linda Moser
Cover design: Judy Forster
Production supervisor: Anne Armeny

 This book is printed on recycled paper.

Library of Congress Cataloging-in-Publication Data

Posner, George J.
    Course design: a guide to curriculum development for teachers /
George J. Posner, Alan Rudnitsky.—4th ed.
        p.   cm.
    Includes bibliographical references and index.
    ISBN 0-8013-0765-1
    1. Curriculum planning. 2. Education, Secondary—Curricula.
3. Education, Elementary—Curricula. I. Rudnitsky, Alan N.
II. Title.
LB2806.15.P67   1994
375′.001—dc20   93-6513
                                                         CIP

4 5 6 7 8 9 10-MA-97969594

To Adrienne, Sue, Becky, Prema, Robin, and Kim

Contents

Figures and Tables

FIGURES

TABLES

Preface

Course Design: A Guide to Curriculum Development for Teachers, fourth edition attempts to bridge theory and practice in curriculum development. Intended primarily for teachers and teachers in training, it presents the concepts and skills of curriculum development and shows how to apply them to actual course planning. The overriding goal of the book is to assist the reader in becoming a flexible and, at the same time, systematic curriculum planner by developing a greater awareness of the important decisions to be made and the alternative courses of action available at each decision point.

Course Design has four principal functions: (1) as a textbook for graduate and undergraduate courses in curriculum development and instructional design or as a supplement to a "methods" course, (2) as a basis for in-service workshops for classroom teachers, (3) as material for individual teachers desiring to increase their professional competence, and (4) as a self-instructional "lab" portion of courses in curriculum development or instructional design. In our curriculum development courses we typically supplement much of the theoretical content by having students develop a course or unit in step-by-step fashion. Students are then able to receive feedback as their work progresses as well as see other students' work.

We begin *Course Design* with a set of guidelines for developing an actual course. By working through this book you will produce a design for an actual course. We guide you through this process by providing relevant design theory, frequent exercises, representative examples, a glossary of terms, bibliographic references, and, finally, sample course designs completed by students. The combination of theory and the process of actually designing a course make *Course Design* a unique approach to learning curriculum development skills.

These materials have been used in beginning curriculum development courses for many years at Cornell University and Smith College. Those enrolled in the courses have been primarily undergraduate and graduate students who plan to teach in public schools, two-year colleges, and nonformal educational settings. The students have designed a wide variety of courses whose diverse subject matter includes beekeeping, propaganda analysis, creative writing, communication media, advanced algebra, developmental psychology, ecology, reading for parents of nonreaders, and hockey. Many refinements and revisions included in the fourth edition have come as a result of student comments and the student-developed course designs.

HIGHLIGHTS OF THE FOURTH EDITION

1. We have greatly expanded the applicability of *Course Design* by recognizing the unique planning requirements facing elementary teachers. The book now includes many more explicit references to elementary unit planning, and these are supported by numerous examples drawn from elementary education.
2. We have thoroughly rewritten and updated chapter 7, "Developing General Teaching Strategies." Extensive and varied examples have been added, and we have included content that reflects the significant contributions of cognitively oriented theory and research.
3. There are three completely new and expanded sample course designs in the appendixes.
4. Our position on the role of behavioral objectives in educational planning has been made clearer and more explicit.
5. In general, we have tried to maintain the basic format of *Course Design* while updating content and references, revising our discussion questions, expanding the number and variety of examples, addressing the needs of elementary teachers, and improving overall quality.

Every time we use this book we think of changes that would improve it. In addition, prerevision and developmental reviews conducted by our editors at Longman supplied us with valuable suggestions for strengthening the text. We are fortunate to have had the opportunity to obtain the advice of such competent and knowledgeable reviewers as the following, and to be able to use this advice for the continuing refinement of what we believe to be a basically sound approach:

Frank Adams, Benedictine College

Kline Capps, Buena Vista College

Roselle Chartock, North Adams State College

Thomas Cherry, Old Dominion University

Lawrence Cohocker, LaSalle University

Larry Hanschaw, University of Mississippi

Herbert K. Heger, University of Texas, El Paso

Mary Jean Herzog, Western Carolina University

Burga Jung, Texas Technical University

John Knipping, Adams State College

Diane Smith, University of Missouri, Kansas City

Bruce Uhrmacher, University of Denver

Phyllis G. Weisberg, Trenton State College

Marilyn Wikstrom, Buena Vista College

A book such as this comes into existence through a process of evolution. The sources of ideas are difficult to identify because they are numerous and have been incorporated into our general orientation to curriculum development. The intellectual source of much of the book stems from the theoretical work of Mauritz Johnson. Although he did not participate directly in the preparation of the manuscript, Johnson's clarity of thought about curriculum and instruction has been both an inspiration and a conceptual guide. Graduate and undergraduate students at Cornell University and Smith College contributed innumerable significant suggestions and many of the examples provided. Colleagues at Cornell and Smith have provided many useful suggestions used to improve the book. We wish to thank the following individuals for their generous permission, allowing us to include their course planning work as examples in *Course Design*:

Michelle Chang, "Immigration"

Elizabeth Clark, "The Inuit of North Alaska"

Leanne Dineen, "World Geography"

Susan M. Etheredge, "A Metric Unit for Grades One and Two"

Bernadette Gaffney, "The Rocky Shore Ecosystem"

Kerry Gaffney, "Colonial America: Social Studies Curriculum for Grade 5"

Erika Hollander, "The Native American Culture"

Kevin Kinneavy, "Coordinate Geometry"

Kelly Nerbonne, "Rivers"

Anne Marie O'Reilly, "Wonders of the Forest Community"

Laura Rochat, "The Sounds of Poetry"

Donna Taylor, "An Introduction to Black and White Photography: From Snap Shot to Art Form" ("The Camera")

Margaret Timmerman, "A Survey of Western Art"

These substantial contributions are greatly appreciated, although any errors or shortcomings are the authors' alone.

CHAPTER 1

Getting Oriented

After completing this chapter, you should be able to:

1. Understand the format of a course planning project and why it has been selected as a focal point for learning the concepts and skills of course planning.
2. Understand the distinction between processes and products of planning.
3. Understand the distinction between curricular and instructional matters.
4. Understand the following terms and their interrelationship: *value, educational goal, curriculum, instructional plan, instruction, actual learning outcome,* and *evaluation* (see the glossary for definitions).
5. Know the three basic needs for course design and be able to perform the preliminary research necessary to begin planning.

THE APPROACH

This book is based on two assumptions about you, the reader. The first assumption is that you want to learn the basics of course design. The second is that you already have in mind or can come up with a particular course that you want to plan.

The first assumption is the critical one. This book can teach you how to plan courses, regardless of subject matter, institutional setting, or educational level. *Course Design* attempts to show you how to get started, to give you a sense of direction in the planning process, to make you aware of what goes into the design of courses and curricula, to help you ask the right questions at the right times, to offer alternatives at each decision point, to suggest some concepts that will serve as useful tools, and to provide examples that can expand the way you think about courses.

The second assumption stems more from the means employed in *Course Design*

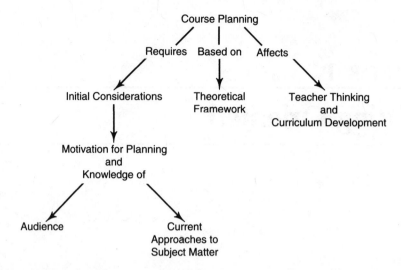

than from the ends. Planning is a process that requires time, energy, and commitment by the planner; learning how to design courses and curricula is similarly demanding. In order to make course planning meaningful to you, we have focused the activities of *Course Design* on a project that consists in the planning of an actual course. The project provides for the application of each concept and skill presented in this book to the particular subject matter, institutional setting, and educational level that interests you.

Focusing the learning activities of this book on your own project has important pedagogical value. If you want to learn the concepts and skills of course planning but do not have a particular course in mind, we suggest that you arbitrarily decide on a course in a familiar subject matter that can serve as a focus.

Keep in mind that the project is primarily a means to an end. The skills and concepts of course planning are primary, and the project is intended to help you acquire them. The steps followed in working through the book do teach how to plan courses, but, given the time constraints usually present, the approach may appear at times too detailed and systematic for actual course planning. This is to be expected. The approach has been designed to teach course planning but not necessarily to guide the course planning process once the skills and concepts have been learned. Learning long division serves as a useful analogy. When we learn long division, we learn a series of specific steps to follow. But once we learn the process, we skip steps and generally divide in a more flexible and intuitive way than when we were learning it.

It is too much to expect a single approach to curriculum development to work always and for everyone. Such factors as audience, setting, subject matter, and grade level place their own particular constraints on teachers. You should feel free to modify our general approach to suit your particular circumstance.

Planning at the elementary school level has its own unique constraints. Fundamentally, elementary teachers tend to plan in unit-sized rather than course-sized sections. Elementary school units vary in scope and duration but typical units may last from two to six weeks and cover topics such as fractions, time, punctuation, myths and fairy tales, animals in winter, oceans, the Revolutionary War, and elections, to name a few.

The emphasis on unit planning is not to suggest that this is the only kind of educational planning elementary teachers can or should do. On the contrary, elementary teachers need to engage in a broader form of planning in which they consider their overall program. Units should be planned in context with other units. Units in a particular content area are preceded and followed by other units; typically, these units are related. The sequence of units is something that should be planned, not simply allowed to happen haphazardly or because publishers sequence their material in a particular way. In addition, units in one content area are taught concurrently with units in other content areas. Teachers should consider which units work particularly well together, which units conflict or are difficult to teach at the same time, and which units may depend on learning in another content area. In any case, steps that may not at first seem appropriate for elementary unit planning can prove crucial for planning that is broader in scope.

The following suggestions may prove helpful for elementary teachers:

1. Intended learning outcomes are likely to be fewer in number. Try to teach a few important ideas and skills well rather than cover too many intended learnings.
2. Some suggested course planning steps such as formulating central questions and sequencing and organizing a course's units may not be appropriate. We suggest that you think about all the course planning steps and consider various alternatives, but do not become a slave to them.

At times we address the particular concerns of elementary teachers, particularly with regard to curriculum organization (chapter 5) and teaching strategies (chapter 7). Appendixes A, C, and D provide three extensive, sample elementary unit plans. At all times, we hope you will use our suggestions flexibly and with imagination. You will not find a prescription in this text for the one right way to develop curricula or the way all curricula should look.

You may need to modify our general approach because different projects have different needs and requirements and thus will have different emphases. Teachers who have taught topics for a long time but have never really considered what particular learnings they were seeking will likely put greater emphasis on clarifying their intended learning outcomes. Teachers wishing to introduce totally new types of courses will have to concentrate on the courses' justification and thus emphasize the rationale. Teachers planning interdisciplinary courses will have to think carefully about how ideas from different disciplines are related. This will likely require a more complex course outline (see chapter 2); perhaps an outline for content from each discipline. Do not think that every component of the design process you encounter in the book requires equal emphasis and attention. Flexibility and adaptation will help make your project more meaningful.

THE PROJECT

If you complete each couse planning step in this book, you will finish with the following products:

1. A *rationale* for the course, including the overall educational goals.

2. A *curriculum plan* describing intended learning outcomes for the course prioritized according to importance, to be expressed in formats that may include the following:
    a. lists of statements and paragraphs
    b. maps of major ideas
    c. flowcharts of skills
3. An *instructional plan* describing what each unit is about, how it fits into the overall organization of units, what learning outcomes each unit is intended to accomplish, and what general teaching strategies could be used in each unit to accomplish the intended learning outcomes.
4. An *evaluation plan* describing behavioral indicators for each high-priority intended learning outcome (main effects), together with a list of some unintended, undesirable learning outcomes (side effects) to be on the lookout for.

You will make other products along the way, such as course introductions, course outlines, and central questions. For the purposes of this book, these are considered instrumental products, used mainly to improve the major components listed above. Instructors using this text in class may or may not require that these instrumental products be part of a final project.

In the appendixes you will find four completed course designs that might give you some idea of our aim.

SOME GUIDELINES FOR GETTING STARTED

Now that you have an idea what this book is about, you can start planning a course as a focal point for learning the basics of curriculum development. Decide on a course you want to plan. In making your decision consider the following points: (1) Your course may run as long as a whole year or it may be as short as a four-week "mini-course." (2) Choose a course for which you know the subject matter well. It is difficult to plan something that is unfamiliar to you. (3) Create a course to answer some educational need, whether it be a learner or a societal need, a "felt" or an "unfelt" need. (4) Don't be afraid to create a unique course; you may want to give a traditional course a different emphasis, combine diverse subject matter, or adjust a course usually taught to one audience so that it can be taught to a different (for example, older, more heterogeneous, more "turned off") audience.

Motivation for Planning

When you begin to plan a course you may have any number of ideas, resources, or restrictions fixed in your mind. You may have received a mandate from an administrative source (for example, the state education department) specifying goals or requiring a certain level of student achievement. An existing course may not be producing satisfactory results. Students may not be taking with them the math they need for next year's work. You may want to implement a new teaching technique and may find the existing course inappropriately organized for such a technique. A school may provide a new language laboratory, a nature trail, a computer terminal, or sophisticated audiovisual equipment that will extend the capabilities of teachers, and courses will have to be created or re-created to use these new resources. Courses at a two-year college may not be attracting students, and new courses may be needed to attract students to the college. Courses previously considered appropriate for a particular kind of student may have to be redesigned as the student population becomes more mature or more heterogeneous. A new middle school may require courses specifically designed for its population and institutional purposes.

All sources for course planning provide "givens" that affect the start of the planning process, and they should be made explicit from the beginning if the course planning process is to proceed in an open and systematic manner rather than on the basis of some hidden agenda.

Audience for the Course

Right at the outset and, indeed, all the way through the planning process a guiding principle should be to consider the students at every stage. It is necessary to consider carefully their maturity, needs, interests, abilities, and knowledge. If you are unfamiliar with the characteristics and background of your intended audience you will have some preliminary work to do before beginning to plan the course. The following resources may help you learn about your audience:

1. Texts in educational psychology covering both the psychology of human learning and human development.
2. Observations or practice teaching at a local school or college with a student population similar to yours.
3. Interviews with teachers who have taught students similar to yours.

We will have more to say about understanding your students in chapter 2.

Current Approaches to the Subject

Another requisite for course planning is a thorough understanding of the subject matter. One part of this understanding is an ability to identify and explain the key concepts and skills in the subject. Another is a thorough knowledge of the details of the subject. Still another is a familiarity with current curricular approaches to the subject matter. This thorough understanding is not easily obtained. Extensive reading, thoughtful writing, and even hands-on experience are typically required. Certainly, reading a single textbook is not sufficient, since such an approach seriously limits one's awareness of alternative viewpoints and does not allow for the development of sufficient depth in the subject. If you are unfamiliar with the current approaches, you may want to do some preliminary work before you begin course planning. The following suggestions may be useful:

1. Collect as many current textbooks and syllabi in the subject as you can. Skim through each of them and study their contents pages in particular in order to get an idea of what is currently being taught in the subject.
2. Try to find out (from texts, teachers, or syllabi) what the students usually study in the subject or related subjects before they get to your course. Also try to determine what they may study in the subject after they complete your course.
3. Talk with teachers in your subject in order to identify topics, approaches to the subject, resources, exercises, and activities that seem to have the potential for stimulating interest.

Course planning begins with and is based on three things: a clearly recognized motivation or source; a recognition of the capacities, needs, and interests of the students; and a familiarity with current approaches to the subject matter.

QUESTIONS FOR DISCUSSION: GETTING STARTED

1. In what general area do you want to plan a course (civis, English, dance, filmmaking, reading, gardening, biology, ecology)?
2. Make a list of courses you have taken (or taught) specifically in this or a related area. How might those courses differ from the courses you want to plan? How might they be similar?
3. Do you have something special in mind for your course (a new technique, a special audience, new equipment)? Describe.
4. What are five questions an interested party might ask about your course?

Course Planning Step 1.1.   Write a brief paragraph describing your course.
With these initial thoughts in mind, it may be helpful to get an overview of *Course Design* before proceeding further with your project.

A FRAMEWORK FOR COURSE DESIGN*

Any systematic approach to course planning must be considered within the context of a theoretical framework. At the least such a framework must identify important aspects of the planning process and must show how these aspects are interrelated. This section presents such a framework.

The basic concept such a framework must deal with is *curriculum*. There are almost as many definitions of curriculum as there are writers, and we do not claim that any one definition is correct. Nevertheless, certain conceptual distinctions are useful in course planning, and certain definitions of curriculum make these distinctions

---

* Much of the following discussion has been adapted from Johnson (1967). The reader is encouraged to read his paper for a deeper understanding of the conceptual framework underlying this book.

important. One such distinction is that between processes and products of planning. Another is that between curricular and instructional matters.

Process-Product

A process consists of one or more events. A product is something produced by a process. Planning is usually a highly complex process, and a plan is the product of that process.

In order to make several points regarding this distinction, let us examine a noneducational but relatively familiar planning situation. A blueprint for a proposed building is a plan developed by an architect. In the planning (a process) the architect considers architectural form, building materials, characteristics of the proposed site, intended use of the building, energy efficiency, and many other factors. The blueprint is the result (a product) of the planning and it guides the process of construction. A blueprint specifies what the product of construction should be but does not specify how the process of construction (the construction schedule) should proceed. This analogy illustrates how a plan may (but does not have to) be for an anticipated process (for example, construction). Also, a complex process such as building houses may be broken down into discrete component processes, such as preparing blueprints, preparing a construction schedule, and constructing the house according to the blueprint.

Curriculum-Instruction

Instruction is obviously a process—a series of events intended to lead to some learning outcomes. As such, it is analogous to the process of house construction. Instruction consists of providing activities, overt or covert, for some content or subject matter. Instructional matters, then, have to do with the nature of the activities and content that make up the process of instruction. The process of instruction is guided by a plan analogous to a construction schedule, termed the *instructional plan*.

It is important to distinguish instruction from curriculum. Curriculum is not a process. Many (if not most) books on education consider curriculum as consisting of experiences or the activities that engender these experiences. But this usage confuses curriculum with instruction. A more precise view of curriculum—and the common understanding of curriculum among laypeople—is that it is what is taught in school or what is intended to be learned. It does not refer to what is to be *done* in school or what is to *happen* in the learning process. Curriculum represents a set of *intentions*, a set of intended learning outcomes. Consequently, curricular matters have to do with the nature and organization of those things we as course planners want learned in our courses. Curriculum development results in a design specifying the desired learnings (the intended learning outcomes); thus, curriculum is analogous to a blueprint or an architectural design. Instructional planning, on the other hand, results in a plan outlining the intended process of instruction; thus, an instructional plan is analogous to a construction schedule. A curriculum and an instructional plan are as different as a design for a new house and a plan giving the steps in its construction. Yet they are related in that a blueprint is a necessary guide for planning a construction schedule.

Curriculum development entails selection and organization of a set of intended learning outcomes. Selecting intended learning outcomes is made more rational by basing them on the educational goals to be served. Educational goals should indicate what the learning should lead to, not what it consists of; they describe intended educational results in much the same way curriculum describes intended learning outcomes. (See chapter 3 for more details on educational goals.) Educational results derive from the complex, interactive, and cumulative effects of actual learning outcomes, intended and unintended, both in school and outside school, in addition to maturation and other forces acting on students. Educational goals describe desired results of the entire educational process. The selection of intended learning outcomes (i.e., curriculum development) represents the best guess as to what needs to be learned to achieve the educational goals. Using our terminology, if a statement is in terms of things to be learned it is curricular; if it is in terms of attributes of the well-educated person it is an educational goal; if it is in terms of teaching strategies, it is instructional.

Thus, the *curriculum* indicates *what* is to be learned, the *goals* indicate *why* it is to be learned, and the *instructional plan* indicates *how* to facilitate learning. None of these three planning processes—curriculum development, goal setting, and instructional planning—results in any learning. Only the instruction process does that.

Figure 1.1 depicts the major processes related to course planning and their resulting products. The arrows in the figure should be interpreted as processes, the boxes as products. Moving from left to right on the chart, one answers various implementation questions. How do we implement our values? By aiming at a particular educational goal. How do we implement our educational goal? By having students learn particular things (a particular curriculum). How do we implement our curriculum? By providing particular activities (that is, a particular instructional plan). Moving from right to left, one answers justification questions: Why this instructional plan? Because instructional planning was guided by this curriculum. Why this curriculum? Because we are aiming at this educational goal. And so on.

Notice in Figure 1.1 that an additional process is included—that of evaluation. For the purposes of this book, evaluation planning will consist of specifying a set of sample indicators that can be used to analyze actual learning outcomes and educational results. The approach used will emphasize evaluation for course improvement rather than for grading individual students.

Although this framework generally clarifies for students the logical relations among educational products and processes, it also misleads in several significant ways. Perhaps the greatest danger in using this framework is that people interpret it as a guide to the *steps* of course design. At times the framework will function adequately as such a guide, but generally it is counterproductive to assume that this conceptual overview is also a procedural model. For example, it is usually wrong to insist on developing curriculum only after goals and values have been specified. Goals and values do underlie our reasons for including particular curricular content, but it is not always necessary to specify those goals and values first. Actually, it is often possible to think productively about abstract topics (such as goals) only after thinking about more concrete matters (such as curricular content and instructional techinques).

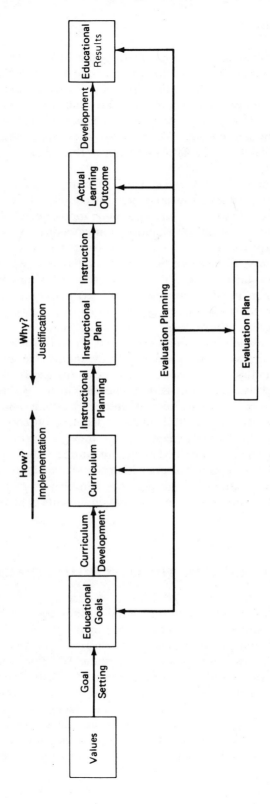

FIGURE 1.1   A curriculum instruction model. (Adapted from Johnson, 1967.)

Therefore, it is important when using the framework to remember that it is a conceptual overview rather than a procedural flowchart of the course design process.

Related to this issue is the assumption by some readers that course design is a fairly straightforward linear process. If anything, we have probably contributed to this belief by depicting a linear framework in Figure 1.1 and by presenting course design in a step-by-step manner. We have obviously oversimplified the process and you should be careful not to fall into the trap of thinking about course design in a strictly linear manner.

A linear approach is one in which each step is completed before the next one is begun. In course design, no steps are ever completed once and for all. Generally, we move to the next step after making a rough approximation because we realize that we will be in a better position to continue our work on an early step with the insights that a later step provides. A course design evolves as a series of successive approximations. In fact, course designs are never really completed. Rather, we "abandon" further planning for the time being. The same can be said of our course planning steps. There is no reason to insist on any degree of finality to a course planning step so long as we remember that we will be returning to that step at a later time equipped with new ideas and clearer thinking.

With this general framework in mind, it may be useful to specify the relationship between process/products and the corresponding chapters of *Course Design*.

Generally speaking, values and educational goals are described in the course's rationale. This component is developed in chapter 3. Curriculum is described, in part, in the course's statement of intended learning outcomes and the conceptual map(s) for the course. The intended learning outcomes are selected and their organization analyzed in chapter 2, and they are further refined in chapter 4. The instructional plan is described in the unit outline of the course developed in chapters 5, 6, and 7. The approach to evaluation is described in the course's evaluation plan, a component of course design developed in chapter 8. Figure 1.2 summarizes the relationships between the model and components of course design as presented in this book.

QUESTIONS FOR DISCUSSION: THE CONCEPTUAL FRAMEWORK

1. What are the advantages and disadvantages of defining curriculum as "an organized set of intended learning outcomes"?
2. Although ends and means are relative, isn't there an ultimate end? What happens when we ask the question "Why?"of an underlying value?
3. What questions (other than "Why?", "What?", "How?", and "Was it successful?") should a course design help to answer?
4. The analogy between curriculum development and the design of houses is not perfect. In what ways does the analogy break down?
5. Do values ever influence curriculum development and instructional planning directly rather than indirectly through educational goals?

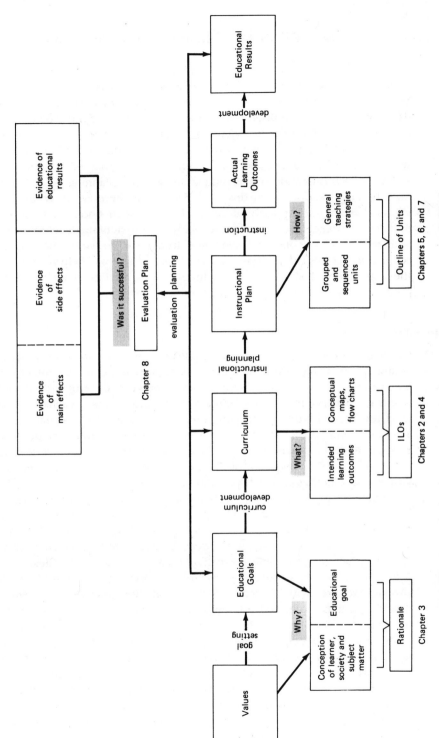

FIGURE 1.2 Relationship between the model and components of *Course Design*.

RELATION OF COURSE DESIGN TO CURRICULUM DEVELOPMENT

The premise of this book is that designing a course or (in the case of elementary grades) a unit is a special case of the more general process of curiculum development. While there may be more to the typical curriculum development process than designing courses and units, this latter process requires the use of many key aspects of curriculum development. Curriculum development, like course and unit design, requires careful consideration of the rationale for the curriculum, decisions about what students should be expected to learn, attention to matters of organization and sequence, determination of teaching strategies, and planning for evaluation. These matters are all addressed in this book. However, there are three other important matters that are not explicitly addressed, because of the book's focus on a course and unit design project as a method for teaching you curriculum development: (1) group deliberation; (2) scope and sequence from year to year; and (3) curriculum adaptation. We hope that discussing these matters here will help you understand how the concepts and skills you learn in this book fit into a more comprehensive preparation in curriculum development.

Group Deliberation

Curriculum development is typically done by teams of people working together on a common project. For example, a curriculum committee in elementary mathematics might spend two weeks each summer for three years developing a school district's K–6 mathematics curriculum. The team might consist of one teacher from each grade level, together with the district computer coordinator, a special educator, a librarian, a principal, and the district's director of elementary education. The process by which curriculum development teams produce a curriculum is termed *deliberation*.

Walker (1971) and Schwab (1970) do address some of these issues. These writers contend that group deliberation is at the heart of curriculum development. Deliberation "treats both ends and means and must treat them as mutually determining one another" (Schwab, 1970, p. 36). Deliberation consists of "formulating decision points, devising alternative choices at these decision points, considering arguments for and against suggested decision points and . . . alternatives, and finally, choosing the most defensible alternative" (Walker, 1971, p. 54). Clearly, this process is less linear than any process delineated step by step can possibly be. Therefore, although we agree with Walker and Schwab that curriculum development can best be described as a "complex and arduous" deliberation task (Schwab, 1970, p. 36), we also recognize the need to provide students a project-centered approach to curriculum study, one that will help the student develop some if not all of the concepts and skills necessary for curriculum development. In addition, since the logistics of college course work will require many of you to work on your course planning projects individually, rather than in groups, after completing this project you will still need to learn how to apply the concepts and skills learned to group work. To the extent that your instructor provides some opportunity for group discussion of project work, you will learn the difference between developing curricula alone and within a group context.

Scope and Sequence

Curriculum development teams of the type described in the previous section typically do not work on courses or units in isolation. They work on a multigrade curriculum. In their work they may depict the curriculum as a matrix in which the themes, topics, or concepts are delineated on the horizontal axis and the grade-by-grade progression through the curriculum is delineated on the vertical axis. Matrices of this sort are termed scope and sequence charts, where the horizontal axis depicts the scope and the vertical axis depicts the sequence. Figure 1.3 is an example of a scope and sequence chart.

In major curriculum development efforts these charts merely summarize more detailed and extensive work on scope and sequence. In such cases the document that describes this work is simply called the "scope and sequence." Figure 1.4 shows one page from an actual scope and sequence. In some school districts it is the scope and sequence that the school board must pass, before one can say that "the curriculum has been adopted by the school district." The scope and sequence, not as a brief chart, but in an elaborated form, is also typically the document that the state education department might send to the school district as the curriculum required by the state.

Although you will not have to deal with grade-to-grade considerations in your design project and will not gain experience in developing scope and sequence documents, many of the considerations involved in producing these documents will be addressed. In particular you will grapple with issues related to content selection and objectives formulation, as well as decisions about content sequence and organization.

Curriculum Adaptation

It is unusual for anyone to develop a curriculum from scratch. More generally school districts and individual teachers adapt an existing curriculum to make it more up to date, multicultural, multimedia, thematic, computer assisted, relevant to students' lives, hands-on, or career oriented (Glatthorn, 1987). Or an existing curriculum may need adaptation in order to bring it into better alignment with state tests or to increase its effectiveness in addressing the needs of certain students, whether they be "at risk" or "gifted and talented." Earlier we discussed many of these motivations for planning as they relate to course design. Here we mention them as a basis for adapting existing curricula, rather than for developing a curriculum from scratch. The point is that although this book approaches curriculum development as a task of course or unit design, this approach might differ from curriculum development work you might face in schools. Although many of the concepts and skills you will learn in this book will be helpful, your work in schools might require you to apply these concepts and skills in a manner that might appear backward, in comparison with the apparent linear progression of curriculum development we advocate in this book.

In order to prepare you for this reality, we discuss several instances of it, in chapter 3 as an issue of "entry point" in planning, in chapter 5 when we present alternative approaches to forming units in your course, and other times when we issue warnings about the apparent linearity of the curriculum development process. Similar

Grade	Strand			
	1 **Physical Health,** **Nutrition, and** **Disease Prevention**	**2** **Sociological** **Health Problems**	**3** **Family Life and** **Emotional Health**	**4** **Environmental,** **Community, and** **Consumer Health**
K	Health Habits; Food Variety; Senses; Care of Teeth—Personal; Feelings—Well/Sick	Uniqueness of Self/ Choices; Safe and Unsafe Substances; Smoking Effects on Self; Kinds of Alcohol	Feeling Special/ Friends; Family Lifestyles; Living and Nonliving Things; Body Parts/Parent Communication; Privacy/Touch; Trusting Feelings/Saying No	Self/Environment; School Health and Safety Helpers; Personal Health Products and Services
1	Growth; 4 Basic Food Groups; Body Parts; Primary and Secondary Teeth; Cause and Spread of Disease	Variety of Feelings/ Decisions and Consequences; Proper Use of Drugs; Smoking Effects on Senses; Effects of Alcohol	Expressing Feelings/ Handicaps; Family Members; Functions of Living Things; Questions about Sexuality; Victim/Offender; Confusing Touch/Support Systems	Community Environment; Community Health and Safety Helpers; Factors that Influence Choices
2	Food, Sleep, and Exercise; Eating Habits; Functions of Body Parts; Care of Teeth—Professional; Communicable and Noncommunicable Diseases	Sharing and Accepting Feelings of Others; Harmful and Helpful Drugs; Smoking Addiction; Alcohol Abuse	Communication Skills/ Handicaps; Family Needs and Support Systems; Gestation/Birth/Dying; Facts and Feelings/Media Messages; Neglect and Abuse; Recognizing Problems/Reporting	Environmental Factors; Responsibilities of Community Health and Safety Professionals; Consumer/Media
3	Maintain Balance/Intake-Exercise; Food Choices; Body Systems (5); Parts of a Tooth; Risk Factors	Risk-taking Behaviors; Media Influence; Decision Making/Peer Pressure	Decision Making/ Handicaps; Family Changes and Responsibilities; Reproductive Systems/Life Cycle; Sexual Problems and Decisions; Feelings and Rights Regarding Abuse; Effective Reporting	Improving School Environment; Responsibilities of Citizens/Training of Health Personnel; Advertising Techniques
4	Overweight/Underweight; Food—Past and Present; Body Systems (4); Tooth Decay; Prevention and Control of Diseases	Coping Skills; Prescription vs. Nonprescription Drugs; Social and Economic Factors; Alcohol Effects on Body Systems	Personality/Relationships/ Handicaps; Families—Past and Present; Puberty/Male and Female Roles; STDs/AIDS; Respect for Self and Others; Uncomfortable Situations/Terminology; Embarrassment/Confidentiality	Types of Pollution; Environmental Health Practices—Past and Present; Consumer Decision Making
5	Body Types; Diets; Interrelationships of Body Systems; Structure of the Mouth; Health Laws and Agencies	Assertive Implementation of Decisions; Effects on Body Systems; Smoking Effects on Body Systems; Laws and Agencies	Emotional Needs/ Stereotypes; Family Roles and Problem Solving; Physical, Emotional, and Social Changes During Puberty; Teenage Pregnancy/Family Communication; Manipulative Strategies of Offenders; Assertiveness/ Helping Friends	Society's Effects on the Environment; Environmental Health Laws; Emotional and Rational Buying

FIGURE 1.3 A scope and sequence chart for a kindergarten–fifth grade health curriculum. (Adapted from the Ithaca City School District Curriculum.)

Health Curriculum - Grade 4

STRAND I   PHYSICAL HEALTH, NUTRITION, AND DISEASE PREVENTION

I-A GOAL: To understand there are many factors that influence the state of a person's health.

Learner Outcome:
Student will:
1. Review physical similarities and differences.
2. Evaluate the interrelationships between body systems in maintenance of good health.
3. Discuss the causes of being overweight or underweight.

I-B GOAL: To understand that certain daily food choices and eating habits are necessary to maintain total health and body growth.

Learner Outcome:
Student will:
1. Identify essential nutrients that help promote one's health.
2. Analyze school lunch program as to meeting daily nutritional requirements.
3. Compare the way the early pioneer family met nutritional daily requirements with present lifestyle.

I-C GOAL: To understand how our senses and body systems help us function.

Learner Outcome:
Student will:
1. Review body systems—muscular, skeletal, digestive, circulatory, respiratory.
2. State functions and identify the parts of the nervous, reproductive, excretory, and endocrine systems.

I-D GOAL: To understand the importance of knowledge, skills, and attitudes appropriate to the promotion of dental health.

Learner Outcome:
Student will:
1. Compare healthy tooth and decayed tooth.
2. Discuss causes of tooth decay.
3. Contrast past dental techniques and habits with today's practices.

I-E GOAL: To understand how behaviors and habits prevent noncommunicable diseases and the transmission of communicable diseases.

Learner Outcome:
Student will:
1. Research the methods developed for the prevention and control of diseases.
2. Describe the chain of infection and how to break it.
3. Identify personnel responsible for maintaining good health.

FIGURE 1.4   One page of a kindergarten–fifth grade health education scope and sequence.

warnings regarding linearity in planning apply to all of the course planning steps presented in this book. For example, rather than begin to develop general teaching strategies from your intended learning outcomes, you might need to modify intended learning outcomes in order to make them consistent with teaching strategies that emphasize a "hands-on" approach to teaching. Eliot Wigginton (1985) provides a detailed account of how to plan a course in a nonlinear, fluid, but purposeful manner as the planner attempts to "make courses do double duty," that is, address the state's list of required competencies and the teacher's or the school's own agenda. His description is full of practical wisdom that any curriculum developer may find invaluable.

CURRICULUM DEVELOPMENT AND TEACHER THINKING

The teaching environment, as Clark and Peterson (1986) note, is characterized by complexity, a fast pace, and unpredictability. Teachers must think constantly about managerial concerns, covering the material, how students are doing, what is coming next, and what has transpired, to name a few. Teachers must respond quickly to a tremendous variety of situations and events (Kindsvatter, Wilen, & Ishler, 1988). In such an environment careful planning can have substantial benefits. However, no instructional plan can anticipate the unexpected. An instructional plan tells teachers what materials to use, what learning activities students should engage in, what sequence these activities should take, and more. But, of course, an instructional plan cannot tell a teacher how to respond to spontaneous classroom interactions. These unpredictable yet commonplace occurrences are significant aspects of instruction and can thus have significant effects on the outcomes of instruction. The ways in which teachers respond to these events depend to a great extent on what and how they are thinking.

A curriculum is commonly thought of as a guide to instructional planning. If it guided only instructional planning, a curriculum would be important but of limited direct significance in day-to-day classroom teaching. However, we have found that the curriculum, or at least the curriculum development process, can also guide teachers in their responses to daily unexpected classroom events. Our experience with *Course Design* is that it has a significant effect on teachers' thinking and on how they act in the classroom. Teachers report that the design process, as a whole, has given them a clear conception of what they want learned and this conception has directly affected their teaching. Teachers find themselves better able to respond to questions and comments in a focused way, to ask pertinent questions, to react to various types of student errors, and to take advantage of unplanned teachable moments. As a result of engaging in the design process, teachers have found that their judgments about their own teaching effectiveness become increasingly based on what and how students learn, not just on how smoothly the day went.

A clear conception of what is to be learned in a course is, perhaps, the major goal of *Course Design*. This clear conception is more than statements of outcomes; it is bound up in a design process that includes justification for learnings and how these learnings will be actualized and evaluated. As you work through the various steps of

Course Design, keep in mind that this process is intended to affect your everyday thinking as well as your planning.

REFERENCES

Clark, C., & Peterson, P. (1986). Teacher thought processes. In M. Wittrock (Ed.), *Handbook of research on teaching* (3rd ed.). New York: Macmillan.

Glatthorn, A. A. (1987). *Curriculum leadership.* Glenview, IL: Scott, Foresman.

Johnson, M. (1967). Definitions and models in curriculum theory. *Educational Theory, 17*(2), 127–139.

Kindsvatter, R., Wilen, W., & Ishler, M. (1988). *Dynamics of effective teaching.* New York: Longman.

Schwab, J. J. (1970). *The practical: A language for curriculum.* Washington, DC: National Education Association.

Walker, D. F. (1971). A naturalistic model of curriculum development. *School Review, 80,* 51–65.

Wigginton, E. (1985). *Sometimes a shining moment: The Foxfire experience.* Garden City, NY: Doubleday.

CHAPTER 2

Setting a Direction

After completing this chapter, you should be able to:

1. Comprehend the meaning and significance of intended learning outcome (ILO).
2. Generate an initial list of ideas for a course.
3. Develop a tentative course outline.
4. Generate one or more central questions for a course.
5. Distinguish ILOs from teaching strategies, materials, activities, and other initial ideas.
6. Identify ILOs implicit in desirable teaching strategies, materials, activities, and test items.
7. Categorize ILOs into skill and understanding categories.
8. Construct a flowchart for a course or a unit.
9. Construct a conceptual map for a course or a unit.
10. Use flowcharts and conceptual maps as a way of expressing ILOs for a course.

GENERATING INITIAL IDEAS

It is important at the beginning of course planning to have something tangible with which to work. The first step is to create a list of "initial ideas." This list may take virtually any form and may consist of words and phrases or sentences identifying subject matter, content areas, specific facts, teaching techniques, and so on. It may contain the names of specific books; it may list other resources. Anything important to

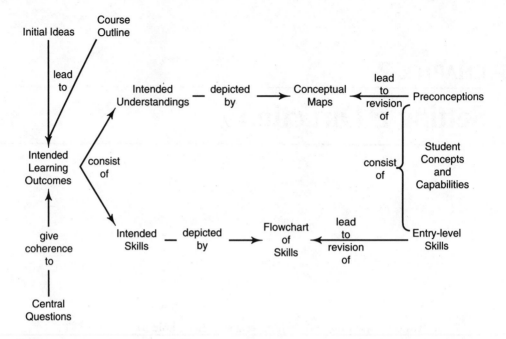

the course should go on an "ideas" list. At this point it is not important that the list be consistent or balanced.

Course Planning Step 2.1.   Jot down any and all ideas you have for your course on a list of initial ideas. The following example illustrates the form these initial ideas may take for an environmental science course. Absolutely no restrictions are placed on this list.

the relationships of various environmental systems

respect and care for the environment

forest succession

ecosystems

food chains

producers, consumers, decomposers

field trips to forest, field, pond

Sapsucker Woods Bird Sanctuary

individual project

plant and animal identification

how one affects environment

pollution

niches

become better individuals

blindfolded walk

build terrarium

nature trail

Once you have made an initial list, your course should be given a title. A title may be creative and novel or it may be traditional. A good way to formulate a title is to consider your list of initial ideas and see if an appropriate title emerges. Planners sometimes have a title for a course in their minds at the outset of planning. If this is true in your case and if this title does not conflict with your initial ideas, use it.

Course Planning Step 2.2.   Give your course a title. To title your as yet incompletely specified ideas, you must consider whether or not these ideas are coherent. This is the primary purpose of supplying a title at this point. It is the first of many considerations of the relationship of the parts to the whole, a consideration that gives an initial focus for the course.

With your initial ideas and tentative title in hand, you are ready to elaborate on your ideas. Developing a tentative course outline will contribute to this ongoing process.

DEVELOPING A TENTATIVE COURSE OUTLINE

A course outline contains the major ideas, components, or topics of the subject you are planning to teach. As mentioned in chapter 1, the task of curriculum development presupposes subject-matter expertise on the part of the planner; and a course outline affords the planner an opportunity to lay out that subject matter concisely. This concise outline will be of help in making sure there are no gaps in the presentation of the subject matter, in making decisions about audience appropriateness, in identifying intended learnings, and in organizing the course content.

Course outlines vary depending on the nature of the course being planned. One aspect of this variation is the outline's degree of detail. Highly detailed outlines may include specific factual information. Less detailed outlines will include only major topics and subtopics. Relatively short units can be described in more detail than complete courses. Another factor to consider in deciding on how much to include is your own knowledge of and confidence with the subject matter. You may find it useful to outline in greater detail topics and/or subtopics for which your knowledge is less thorough.

The best way to produce a tentative course outline is to consult several good resource books on the topics. Some of your initial research on current curricular approaches will be relevant here (see page 5). The outline should be written as you peruse these references. Do not worry about course planning decisions at this point. The purpose of the outline is to acquire, update, or refresh your knowledge, to make sure that important content is not inadvertently omitted, and to make explicit the relative importance of topics and subtopics. Including information in your outline does not mean that you must include the information in your course. Teachers report that the "extra" content on an outline is often very helpful in answering student questions that go beyond content contained in the lessons and in coming up with suggestions for topics that students may be interested in pursuing on their own. Outlines, like all aspects of course design, are never finished. You will always find new resources and acquire new information. Outlines should be regularly updated and fleshed out. After you have taught a unit several times, the outline should be quite detailed. The Inuit unit outline, included as an example, is an initial outline, prepared before the unit was taught for the first time.

Content Outline—the Inuit of North Alaska

  I. Geography
    A. History of glacial ice cap. (In Pleistocene times the massive accumulation of water in the glacier ice caused a lowering of the sea level, permitting a few hardy animals to cross the Bering Strait from Asia to America.)
    B. Van Allen belts
      1. Radiation
      2. Aurora Borealis
    C. Arctic land mass
      1. Location on a globe
      2. Physical characteristics
        a. Permafrost
        b. Perennially frozen topsoil
        c. Vegetation
      3. Climate
        a. Seasons
        b. Arctic days and nights
        c. Weather
        d. Temperatures
      4. Inhabitants
        a. Mammals
        b. Birds
        c. Insects
    D. Arctic Ocean
      1. Physical characteristics
      2. Inhabitants
        a. Mammals
        b. Fish
  II. Ecosystem
    A. The food chain
      1. Producers
      2. Consumers
      3. Decomposers
      4. Niche
    B. Habitats

C. Adaptations
    1. Plants—Arctic plants must retain enough heat to enable photosynthesis to take place (43°). They do it in the following ways:
        a. Small leathery leaves
        b. Clumping
        c. Hairy leaves and stems
        d. Large root systems to reserve supply of carbohydrates
    2. Animals
        a. Some animals such as the musk ox have adapted long fur.
        b. Some animals have adapted shorter appendages with less surface to radiate away body heat.
        c. Some animals have adapted a thick undercoat.
        d. Some animals have adapted hair that is thicker at the top and traps body heat.
        e. Some animals change the color of their fur. Cells that formerly contained pigment contain air that holds body heat.

III. Humans
  A. Food
    1. Food gathering
        a. Berries
        b. Pemmican
    2. Hunting
        a. Aboriginal technology
          (1). Transportation
              (a). Umiaks and kayaks
              (b). Sleds
                  (i). Dogs
                  (ii). Harnesses
          (2). Weapons
          (3). Trading
        b. Western technology
  B. Clothing
    1. Function
        a. Summer dress
        b. Winter dress
    2. Labor intensive vs. cost intensive
  C. Shelter
    1. Sod
    2. Skin
    3. Wood
    4. Snow
    5. Stone
  D. Culture
    1. Language
        a. Storytelling

    b. Poetry
    c. Literature—myths and legends
  2. Art
    a. Masks
    b. Carving
    c. Printmaking
    d. Stitchery
  3. Religion
    a. Magic
    b. Shamans
    c. Amulets
  4. Games

The exact sequence of the topics in the outline is not particularly important at this stage. Decisions about whether particular content is appropriate for the intended audience need not be made now, unless these decisions are obvious. Of far greater importance is the outline's inclusiveness and that the format adequately represents the relative importance of the subtopics under each topic.

Courses that do not focus on traditional subject matter will have to have outlines suited to their content. The teaching of reading, writing, typing, or instrumental music, to name a few, are typically performance-oriented courses. A course outline for subjects like these should break down the overall performance into subtopics that can be separately addressed. A reading unit, for example, could be divided into the following subtopics: decoding using phonic cues, decoding using the context, decoding by structural analysis, reading for literal meaning, making inferences for news articles, and so on. Regardless of course type, an outline of the course is the planner's first chance to think systematically about the substantive elements of the subject.

Course Planning Step 2.3.   Develop a tentative course outline.

INTENDED LEARNING OUTCOMES (ILOs)

The primary product of this planning phase is a stated set of *intended learning outcomes*, or learning objectives. An intended learning outcome is a statement of what the student is to learn. It may be a statement about facts, ideas, principles, capabilities, skills, techniques, values, or feelings. A set of ILO statements may be altered, reconsidered, and refined, but it is an important part of almost every step in course planning.

Since the notion of ILO is crucial to all that follows, let us examine it in more detail. The use of the word *intended* emphasizes control and direction in the educational process. A course may result in many outcomes, and some of them may be quite accidental, whether good or bad. Course planning does not proceed on the hope of accidental learning but with lucid, stateable intentions. The word *learning* is again used advisedly, for it emphasizes that the major purpose of planning a course is to affect student learning. Courses are for students, not for teachers or for testers. A student may learn more or less than a teacher has actually taught. Much of the content taught (for example, the use of examples) may be only instrumental for the learning of particular concepts, principles, attitudes, and skills. Similarly, for one reason or another a student may or may not meet the requirements of a certain test and still may have learned what was intended. Finally, the word *outcome* indicates that our major concern is what the student will gain after completing the course.

The next step in developing a focus is selecting intended learning outcomes from the initial list of ideas and the course outline; other ILOs will be added later. The process of selecting important material to be learned is, in part, a process of "drawing a ring" around the course's learning objectives. This consists of deciding what the course will and will not be about. After this decision has been reached, the material can be further specified so that all the learnings important to the course are included.

Identifying ILOs

The first step in the process of selecting intended learnings is to decide which items on the list of initial ideas and in the course outline represent intended learning outcomes. These ILOs may be facts, ideas, theories, or other types of information that the student is expected to learn as a result of the course. Ecosystems, food chains, the causes of World War II, and the characteristics of a good diet are examples of content to be learned. ILOs may also be skills, competencies, or values. Touch typing, math computation, clear speaking, and proper grammar are examples of skills to be learned. Intended learnings may also include values such as respect for the environment, for honest advertising, and for the rights of others. Specific teaching strategies are not intended learning outcomes. Special materials, such as particular books, filmstrips, videotapes, or programmed instruction units, are not intended learning outcomes. We must also leave out field trips, group projects, and oral reports. Nevertheless, all these things must be examined carefully to ascertain what specific intended learnings they suggest. For example, if a field trip is on the list of initial ideas or in the course outline, consider why a field trip is important. What will students be expected to learn from the trip (for example, an ability to apply ecological concepts in a natural setting)?

An ILO comes into being because you think an item in your list of initial ideas or course outline is something to be learned. Use your judgment and imagination. Do not omit potentially important ILOs because an item "doesn't look like an ILO." Some ILOs are obvious and explicit; others, however, are implicit and require thinking if they are to be identified. It is better to have too many rather than too few ILOs. Later course planning steps will help you refine your ILOs.

Exercise 2.1. *   The lists below represent what might be lists of initial ideas. Identify obvious and explicit ILOs in the lists with a check mark.

1. Creative Cooking
types of kitchen tools
the student knows what a frying pan is for

---

* Answers to Exercises appear at the end of each chapter.

Rombauer's *Joy of Cooking*

ability to test cake to see if done

trip to local restaurant

how to bake bread

cooking not a specifically female thing

desserts

knowledge of menu planning

manual cooking skills: kneading, sautéing, flipping crepes, stir-frying

how to plan before you cook

meats

vegetable protein

each student prepares own dish—bring-a-dish meal

safe use of knives

2. English Grammar and Composition
complex and compound sentences

parts of speech (verb, noun, article, adjective, adverb, etc.)

correct punctuation

recognizes sentence fragments

choice of words

learns from reading

appreciates own good writing

uses commas with nonrestrictive relative clauses

avoids run-on sentences

doesn't use dialectal forms in formal writing

use of exercises as teaching device

assign compositions every week

short stories

spelling tests weekly

3. Social Studies
small-group discussions

knowledge of what constitutes an institution

institutions are self-perpetuating

enlightened self-interest in relationship to society

essay on democratic vs. autocratic institutions

cooperatives

media as used by social forces

recognizes institutional interests

extensive use of library sources

films

types of institutions: social, religious, commercial

how institutions change

4. American History—The Post-Revolutionary Period
knows significance of the dates: 1776, 1803, 1812

Jefferson, Adams, Madison

debates

understands the causes of the War of 1812

can describe the attack against Tripoli

can describe why Hamilton accepted a duel with Burr

film: *The Burr Conspiracy*

the U.S. Constitution

economic trends

America takes her place among the nations of the world

the situation with Britain and France at the time

projects

the Embargo Act of 1807

description of the burning of Washington

knows the origin of the national anthem

Exercise 2.2. In Exercise 2.1 you selected the ILOs already apparent in the lists. For this exercise, go back to the lists and develop possible ILOs that are implicit or suggested rather than explicit.

Course Planning Step 2.4. All ILOs, either explicit or implicit, in your list of initial ideas and course outline should now be written on a separate list, "the list of ILOs." (See appendixes for additional examples.)

Categorizing ILOs

For the purposes of curricular and instructional planning, it is often useful to categorize learning into types. Categorization is useful because different types of learning require different types of instruction, different considerations when sequencing and organizing the course, and different types of evaluation. At this point in the planning process, ILOs are grouped into two categories: skills and understandings. Generally speaking, understandings comprise the information and beliefs with which we think. Understandings can be thought of as "knowing that" (including "knowing" in a deep sense, not just memorizing). Ideas, concepts, facts, principles, theories, and generalizations are some of the things that can be known. Skills can be thought of as "knowing how." Skills are things students are able to do at the end of a course. Skills include mental abilities, such as problem solving, reading, arithmetic computation, interpretation, analysis, application; and physical abilities, such as bicycling and ball throwing.

For most courses, some balance between skills and understandings is desirable. A course stressing only skills is more characteristic of training than of education. Such a course aims at having students learn how to do things but not at learning the principles behind what they are doing. For example, a good physical education course teaches the rules of the game and the basis for good sportsmanship. On the other hand, a course stressing only understandings may equip students with a set of ideas but may leave them without any competencies. A course of this type may not provide students with the ability to use what they have learned. A good English literature course, for example, teaches the skills of literary criticism.

Course Planning Step 2.5.   Categorize your ILOs into skills and understandings.
This is the first time in the planning process that items are categorized under specific headings (skills/understandings), but you will be called on to perform this type of operation again. This is a part of the process of giving your course direction and assists you in planning and determining such things as completeness and balance. This categorization is not just an exercise, but an instrumental step in the planning process.

FORMULATING CENTRAL QUESTIONS*

Initial ideas, a course outline, and a list of tentative ILOs describe the scope of your course. Central questions, questions that are fundamental to the course and that identify the focus of the course, help to give these elements coherence. In order to develop central questions, formulate the most important questions addressed in the course. Different courses have different focal points and, therefore, different types of appropriate central questions. In some cases the central questions can be answered correctly by a student successfully completing the course. In other cases, such as those in philosophy or literature, the questions may be open-ended, and the student who completes the course should be able to deal with these questions independently, rather than be able to answer them correctly. Courses range from ones emphasizing understanding and appreciations, to those emphasizing problems or decisions, to those emphasizing skill acquisition and personal growth.

Inquiry Orientation

In general, an inquiry orientation aims at understanding. In some inquiry-oriented courses the teacher and students explore topics in a search for underlying reasons for, meanings of, or implications of events. Inquiry-oriented courses might also investigate the structure or function of living things, objects, systems, or social organizations. Or

---

* We are indebted to the work of Gowin (1970) for this idea, although he used the term *telling questions*.

they might study the meaning of particular concepts, such as humanity, reality, truth, or equality. Inquiry-oriented courses would be best summarized by questions such as the following:

What is X?

What are (or were) the causes of X?

What are the implications of X?

What is the structure (or function) of X?

What does X mean (what is its nature or essence)?

Why does (did) X occur?

How does (did) X happen?

These general questions are intended only to suggest the form some central questions might take, rather than to limit you in formulating central questions for your course.

Appreciation Orientation

Appreciation-oriented courses help the student develop taste, whether that taste is in literature, music, fine arts, dance, or theater. In such courses students typically experience art through reading, viewing, listening to, or participating in the creation of an art product. While doing so, students develop personal preferences and also learn the criteria that experts use in critiquing a piece of art. Central questions for such courses are of the sort, "What do I like, and why do I like it?"

Problem Orientation

Some courses focus on developing the students' ability to solve problems. For example, philosophers of science have described the training of physicists as instruction in how to categorize physical phenomena (such as pulleys) as a type of problem (an equilibrium-of-forces problem), and how to solve a variety of these problem types. Mathematics (for example, elementary algebra) can be similarly characterized, though being problem oriented does not mean that a course cannot also be inquiry oriented. The range of courses that focus on problems is very broad. Business courses focusing on management problems, interdisciplinary courses focusing on environmental problems, psychology courses focusing on coping with personal problems, and courses aimed at teaching general problem-solving methods represent only a sample of possibilities. In problem-oriented courses, the central questions would be of the type, "How does one solve problems X, Y, and Z?" A listing of the major problems or problem types is probably the best central question format for these courses.

Decision Orientation

Decision-oriented courses provide the student with information or frameworks on which to base decisions, and sometimes even with a step-by-step method for arriving at a decision. Decisions such as what career to pursue, what types of energy conservation measures to take, and what kind of used car to buy are typical. Included here would also be courses aimed at helping individuals with moral decisions. Some courses allow the decisions to be open-ended, whereas other courses assume a prespecified decision. A course in car buying may or may not be biased toward fuel efficient cars but a drug education course is very likely to be biased toward a decision not to use (or, at least, not to abuse) drugs. Decision-oriented courses are best represented by central questions that simply list the decisions.

Skill Orientation

Still other courses are most appropriately described as skill oriented. A skill orientation emphasizes improving performance in carrying out physical tasks. Skill-oriented courses emphasize "how to do it," whether "it" is driving a car, typing, or playing ice hockey. Central questions for such courses will typically be of the type, "How does one (or what is the proper way to) do X?" Often such questions include qualifiers for X such as "safely," "efficiently," "critically," and "with good sportsmanship."

Personal Growth Orientation

Though not entirely distinguishable from some of the other orientations, a personal growth orientation attempts to help the student define a personal goal (typically a psychological state, such as "self-actualization") and then to develop ways to work toward that goal. Such courses are usually grounded in theories of psychological counseling. Appropriate central questions are of the sort, "What are my goals and how do I work toward them?"

It should be obvious that any real course is unlikely to represent only one of these types. Some courses might even be inquiry, appreciation, problem, decision, skill, and personal growth oriented all at once. The important point is that your central questions should reflect the central concerns of *your* course. How many and what kinds of central questions naturally depend on the course. The following course titles accompanied by central questions serve as illustrations:

1. Driver Education
What is the proper way to drive an automobile safely?

2. American History 1700–1800
What political, social, and economic forces shaped America during this period?

What was "revolutionary" about the United States?

3. Environmental Science
How should I, as an individual, interact with my environment in a mutually beneficial way?

What elements make up an ecosystem, and what is the nature of their interaction?

4. Philosophy

What is the nature of reality?

How do I give meaning to my life?

5. Social Studies (from Man: A Course of Study)

What is human about human beings?

How did they get that way?

How can they be made more so?

Central questions do not include all the interesting or important questions for a particular course, but they should concern what is most fundamental to it. Central questions represent the "heart" of a course and are sometimes referred to as "essential" questions (Wiggens, undated). They are the questions that, once discovered by a student, serve as the focus for study. That is, a student who discovers a course's central questions might remark, "Aha! Now I see what this course is about. Now I see what the purpose is."

Obviously, the more central questions you specify, the less focused your course will appear. If you have a large number of central questions (more than five), you might attempt to organize them into major questions, each with associated subquestions. Such a procedure will maintain the scope of your course, while forcing you to examine its coherence.

One way to generate central questions is to imagine that you are developing a final examination for your course consisting of less than six essay questions. What would these questions be? This might be a good time to write out your ideal answers to these questions.

Course Planning Step 2.6.   Examine your list of initial ideas, ILOs, and tentative course outline and write down the central questions that give coherence to your course. Now reconsider and expand your ILOs in light of these questions.

Thinking about central questions at this stage of course planning should help you in identifying the central or unifying theme of your course. You may find that your course will need revision in order to achieve a focus. In general, thinking about central questions is another way to evaluate and continue to develop your course. These questions are only one of several tools you will be taught for thinking about your course.

QUESTIONS FOR DISCUSSION: CENTRAL QUESTIONS

1. What do your central questions tell you about the focus of your course?
2. Are one or two of your questions the *real* focus of your course and the others secondary or subquestions? From your list of central questions, which ones truly represent the "heart" of your course?
3. What would be unacceptable answers to some of your central questions?

4. What kinds of questions are you asking? Are you more interested in "where" and "when" or in "why" and "how"?
   a. If you are more interested in "where" and "when" questions, what does that suggest about your course?
   b. If you are more interested in "why" and "how" questions, what does that suggest about your course?
5. What are some of the evaluative words you have used in your questions (*good, bad, useful, beneficial, harmful, efficient, growth, interest*)? What does this suggest about your course?
6. Are there some central questions that might appear relevant to your course, but which you would reject? Explain why you would reject them.
7. To what extent do these questions take the *student* into consideration? The *society* in which the student lives? The *subject matter?*
8. Show your questions to an expert in the field. Does the expert agree with your focus? How do you account for any discrepancies?

Although central questions, lists of ILOs, and course outlines are useful tools for thinking about the scope and coherence of your course, they are not sufficient. More schematic tools such as charts are needed. Two schematic tools will be discussed in this chapter: conceptual maps and flowcharts. Conceptual maps are appropriate for representing understanding; flowcharts are most useful for analyzing skills.

CONCEPTUAL MAPS

The technique you will learn in this section is called conceptual mapping. You already know about maps as diagrammatic representations of geographical regions. Maps of this type show where you are in relation to other geographical points. For example, road maps help you to "get your bearings and to proceed to your destination" (Anderson, 1979, p. 17). Conceptual maps are like road maps, but they are concerned with relationships among ideas, rather than places. Conceptual maps also help you to "get your bearings" in designing a course—to clarify the kinds of ideas you want taught—so that you can proceed toward your destination of real student learning.

This is the first stage of conceptual mapping. Here we will focus on identifying key ideas and arranging them in a reasonable pattern. In chapter 4 we will elaborate on this technique further, identifying and representing specific relationships among ideas. You may want to continue with the discussion of maps in chapter 4, temporarily skipping chapter 3.

In a conceptual map, ideas are depicted as related to one another. These ideas include concepts, theories, facts, rules, propositions, principles, and generalizations. Maps may depict relationships among ideas as simple or complex, clear or indefinite.

Figure 2.1 is a simple map. It is definite and clear but gives us only limited information. The first thing the chart indicates is that each labeled node represents a subcategory under the category "cooking with heat." Reading down from the top of the chart shows us that there are two major subcategories for "cooking with heat," one using the stove top and one using the oven. If the oven is used, two methods can be

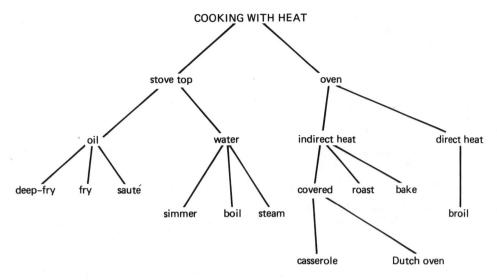

FIGURE 2.1 Cooking with heat.

employed: indirect heat and direct heat. This is a hierarchical map. It specifies only two things, but it does this definitely and exhaustively: subcategory identification and membership. For example, simmer, boil, and steam are all members of the subcategory water. Likewise, oil and water are members of the subcategory stove top. This method of mapping is simple, definite, and complete. It specifies precisely every relationship it sets out to show. Nevertheless, it is important to note that many other relationships are not specified. For example, the relationship between bake and roast is seen here only as membership in the same subcategory. Likewise, the similarity of boil to deep-fry is not shown in the diagram. This simple hierarchical diagram simply does not have the capacity for showing these relationships. A hierarchical diagram is a graphic presentation of conceptual structure in terms of the relationship of classes to constituency.

But maps do not have to be hierarchical diagrams. Ideas may be related in ways other than class membership. One idea (a) may *cause* another (increased inflation is one *consequence* of government spending), (b) may be compared with another with regard to magnitude (the amount of solar radiation the earth absorbs *equals* the amount it radiates), and (c) may be a *property* of another (hurricanes have *high* winds and torrential rains). These are only examples of the many possible relationships among ideas.

For example, Figure 2.2 is a conceptual map for a social studies unit on rice growing. Instead of a hierarchical arrangement, causal relations seem more appropriate for this content. According to this map four factors affect rice growing: fresh water, a flat area, fertile soil, and warm temperature. Other concepts could be added through more detailed analysis. For example, irrigation could be added between "river or lake" and "supply of fresh water." Collins (1977) discusses in detail how such a map could guide the teaching of a student using Socratic questioning.

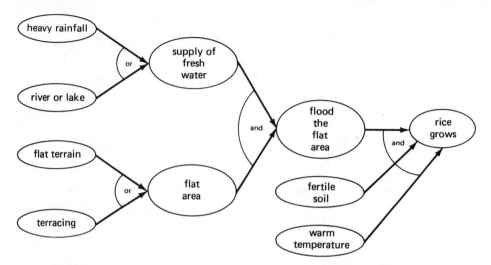

FIGURE 2.2   The causal factors affecting rice growing. (Adapted from Collins, 1977.)

When you construct a conceptual map you do not have to choose which one of the many possible relationships your map will feature. A map may employ several kinds of relationships. For example, Figure 2.3 illustrates three factors that *influence* freshwater habitats, and two *aspects* of the adaptation of freshwater inhabitants to their habitats.

Obviously, the kinds of relationships featured in your conceptual map will depend primarily on the subject matter and the relationships within that subject matter that concern you as a planner. Accompanying a map with a brief explanation is one way to clarify or highlight a map's relationships. Making those relationships more specific and explicit will be one of the topics treated in chapter 4.

One issue that almost always surfaces when constructing maps concerns the appropriate level of detail. Using our earlier comparison of conceptual maps with geographical maps, we might think of a map as a "view" of the "conceptual terrain" in a course. In a sense, there is a trade-off between the level of detail (the "resolution") and the scope (the "field of vision") of information included in a particular view of the terrain. The broader the field of vision we wish for our view, the less resolution we can provide. Similarly, the higher the resolution of our view (the "finer grained"), the more restricted our field will be.

It is very difficult to represent all the major concepts of a course on one map. Instead, a series of maps with varying degrees of detail is probably a more fruitful approach. This approach is similar to that followed in atlases. A world atlas might contain maps of the world, maps of continents, maps of countries, and even maps of provinces and states. Maps of states may even contain "inserts" depicting major cities within a state. Although the level of complexity of an atlas is far greater than the complexity of a conceptual map for a course, the general approach may be useful. For example, some students have found it useful to construct a general conceptual map

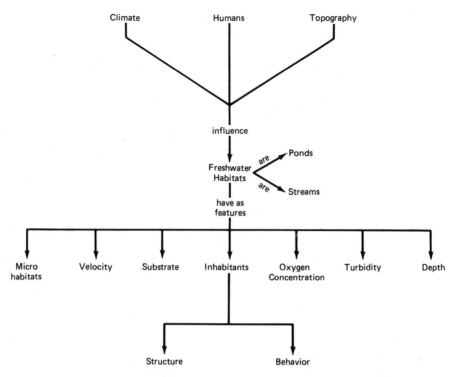

FIGURE 2.3   A conceptual map for a course on freshwater habitats.

for their course, then to detail portions of their general maps for each of their units or even for each of their lessons.

Many teachers with whom we have worked have found two metaphors helpful in creating their conceptual maps. The first is that a map is like a dinner conversation. Many dinner conversations at which a schoolchild is present have a familiar pattern. "What did you learn in school today?" is often answered by "Nothing." "Nothing? You spent all day in school and you didn't learn anything?" Perhaps after some prodding a parent finds out about a playground or lunchroom event of significance. The conceptual map fits into this conversation in two distinct ways. The map with an accompanying explanation is the kind of information that a teacher could send home to help parents focus a conversation on ideas being covered in school. (See Figure 2.4 on p. 37 for example.) Rather than ask a general question about what was learned in school, parents could ask questions like the following: "What are you learning about the plants and animals of the rocky shore?" "How do living things adapt to this environment?" "What are the important characteristics of the environment?" Another way of thinking about the dinner conversation metaphor for a conceptual map is that the map outlines what a student who has successfully learned the important ideas of the unit would say instead of "nothing." The conversation could go as follows:

PARENT: What did you learn in school today?

STUDENT: Well, we're learning about the rocky shore ecosystem.

PARENT: Really? Tell me about it.

STUDENT: I know a lot about it. What do you want to know?

PARENT: Well, I don't know anything. Better start at the beginning.

STUDENT: Living things must adapt to their physical environment to survive. The rocky shore presents real physical challenges for living things. . . .

Thus a conceptual map can be conceived as a framework for a dinner conversation between parent and student.

The second metaphor that teachers have found helpful is that of a story. In many ways teaching is like storytelling. While we use examples, activities, assignments, and other learning activities, our goal as teachers is to convey a story or underlying theme. The conceptual map sketches out the story or theme. How detailed the story should be depends greatly on the age and sophistication of the learners. By helping us see the story we want students to learn, a map frees us from the constraints of specific content and thus enables us to tell the story more effectively. The adaptation of living things to their environment is such a story. The Rocky Shore unit began with a slide show that contrasted successful and unsuccessful adaptation. A field teeming with dandelions was followed by the image of a bristlecone pine that has not had an offspring in over 1,000 years. A herd of caribou on the tundra was followed by hatching Galapagos turtles being picked off by predators on their way to the water. The show continued, its point being to set the stage for the specific story of the rocky shore. Teachers sometimes mistakenly think that the ideas included on a conceptual map are to be taught directly. For elementary teachers this sometimes creates an image of heavy-handed instruction. The fact is, one teaches ideas through engaging and appropriate use of specific content. The story or theme is what ties the specifics together. Teachers need to refer to the theme or story to lend coherence to the material being taught. In creating a conceptual map many teachers have been helped by thinking of it as a device that lays out the story line. This has helped them keep the specific content to a minimum and instead focus on the unit's major underlying ideas.

The Rocky Shore map, Figure 2.4, and accompanying explanation was designed for a sixth grade science unit. The map shows that the ideas central to understanding an ecosystem include knowing the physical characteristics of that environment and knowing what lives there. The map also shows that it is the adaptive relationship between organism and environment that is the key to understanding the ecosystem. Below adaptation are concepts that will help students think about and understand the ways in which living things adapt to their environment. It is worth noting that this basic conceptual structure could be used to study any ecosystem, not just that of the rocky shore. The details would change but the fundamental ideas and their relationship would stay the same. There is often a fine line between enough and too much specific detail on a conceptual map. Maps are not supposed to be course outlines in two dimensions. The Rocky Shore map could include some specifics about this particular ecosystem. Waves and tides, for example, are crucial features of the physical environment of the rocky shore. Organisms of this ecosystem with some distinct adaptations that relate directly to physical conditions could be mentioned.

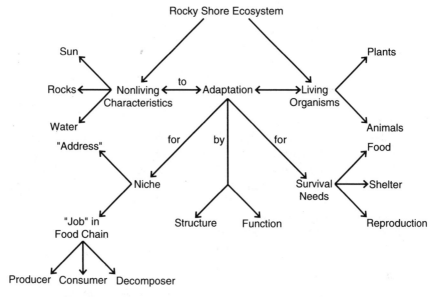

FIGURE 2.4 A conceptual map for a unit on the rocky shore ecosystem.

Explanation of Conceptual Map

The rocky shore ecosystem of the North Atlantic coast boasts unique characteristics because it is a "border ecosystem"; it exists where land and water meet. Water movement, including tide changes and wave patterns, is the most prominent of these characteristics. This movement has both beneficial and detrimental effects on the living and nonliving members of the shore ecosystem. The continual wave movement consistently replenishes the oxygen and nutrients in the rocky shore ecosystem but, at the same time, it challenges the survival of many of the living members of the ecosystem with its damaging strength.

The sunlight present in the rocky shore ecosystem changes with the weather and with the tides; although the water level never reaches a height greater than 6 to 8 feet, a larger amount of sunlight will reach the shallower areas and will ultimately affect the algae growth in the area. While this aspect of sunlight is beneficial to the ecosystem, the tides will eventually go out and there will be no water boundary between the rocky shore and the sun. Many of the living members uncovered at low tide must survive the drying effects of this change.

Survival by the living organisms in this ecosystem is a constant challenge. The ease with which an organism adapts to this environment determines its ability to obtain its survival needs: food, shelter, and reproduction. By adapting in both structure and function, an organism can take from this environment what it needs and, simultaneously, defend itself from the negative aspects of the environment. Organisms have various ways in which they meet their survival needs and, in doing so, they find a unique niche in the ecosystem.

This niche determines the activity that the organism performs in the food chain of the ecosystem. The food chain is the primary method by which all organisms divide the available resources of the environment. All the organisms in an ecosystem depend on one another for this distribution of resources; they are thus dependent on one another for the conditions of life. The niche also defines the place in which the organism spends its adult life. In the rocky shore ecosystem, the "addresses" of various organisms are clearly determined by the tidal divisions. The subtidal region is that area of the rocky shore that, except at the lowest tides, is completely submerged in water. The intertidal zone is that area of the shore that is constantly wet by wave movement and is covered by water twice each day during high tide.

The teacher using this unit can and should use this conceptual map as a general outline for an ecosystem. Maintaining a consistent conceptual framework for all ecosystems will enable students to compare and contrast characteristics of other ecosystems studied. This map should also serve as an anchor upon which other more complex additions can be made.

The highest priority relationships (intended cognitions) represented by this conceptual map are:

- Ecosystems consist of the living organisms and the nonliving characteristics present.
- The nonliving characteristics determine that to which the living organisms must adapt.
- Living organisms adapt by structure and function in order to find a niche and obtain survival needs (food, shelter, reproduction).
- The living organisms must divide the available resources and are dependent on one another to do so.
- The food chain is the primary way in which living organisms divide these resources.

Course Planning Step 2.7.   Analyze the important terminology contained in your skill and understanding ILOs and course outline, and list all terms you feel are representative of the major ideas you want your students to understand.

The following list of words might represent the major ideas in one teacher's physics course on mechanics:

Mechanics	Direction
Kinetics	Force
Dynamics	Mass
Particle	Rest
Body	Acceleration
Motion	

Course Planning Step 2.8.   Arrange the list of words signifying ideas and add interconnecting lines until you have a diagram or set of diagrams illustrating the interrelationships among the ideas particular to the course. Add any ideas that you feel are needed to make your map(s) meaningful and complete.

Figure 2.5 shows the arrangement of terms produced by one university faculty member. Other "correct" arrangements are possible.

Course Planning Step 2.9.   Evaluate the map(s). Have you depicted major relationships clearly? Can the map(s) be simplified and still effectively communicate the relationships you consider most important?

Conceptual maps are useful for thinking about your course. In fact, mapping is an important step toward acquiring a clear conception of what you want learned. Understandings are, in many ways, more adequately expressed as a map than as a set of ILO statements (to be discussed further in chapter 4). Knowledge has meaning in context and part of context is how ideas are interrelated. These interrelationships can be, at least partially, expressed by a map.

Maps can illuminate many important issues at this stage of planning. (See Novak & Gowin, 1984; West, Farmer, & Wolff, 1991.) For example, a map that includes only discrete and specific facts may indicate a need for more inclusive ideas. On the other hand, a map may show only inclusive and abstract ideas without the applications and examples that make these ideas understandable and useful. Noticing that a map lacks relationships among certain ideas may point out the need for additional ideas to make those relationships possible. These are only a few examples of the information a conceptual map may provide during planning.

As a sort of shorthand representation of a teacher's conceptual ILOs, maps often prove useful during instruction. Knowing how ideas relate should help teachers to respond to questions and comments in a more focused way. Remarks made by students can be seen as instances of a concept, and the teacher can try to help students understand the desired relationships. A teacher's cueing, questioning, and supplying of new information is apt to be more targeted when accompanied by a clear notion of the ideas and relationships the teacher wants learned. (See Collins, 1977, for several useful examples.)

The mapping process is flexible and a map for any given set of concepts can take many forms. Too often teachers worry about the "correctness" of their maps. Correctness is a secondary concern here. You, the teacher, will be teaching the course, and you undoubtedly have some view of the relationships among the course's ideas. Whatever framework you possess is likely to affect your teaching. Mapping allows you to make this framework explicit, revise it, and, generally, be more conscious of it. Therefore, in constructing a conceptual map, your initial attempts should be made with the goal of getting this framework on paper and with the expectation that the framework will require revision. Relating all the important ideas in a course in two dimensions is a difficult task. However, mapping is usually worth the effort and will prove useful in thinking about and planning your course.

QUESTIONS FOR DISCUSSION: MAPPING

1. If your map has lines connecting terms, do the lines mean different things? What do they mean?
2. Compare those terms that are connected to many other terms with those terms connected to just one other term. Does this comparison help you identify the important or central ideas in your course?

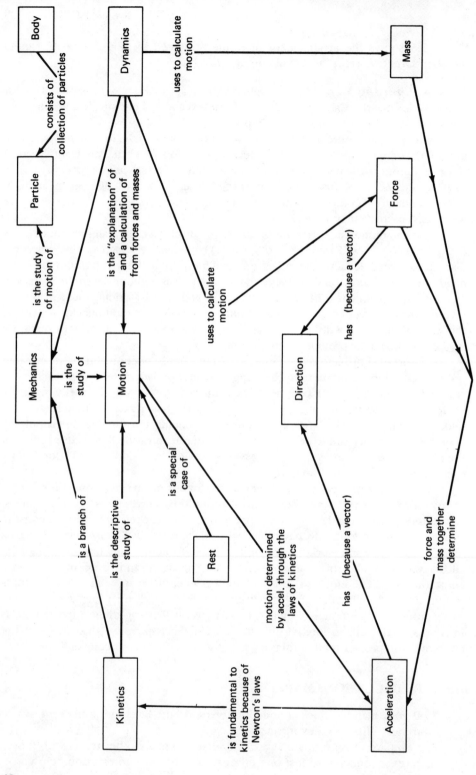

FIGURE 2.5 One possible arrangement of physics terms. Note the advantage to the reader when the mapmaker labels the arrows. (Adapted from Champagne, Klopfer, Solomon, and Cahn, 1980.)

3. Was your map instrumental in finding any new ILOs?
4. Do you feel your course lent itself well to mapping, or did you find mapping inappropriate? How do you account for this?
5. Would your map help students find their way through your course? If so, you might want to use it as a handout, a kind of two-dimensional course outline.
6. Show your map to an expert in the field. Does the expert understand and agree with you regarding your map? Are any changes in order?

FLOWCHARTS

Arithmetic computation, reading, writing paragraphs, editing films, and parking a car are all complex skills in the sense that they each require a set of subskills and understandings for their performance. If we want to teach any of these skills we must do so by teaching the necessary subskills and understandings. Therefore, it is important to identify the components of these complex skills. So long as important aspects of a desired skill remain unidentified and untaught, achievement of the skill will be impeded. Identification of subskills and understandings enables them to be specified as course ILOs and subsequently taught using appropriate teaching strategies.

One tool for identifying such subskills and understandings is a cognitive task analysis utilizing flowcharts. Let us look at an example.

$$3/5 + 1/5 = ?$$

Try to solve this problem and analyze your thinking process at the same time. That is, think the steps through aloud as you do each of them. Note what you are doing and compare it with the flowchart in Figure 2.6.

Now look at this more difficult problem.

$$3/5 + 2/15 = ?$$

Again analyze your thinking process by verbalizing the steps you follow in solving it. A more general procedure for solving such problems is depicted in Figure 2.7. According to this more complex and generalized flowchart, these two problems require the addition of fractions that can be represented in a general form as:

$$a/b + c/d = ?$$

In the first problem $b = d$ (both are 5) so we can add a and c (that is, $3 + 1$) and get 4/5 as an answer. Notice, however, that this flowchart begs the question of how we add 3 and 1. Do we count on our fingers, or in our heads, or do we just know the answer? Clearly, these analyses can be performed at different levels of depth.

In the second problem $b = d$, but d is a multiple of b (15 is 3 times 5). As in the first problem, each step in the procedure could be reanalyzed as a subskill for which

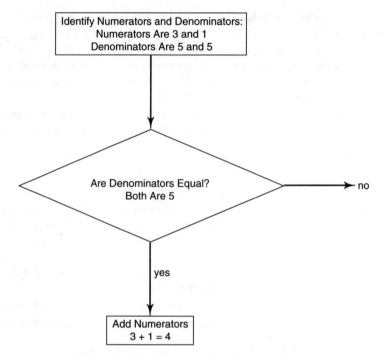

FIGURE 2.6   Procedure for addition of fractions with
like denominators.

we could identify additional and necessary subskills, facts, principles, etc. The depth
of our analysis will depend on what learning outcomes we can assume our students
have already achieved.

In a similar way we could analyze each of our skill ILOs by asking the question,
"What do I go through when I perform this skill, and, specifically, what skills and
understandings does the ILO entail?"

This analysis could be done at a general level for the whole course by analyzing
the course's ILOs. For example, Figure 2.8 presents the skills and understandings
entailed in playing a game of ice hockey. Then, at a more specific level, each of the
skills in this general flowchart could be analyzed in greater detail.

In the analysis of most skills, the skills (or "tasks" as they are typically called) can
be best described in terms of a series of internal and/or external actions performed on
available information. Many cognitive psychologists distinguish between data or
"information" and the operations or actions we perform on the data, termed
"processes." These psychologists are concerned with how humans act on (process)
data (information); thus, they use the term *information-processing analysis.*

There are several additional points to keep in mind as you construct flowcharts
for your skill ILOs:

1. Many of the subskills you identify during the analysis may be internal
thought processes rather than observable behaviors. This is to be
expected.

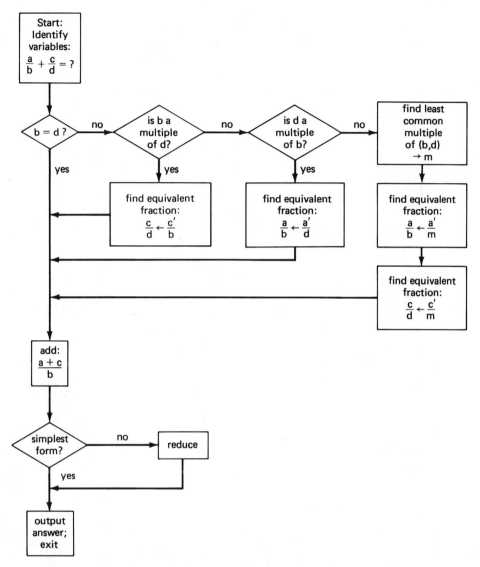

FIGURE 2.7 Procedure for addition of fractions. (Adapted from Greeno, 1976.)

2. It is usually best to think of the steps in the procedures as occurring serially (one at a time).
3. The analysis should include the identification of both understandings (information and data) and other subskills (processes or operations on the data).
4. Any flowchart represents a hypothesis regarding the processes and information necessary in performing skills. There is usually more than one possible flowchart for a skill. Which of several candidates is correct is a

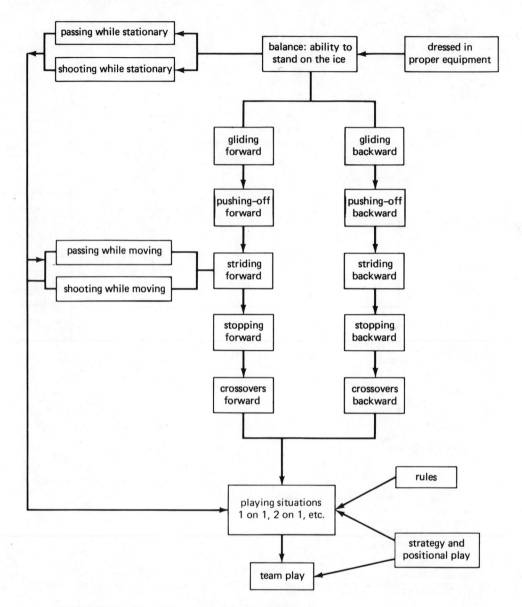

FIGURE 2.8 Flowchart of skills for ice hockey.

matter for psychological research. However, the one you construct should be consistent with your own introspective experience when you ask yourself, "What do I go through when I perform this skill?"

5. As a set of subskills and understandings that need to be taught in the pursuit of a particular skill ILO, a flowchart can be considered an expression of intended learning outcomes.

6. A flowchart is only one way to represent the subskills and understandings necessary for the performance of a skill. Skills that are very complex or not highly structured do not easily lend themselves to flowcharting. Nevertheless, these skills can and should be analyzed. As an alternative to flowcharting, the subskills and understandings resulting from this analysis can be expressed as a list. Skills that are not complex need not be analyzed at all.

Course Planning Step 2.10. Construct a flowchart or list of subskills and understandings for any of your ILOs representing complex skills.

FINDING OUT WHERE THE STUDENTS ARE

The charts and lists developed up to now have been concerned with your view of what the course should cover, what students should learn, and what questions students should address. Now we will reconsider your view of the course in light of the students' capabilities and conceptions.

Preconceptions

Of course, we would not want a course to cover the same ground as previous courses, except for review purposes. But the fact that students have or have not been exposed to certain ideas does not tell us what they do or do not understand. In fact, students' existing knowledge is not typically an all-or-nothing situation. Students do not come to any of a course's topics completely empty-headed. They may not know the terminology or have a precise understanding of the topic, but they usually have some ideas about it. Whether the course includes the study of how plants get their food, how to write an academic essay, the meaning of a fraction, the dangers of drug abuse, or how to "head" a soccer ball, students typically come to most courses with well-developed preconceptions.

Although much of the research on student preconceptions has been conducted in science education (see Driver, 1983; Resnick, 1983; Eylon & Linn, 1988; Osborne & Freyberg, 1985), there is enough research to suggest that students generally are not empty vessels into which we pour knowledge. Instead, they actively try to make sense of their experience (including classroom experience) based on what they already know or believe. When students' preconceptions are either incorrect or only partially true, instruction may become a task of changing people's ideas rather than instilling fresh knowledge.

Before we can adjust a course's ILOs and instructional method to the students, we must know in fairly specific terms what particular students know or believe about the topics we intend to teach. The best way to find out this crucial information is to talk with them in open-ended interviews and group discussions, asking them for their explanations or descriptions while listening to them very carefully. In these diagnostic settings, we can find out the extent to which their views are idiosyncratic or common to the other learners; whether their ideas derive from prior instruction, mass media, life experience, or their own "spontaneous reasoning" (Viennot, 1979, p. 205); and possibly how deeply held their beliefs are and, thus, how difficult they will be to change. The work of Nancie Atwell provides detailed accounts of how teachers can observe and listen to students to assess their present levels of understanding and their needs (see Atwell, 1987; 1991).

Without the opportunity to study students directly, the course planner has to settle for secondhand knowledge, for example, the observations of experienced, perceptive teachers. Although there are times when this type of information must suffice, firsthand knowledge of students gained from observations and discussions both inside and outside of the classroom is highly preferable.

It is important to find out what students know because the course planner can determine not only which of their ideas the course needs to correct or extend, but also what resources students can bring to their understanding of the new material. The course can act as a bridge between what students already know and what the course planner wants them to understand. Analogies, metaphors, and examples are some of the instructional devices teachers use as bridges between familiar and unfamiliar ideas. We used the analogy between course design (unfamiliar) and building construction (familiar) in order to introduce this book in chapter 1. Without knowing what students understand and what experiences they have had, teachers may use these potentially powerful strategies inappropriately and ineffectively.

One way to represent students' preconceptions is to construct a conceptual map describing which ideas and which relationships between ideas students seem to understand. In fact, you might try giving students a list of words representing the major ideas in the course after you complete Course Planning Step 2.7. You could then ask the students to try to complete Course Planning Step 2.8. While the students talk you through their maps by explaining the relationship between each pair of connected words, you develop a stronger sense of their understandings, misconceptions, and gaps in knowledge about the subject matter. As a result, you are in a better position to decide what aspects of the course need to be added, omitted, delayed, and emphasized.

Course Planning Step 2.11. Revise your course outline and ILOs in light of what you have learned about your students' existing knowledge.

Entry-Level Skills

Much of the previous discussion about preconceptions is also applicable to skills students bring to courses (their "entry-level" skills). Students base their approach to the learning of new skills on their current repertoire of skills. This fact suggests a view of students' current skills both as obstacles to learning (things to unlearn) and as foundations of new learning. Giving students tasks to perform and carefully observing their performance are the best means for diagnosing the skills they have and thus for determining the starting point of the course. (See Kemp, 1985; Eby, 1992; Barell, 1991.)

The flowcharts developed in Course Planning Step 2.10 provide one basis for this diagnosis. You can use these flowcharts to identify which of the subskills students can and cannot perform, which ones need some polishing, and which ones are performed incorrectly. As in the case of preconceptions, this diagnosis provides an informed basis for reexamining the course outline and ILOs.

Course Planning Step 2.12.   Revise your course outline and ILOs in light of what you have learned about your students' entry-level skills.

You now have a course outline, a list of ILOs, a set of central questions, one or more flowcharts, and one or more conceptual maps that, taken together, represent the skills and understandings to be acquired by students in your course. These lists and charts represent what you intend the student to learn and will be the foundation for a large part of subsequent course planning. They will influence the selection of materials, the design of teaching strategies, the development of evaluation techniques, and even the actual process of instruction. While there will be many opportunities to revise and edit them, it should now be clear how crucial they are to the process of course planning.

Course Planning Step 2.13.   Look over your ILOs and think carefully about them. Review the process by which you developed them. Make any changes you think are appropriate at this time.

RELATED MATERIAL

This chapter completes the initial phase of selecting and clarifying statements of intended learning outcomes. The criterion of clarity for this phase is whether or not the ILO statement communicates clearly to you, the planner. The second phase of this process is the subject of chapter 4, where a great deal more attention is given to the clarification of ILO statements. The criterion of clarity in chapter 4 is whether or not the ILO statement communicates clearly to other planners, to teachers, and to students.

Chapter 8 shows how to translate each type of ILO into behavioral indicators that can be used to determine if the course's intended learning outcomes have actually been achieved. One criterion for an adequate behavioral indicator of an ILO is whether or not it is observable.

But before proceeding further with course planning on the basis of the ILOs you have produced so far, chapter 3 asks you to give some thought to justifying these ILOs and thus giving your course an overall purpose.

ANSWERS TO EXERCISES

Answers to Exercise 2.1

1. *Creative Cooking*
the student knows what a frying pan is for

ability to test cake to see if done

how to bake bread

knowledge of menu planning

manual cooking skills: kneading, sautéing, flipping crepes, stir-frying

how to plan before you cook

safe use of knives

2. English Grammar and Composition
correct punctuation

recognizes sentence fragments

appreciates own good writing

uses commas with nonrestrictive relative clauses

avoids run-on sentences

doesn't use dialectical forms in formal writing

3. Social Studies
knowledge of what constitutes an institution

enlightened self-interest in relationship to society

recognizes institutional interests

4. American History—The Post-Revolutionary Period
knows significance of the dates: 1776, 1803, 1812

understands the causes of the War of 1812

can describe the attack against Tripoli

can describe why Hamilton accepted a duel with Burr

knows the origin of the national anthem

Answers to Exercise 2.2

1. Creative Cooking
recognizes and names types of kitchen tools

believes that cooking is not a specifically female thing

knows how to prepare desserts

knows how to prepare meats

understands the importance of vegetable protein

2. English Grammar and Composition
distinguishes between complex and compound complex sentences

recognizes and names parts of speech in a sentence

carefully chooses words when writing

3. Social Studies

knows that institutions are self-perpetuating

understands how cooperatives operate

recognizes that media are used by social forces

distinguishes among the types of institutions

knows how institutions change

4. American History

understands the role played by Jefferson, Adams, and Madison in shaping early America

familiar with U.S. Constitution

explains the economic trends occurring in early America

understands America's relationship with Britain and France

comprehends the impact of the Embargo Act of 1807 on trade

REFERENCES

Anderson, T. H. (1979). *Techniques for studying textbook materials in preparation for taking an examination.* Urbana: University of Illinois at Champaign-Urbana, Center for the Study of Reading.

Atwell, N. (1987). *In the middle: Writing, reading and learning with adolescents.* Portsmouth, NH: Heinemann.

Atwell, N. (1991). *Side by side: Essays on teaching to learn.* Portsmouth, NH: Heinemann.

Barell, J. (1991). *Teaching for thoughtfulness: Classroom strategies to enhance intellectual development.* White Plains, NY: Longman.

Champagne, A. B., Klopfer, L. E., Solomon, C. A., & Cahn, A. D. (1980). *Interactions of students' knowledge with their comprehension and design of science experiments* (LRDC Publication No. 1980-9). Pittsburgh: University of Pittsburgh, Learning Research and Development Center.

Collins, A. (1977). Processes in acquiring knowledge. In R. C. Anderson, R. J. Spiro, & W. E. Montague (Eds.), *Schooling and the acquisition of knowledge* (pp. 339–363). Hillsdale, NJ: Lawrence Erlbaum Associates.

Driver, R. (1983). *The pupil as scientist?* Milton Keynes, U.K.: The Open University Press.

Eby, J. W. (1992). *Reflective planning, teaching, and evaluation for the elementary school.* New York: Macmillan.

Education Development Center. (1968). *Man: A course of study.* Cambridge, MA: Author.

Eylon, B., & Linn, M. C. (1988). Learning and instruction: An examination of four research perspectives in science education. *Review of Educational Research, 58*(3), 251–301.

Gowin, D. B. (1970). The structure of knowledge. *Educational Theory, 20*(4), 319–328.

Greeno, J. G. (1976). Cognitive objectives of instruction: Theory of knowledge for solving problems and answering questions. In D. Klahr (Ed.), *Cognition and instruction* (pp. 123–159). Hillsdale, NJ: Lawrence Erlbaum Associates.

Kemp, J. E. (1985). *The instructional design process.* New York: Harper & Row.

Novak, J. D., & Gowin, D. B. (1984). *Learning how to learn.* Cambridge, U.K.: Cambridge University Press.

Osborne, R., & Freyberg, P. (1985). *Learning in science: The implications of children's science.* Portsmouth, NH: Heinemann.

Resnick, L. B. (1983). Mathematics and science learning: A new conception. *Science, 220,* 477–478.

Viennot, L. (1979). Spontaneous reasoning in elementary dynamics. *European Journal of Science Education, 1*(2), 205–222.

West, C. K., Farmer, J. A., & Wolff, P. M. (1991). *Instructional design: Implications from cognitive science.* Englewood Cliffs, NJ: Prentice Hall.

Wiggens, G. *Toward a more thought-provoking curriculum,* undated publication from the Coalition of Essential Schools, Brown University, Providence, RI.

CHAPTER 3

Developing a Course Rationale

After completing this chapter, you should be able to:

1. Understand the relation between a rationale and a set of ILOs.
    a. Know that a rationale guides curriculum development by providing overall direction.
    b. Know that a rationale serves to justify a set of intended learning outcomes.
    c. Know why a particular rationale may justify many different sets of ILOs and a set of ILOs may be justified by many different rationales.
2. Know that a rationale incorporates a set of values within three frames of reference (that is, the learner, the society, and the subject matter), to gether with a statement of educational goals. This knowledge should include an understanding of how each frame of reference provides distinct bases for justifying the educational goals.
3. Construct a rationale for a given set of ILOs. This rationale should include all component parts.
4. Analyze a statement of the rationale for a course into its component parts, determine whether or not the goals are well stated, and identify the values and assumptions implicit in the statement.

"Why do we have to learn this stuff?" "What good is this going to do me?" "This is a waste of time, I'm never going to use this!" Such expressions, if not frequently voiced by students, are frequently thought by them. And answers all too often are not readily available or are unsatisfactory to both students and teachers. This lack of purpose and justification is also reflected in the conduct of a course. As a teacher, you should always be thoughtful about your work, able to articulate your goals and to justify the

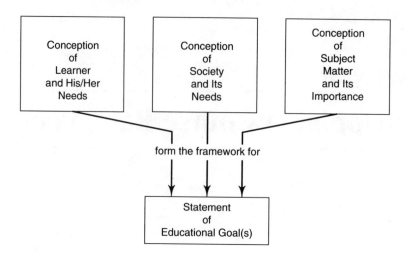

time and resources spent striving for those goals. This chapter is about justification. It is not just an exercise in rationale writing but a framework for dealing with the "why" questions that could and should be asked about the course.

A course rationale is a statement that makes explicit the values and educational goals underlying the course. The rationale serves the purpose of justifying the learnings that students are to acquire during the course as well as justifying the methods and procedures employed in teaching the course. The rationale also serves the related purpose of guiding the planning of other course components. The values and educational goals expressed in a rationale reflect the rules and expectations that will underlie the way the course will be taught; they express the emphasis and tone that the teacher will give to the course. Last, the rationale serves as a check on the consistency of the various course components in terms of these values and goals. The values and goals expressed in a rationale are related; that is, goals are desirable only as they reflect certain values of the planner.

VALUES AND ASSUMPTIONS

As any parent of a preschooler knows, the answer to a "why" question can be followed by another "why" question *ad infinitum.* Although an educational goal answers the "why" question for a given set of ILOs, we can always ask the question "why these educational goals?" and follow the answer to that question with another "why" question. Our answers to successive "why" questions are framed in terms of more and more basic values and assumptions regarding education and, ultimately, life in general. Rarely do course planners examine these basic values and assumptions; nevertheless, they underlie the course's rationale.

The values and assumptions underlying the rationale concern the role of the individual in society, the societal role of education, the nature and purposes of society and human beings, the relation of the future to the present, the question of what knowledge is most useful, and the purpose for which it should be useful.

QUESTIONS FOR DISCUSSION: VALUES AND ASSUMPTIONS*

1. Individual–Society

    Is education an investment that should pay off to the society, or is its main purpose to increase self-realization? Are there other purposes that education fulfills?

    What is the individual's proper role in society—passive participant, rebel, agent for encouraging rationally directed change, middle-class conformist, rugged individualist, warrior, peaceable resister, employed person, parent, competitor, cooperator?

2. Societal Role of Educational Institutions

    Is it the job of educational institutions to perpetuate present society or to encourage a restructuring of society? If the latter, what direction should the restructuring take?

3. Societal Purposes

    What is it that makes a good society? Are free enterprise and capitalism as we now know them essential to democracy?

    What constitutes progress—technological advances, increased gross national product, improved social conditions, increased knowledge?

4. Present–Future Orientation

    Is education preparation for adulthood or should education help individuals live their present life to the fullest? Is the future predictable? Can it be used as a basis for planning?

5. Gratification of Needs

    Should needs be gratified when they arise or should gratification be delayed?

6. Termination–Recurrence of Education

    Should education terminate or should it recur throughout life as needs arise?

    Should education before adulthood be devoted to the pursuit of individual interests rather than provide basic skills? Can the individual afford to wait for these basic skills?

7. Utility of Subject Matter

    Is a subject matter useful if it enables the individual to solve a relatively narrow range of problems and perform a relatively narrow range of skills?

    Is a subject matter useful if it influences the way an individual experiences things, as the arts often do by enriching the individual's imagery?

    Is a subject matter useful if it enables an individual to interpret the world by providing concepts for use in processing information?

    Is a subject matter useful because it is helpful to adults in today's world? because it will probably be of use to the individual in the future?

---

* Adapted from Grobman (1970, pp. 107–108).

because it will be of use in further learning? because it can be applied in everyday practical situations?

Which is of more utility, an exposure to, and an understanding of, the popular culture or the classics?

8. General–Specialized Education

Are liberal studies less or more useful to those secondary school students least likely to pursue them further in college?

As the level of necessary training increases with an increasing technology, does the level of general education required to profit from training (and probable retraining) increase or decrease?

These questions are obviously difficult for an individual to answer, let alone for a group of individuals to achieve consensus on. No wonder, then, that value differences and disputes about goals underlie much of the debate about what our educational institutions should teach (see Goodlad, 1984; Pai, 1990; Powell, Farrar, & Cohen, 1986). Although it would be overly ambitious to attempt a conclusive answer to these questions, a careful consideration of the purposes and significance of a particular course at this point in planning can contribute greatly to the coherence and validity of that course.

RATIONALE AND ENTRY POINT IN PLANNING

Logically, the rationale comes first in course planning. This is the often-cited position taken by Ralph Tyler (1950).* Nevertheless, other factors may influence what comes first in course planning. The "entry point" (that point at which the actual process of course planning begins) may be determined by any number of considerations. As we mentioned in chapter 2, motivation to develop a course may come from a mandate or a philosophy. A grant, materials, the availability of an expert, or physical facilities such as a laboratory or special audiovisual equipment may suggest that the course planning process be begun.

In the absence of other compelling factors, the statement of the rationale fits best as a course planning step immediately after the initial thinking about ILOs and before the step in which ILOs are refined. This is true for several reasons. First, anyone planning a course has a notion, however vague or unarticulated, about the overall aims of the course. The task of clearly articulating this rationale is best accomplished after some thought has been given to the particulars of the course. Second, a well-articulated rationale provides a guide to the refining of course ILOs as well as to other steps in the planning process. This guide can serve to help keep the course components consistent and focused. In the writing of a rationale you will probably make decisions or confirm implied aims. Subtle or even major alterations in your viewpoint may make some ILOs no longer consistent with the rationale. In this case, it will be most appropriate to consider the ILOs a second time. In any event, a carefully

---

* But note that Tyler (1975) recognizes the need to be flexible with regard to entry point in planning.

constructed rationale, one that accurately represents your overall purposes and shows how the ILOs express those purposes, is essential in helping you to refine your ILOs.

COMPONENTS OF A COURSE RATIONALE

Every person holds values that express conceptions of people, practices, and institutions, as well as other aspects of that person's world. A course rationale, if it is to be useful and complete, should express a planner's values at least in terms of the learner, the society, and the subject matter. These valuative considerations, expressed in a rationale, are the "determinants" (Gwynn & Chase, 1969), "sources" (Tyler, 1950; Zais, 1976), "influences" (Tanner & Tanner, 1980), "data-sources" (Goodlad, 1966), "platform" (Walker, 1990), or "criterial sources" (Johnson, 1967, 1977) for the course. Historically, a major curriculum issue has been what values shall underlie the purposes of American education. Proponents for a society-centered, child-centered, or subject-matter-centered curriculum have at times opted for their value position to the exclusion of all others. Our view is that course planners must give careful consideration to all three of these value areas, although a completed rationale might emphasize only one or two of the areas.

The Problem

A rationale begins by presenting the problem or situation that the curriculum is intended to address. Curriculum development arises out of a desire to solve some practical problem. A practical problem (as contrasted with a theoretical problem) "arises when someone identifies conditions that they want to ease or eliminate" (Walker, 1990, p. 162). Formulating the problem that drives your curriculum, or as Vickers (1968) puts it, "appreciating the situation," is not a simple matter. As Walker has argued, "a completely adequate posing of a problem offers a model of the problem, which explains its symptoms, origins and causes, and an interpretation of the problem's significance, which explains why this problem deserves attention and cannot be lived with anymore" (Walker, 1990, p. 171). Clearly, your rationale will not be able to express a complete posing of the problem. However, the more completely and adequately you formulate the problem, the more likely your curriculum will address it.

The Learner

Values regarding the learner express conceptions of what individual learners are like and what they need. Smith, Stanley, and Shores (1957) identified two variations in conceptions of learners. The first one emphasizes education that prepares the individual for achieving maximum social and economic success. The second conception views individual needs and interests in terms of developing a well-balanced person. These two sets of values would probably underlie different sets of educational goals. The debate about "cultural literacy" highlights this issue (see Bloom, 1987; Hirsch, 1987; Ravitch & Finn, 1987).

Expressing a conception of the learner gives you the opportunity to deal with the issue of the individual learner's unique interests, abilities, learning style, and needs. It is important to specify the intended audience for the course and what you assume to be their unique needs and interests. The following examples illustrate conceptions of the learner as expressed in actual course rationales.

Literature, High School: Students may be seen as people working through life, looking for satisfaction, for pleasure, and for value. Every person needs to find beauty and meaning in the world. Beauty and meaning—these elements make the world more enjoyable in good times, more tolerable in bad. The worst situation is seeing life devoid of sense and without aesthetic pleasures. Many studies provide access to beauty and meaning (including science and religion, for example) but the study of literature, because it may be written about anything (including science or religion, for example), affords the student a direct and broad approach. Not every student may find interesting questions or tentative answers in literature, but if a literature course opens that form of art and knowledge (often depreciated in our technological society) to a few students, it is worthwhile. For young people trying to make sense of the world and themselves, reading works of literature may provide some insights. This means that students must have the opportunity to bring their own meanings to the text; a course that depends on the use of secondary sources and simply presents literature as others have read it will distance the works from the students.

Basic Math, Ninth Grade: Basic math is intended to help the individual gain self-confidence through success in math and take pride in the ability to meet or exceed societal standards for performance, including job-related uses. Most important, a knowledge of mathematics increases an individual's versatility in communicating with others, and in understanding the world through observations and through the media.

The Society

The assignment of societal values might involve informed voting, environmental awareness, rapid social change, racial intolerance, uncontrolled technology, and so forth. Values with respect to the society concern conceptions of social responsibilities or societal constraints and how the course can help the individual meet these responsibilities or deal with these constraints. The attitudes, knowledge, and skills learned in a course are, from this perspective, those required for participation in the social group.

Societal values vary and may be directed toward socialization, preservation of the social order, or preparation for citizenship. Bilingual and multicultural education are two very important societal values having significant effect on the curriculum (see Ambert & Menendez, 1985; Banks, 1988). Occupational or vocational preparation is a societal value when implemented as a means to supply the work force with the skilled people needed by society at any particular time. Conceptions of society also include those views that express the need for a restructured social order or the "destructuring" of present institutional arrangements. Whatever conception of society is implied by your course, it should be articulated in the course rationale. It should make clear your explanation as to why the course goals are of value to society. The following examples are illustrative of conceptions of society as expressed in actual course rationales.

> *Indian Music, High School:* The United States is a young nation. Speed and practicality are her watchwords. There is no time for waiting. Instant tea, instant success, instant art, instant culture, instant salvation . . . these are the hallmarks of life here. The stress is more on "reaching outness," and "out-goingness" than on introspection or self-knowledge. A dash of orientalism through the music of India, if made available to the young, may inject a badly needed counter-influence to the speed of life here.
>
> *English for Speakers of Nonstandard English, High School:* If these symptoms (reading problems) do not have a pathological cause, perhaps the problem is social in nature. The job situation is one example that points to this possibility. Studies have demonstrated a high correlation between reading failure and supposed "speech irregularities," especially extraordinary slurring and deletion of consonants. And statistics indicate that candidates for employment who do not speak "standard English" (and, therefore, cannot read "standard English") are shunned by the nation's employers. Clearly, this is a social judgment, since many jobs do not entail reading or writing.

Although most courses serve both individual and societal needs, the distinction between the two is important and may reflect significantly different curricular emphases. For example, an occupational education course may view work or a career primarily as a means to self-sufficiency and self-fulfillment and thus respect individual purposes and lifestyles. However, another occupational education course may view as its primary purpose the supplying of society with workers in the proper number and with the proper qualifications. Such a course may attempt to produce an "organization man" and may derive its curriculum solely from labor data and task analyses. Some courses (for example, literature and art) may aim exclusively at self-fulfillment with society receiving only the indirect benefits attributable to being populated by fulfilled individuals. Other courses (for example, social studies) may aim solely at "good citizenship," with the individual receiving only those benefits that all citizens gain from living in a stable or progressive society. Whatever the emphasis, the rationale should clearly indicate the planner's values with respect to the individual learner and to the society in which the learner lives.

The Subject Matter

The conception of the subject matter is the third area of values that needs explication in a course rationale. Values with respect to subject matter reflect the way you are approaching a particular subject and your conception of why that subject matter and that approach is significant enough to warrant a course. The rationale may stress the importance of a particular topic or discipline. Ancient history as the vehicle of our cultural heritage, mathematics as a necessary way of ordering the physical world, and literature as a storehouse of humanity's great thoughts are examples of the manner in which a rationale may treat subject matter. The balance of nature in science, the inquiry approach to history, and the Renaissance as the most magnificent period in art are examples of approaches to subject matter that might be justified in the rationale.

A rationale should express the value of the subject matter to its particular audience. Tyler (1950, pp. 27–33) asks, "What can this subject contribute to the education of young people who are not specializing in it?" In part, your answer to this question will express the value of the subject matter.

The following examples illustrate conceptions of subject matter expressed in actual course rationales.

Poetry Unit, High School: Poetry is the speech of a man speaking to men, in the words of the poet William Wordsworth. In a sense, at its inception, language itself was poetry. The poet Karl Shapiro states, "Poems are what ideas feel like." And in this light, every word at its birth is a new flash of poetry by which an individual sees a thing in a new way. Thus, poetry has always been a method of discovery as well as a way of knowing. What we seek to know through poetry is the world and ourselves, perhaps mainly ourselves.

Filmmaking, High School: This course attempts to introduce the language of film in much the same way that a parent might introduce a child to English; the course focuses on the problem of getting the student to speak. Thus, the course is more interested in helping students *express* themselves adequately through film than it is, say, in filling their heads with notions of proper cinematic diction or syntax. Just as a parent might steer a child away from obviously incoherent phraseology, this course will attempt to steer the student away from the use of unintelligible images or image groups.

Thus the rationale should include a description of what the course is about. However, equally important is a description of what the course is not about.

Wildflowers Unit, Sixth Grade: This should *not* be considered a course in floral biology or botany. The children will be studying wildflowers as organisms—not the flower as the reproductive part of a plant. Therefore, parts of a flower, pollination, and seed formation are not covered in great detail. Rather, the emphasis is on ecological relationships and man's interest in wildflowers. (If the other topics are to be covered, the course will have to be expanded considerably.)

As the conceptual map at the beginning of this chapter shows, conceptions of the learner, the society, and the subject matter form the framework for the course's educational goals.

The Educational Goal

Goals found in a course rationale should be educational goals. In considering what distinguishes educational goals from other types of goals, it is useful to consider the distinctions Zais (1976) makes. Zais distinguishes between curriculum aims, goals, and objectives. Aims are described as "life outcomes, targets removed from the school situation to such an extent that their achievement is determinable only in that part of life well after the completion of school" (p. 306). Goals refer to "school outcomes," which are long range and reflect schooling in general rather than specific levels of school. Objectives are viewed as specific outcomes of classroom instruction. Zais's description of goals and objectives corresponds closely to our notions of educational goals and ILOs, respectively. The goals expressed in a rationale should capsulize the intentions of the course and thus should be more general and inclusive than learning objectives (that is, ILOs); yet they should remain school related, the cumulative effect or result of many learnings. Goals describe anticipated educational results. *Goals are attributes or characteristics of the well-educated person rather than the specific skills or knowledge that constitute that education.* Furthermore, the educational goal stated in the rationale must be consistent with the planner's conception of the learner, the society, and the subject matter.

The following guidelines should help you to state appropriate educational goals:*

1. Educational goals should describe the desired product. What units should be offered, what instructional procedures should be used, and what environmental conditions should be maintained to achieve those results should be determined later. This means that a statement of goals should not advocate the "opportunities" to practice this or experience that. It should describe the consequence of such practice and experiences, preferably in general terms of what the students should be like as a result of education.

2. Educational goals should be stated as desirable characteristics attributable to *learning*. Educational institutions may well be expected to achieve certain social goals, such as racial balance, reduction of dropout rate, and nutritional supplementation, but these are not *educational* goals because they are not achievable through learning.

3. If more than one goal is stated, priorities should be indicated. If all goals cannot be fully achieved, which goals should be given preference?

4. The goals should indicate what each *individual* should derive. Let society's benefit be indirect and implicit. Individuals with certain characteristics result from education. They, not the schools or colleges, will create the good society. Let not the "good citizen" be a stereotype; the properly educated *individual* is the best kind of citizen a democracy can have.

5. The scope of educational goals is an important consideration. Goals should not be so broad that they give purpose and justification to anything and everything and thus mean nothing. A statement such as "a person needs to be well educated" provides no guidance, purpose, or meaningful justification for any set of learnings. On the other hand, goals should not be as narrow as ILOs. A statement such as "a person should know the names of the major world capitals" is too restrictive to serve as a justification; it is more appropriately an ILO. Considering the proper scope for educational goals is a way to make sure that the rationale is

---

* Adapted from Johnson (1972, pp. 4–8).

more than educational rhetoric. Goodlad (1979) and Walker and Soltis (1992) provide excellent discussions of the issues involved in formulating goals as well as many examples.

The following are examples of brief goal statements extracted from actual course rationales.

This course is designed for adults who are active in local voluntary organizations and is aimed at improving their confidence and skill in dealing with their local mass media.

Specifically, this course will provide good management and personnel for the parts function of the machinery business. Furthermore, this course will provide customers who are more knowledgeable as to what the parts function of a machinery dealership should be, so that they can make intelligent choices as to which dealerships to deal with.

The purpose of this course is not immediately to reject or regard as suspicious everything we read, but to learn how to understand the implications of what we read.

The curriculum hopes to provide parents with the necessary incentives to cultivate advantageous reading environments at home.

SUMMARY

Logically a rationale comes first in course design, but other considerations may put it in a different position in the actual planning procedure. In the absence of other compelling factors, the rationale should follow the initial thinking about ILOs (which it serves to justify) and should come before the refinement of ILOs (for which it acts as a background).

A rationale contains a general statement of educational goals. Conceptions of the learner, the society, and the subject matter form the framework within which the planner articulates these goals. The rationale serves as a guide and a check for all later steps in course planning.

A Sample Rationale

The following example is an actual course rationale developed by a teacher in training. It is not perfect, but it does illustrate one approach used in course rationales.

*Writing from Experience, a One-Semester Course for College Freshmen.**
Individuals who know who they are in a deep and secure way will be able to lead lives that are meaningful to themselves and probably useful to other

---

* This rationale is taken from a course design produced as a term project by Carol Lamm, Cornell University, 1974.

people. Education should encourage the growth of people in this direction of self-knowledge, self-confidence, and self-direction; it should not force people to grow in ways that are twisted or unnatural for them.

One place where many students are "twisted" is in traditional English classes. In reading literature, students are all too often forced to accept, without believing, a more mature and sophisticated interpretation of the work than they ever could have developed on their own, and which they find far-fetched. Their need to look into and explain their own responses to written work in any depth is usually ignored. Students are forced to write about things about which they know very little and sometimes care less; thus they develop the ability to hedge and a sense that writing—at least as far as they are concerned—is a matter of super-ficialities.

Writing from Experience is a course whose purpose is putting students in touch with their own thoughts, feelings, and experiences, and encouraging them to develop their sense of themselves, through writing and through reading other students' work.

Writing is a way of helping people think clearly. Almost all people who use writing regularly and seriously will say that writing helps them clarify their thoughts. Their descriptions of the process differ—some speak of fragmented thoughts on a topic coming together on paper; some of metaphors that suggest new possibilities; some of rough drafts whose ambiguities force the writer to rethink what he wants to say. In any case, good writers find a real connection between clear writing and clear thinking.

Similar processes take place when writers deal with their feelings as when they deal with their ideas. Since feelings cannot always be laid out as explicitly as ideas, a writer may have to work toward a kind of clarity that is not entirely verbal; he may have to establish a personal symbolism to deal with his feelings, for example, or he might find that he can best communicate by presenting a situation in a new and different form. However he writes about his experience, though, the writer uses writing to discover and develop himself in a way that goes below the surface.

QUESTIONS FOR DISCUSSION: SAMPLE RATIONALE

1. Having read the rationale, discuss how it conceptualizes the learner, the subject matter, and the society.
2. Is equal emphasis placed on all three considerations? If not, which conception is emphasized?
3. What are the educational goals stated in this rationale? Does it seem to strike a balance between generality without being grandiose or elusive, on the one hand, and specificity without being trivial, on the other?
4. What kind of course does this rationale imply? See if you can describe the

ILOs and the instructional plan that might follow from it. How would this course differ from other possible freshman writing courses?

5. What assumptions does the rationale make with respect to the role of the individual in society, the societal role of educational institutions, the nature and purposes of society and of human beings, the relation of the present to the future, the question of what knowledge is of most utility and the purposes for which it should be useful? What would you like to ask the planner about her course in order to identify these assumptions?

Exercise 3.1.   Below are four sets of statements, expressions, or words. Each set represents initial thinking about ILOs, and each set is for a different course. Read each list, then consider what a rationale for a course based on each list might include. Formulate for yourself (not necessarily in writing) conceptions of the individual, the society, and the subject matter, as well as goals that may be included in such a rationale. Last, try to justify these courses with another rationale that differs from the first and determine the ways in which the alternative rationale implies a different kind of course.

1. Child Raising

rewards	protection from the cold world
discipline	overprotection
attention	the spoiled child
sister/brother	permissiveness
older/younger	imagination
family get-togethers	stifling the child
privacy	home medical care
fights	"shut up" and "you're really bad"
everything begins at home	divorce
good citizenship	child abuse
fights between parents	

2. Team Games

football	team games vs. individual sports such as swimming and running
practice	
good physical well-being	praise/cheers
part of a health program	pride
physical coordination	injury
taught by games	medical attention
a healthy body and a healthy mind	teamwork
lacrosse	the need for play as a part of growth
baseball	

3. Consumer Buying

bargains

what is a bargain? (It's not a bargain unless you need it)

buy in season

be sure to buy the sales sensibly

quality vs. quantity

buying on time

guarantees

where can you haggle over the price?

waste not—want not

making use of leftovers

our sometimes wasteful economy

returnable bottles

recycling

tools can be an investment

using the public library

4. The Environment

pollution

food chain

ecology

balance of nature

cows

insects

role of the predator

industrial waste

farming in India

the pond

life cycles

human beings in relationship to their environment

people should be aware of the consequences of their actions on the environment

field trip

RATIONALES FOR ELEMENTARY SCHOOL UNITS

Many people planning elementary units find a complete rationale for each unit unnecessary. The term *rationale* as explained in this chapter is more descriptive of the justification needed for a semester's or full year's worth of planning. For an elementary unit, we suggest that you consider including an "introduction." An introduction should contain the following: (1) educational goals for the unit; (2) where the unit fits into the overall curriculum, that is, what should precede or follow it and how it fits in with the rest of the year's work; (3) your view of the learners, what they should know going into the unit, and why this content is interesting and appropriate; and (4) comments or suggestions that convey the manner in which the unit should be taught. The introduction is your chance to tell others what you might say to them if they were going to teach your unit. You should certainly use this opportunity to think about your goals and values. You may want to write the introduction to your unit as a final course planning step.

Course Planning Step 3.1. Write a rationale for your course on the basis of your initial ideas and your thoughts about the course's focus. The rationale should clearly state the course's educational goals within the framework of the learner, the society, and the subject matter.

It is easy to get lost in the forest amongst the trees. One of the dangers in paying too much attention to the components of a rationale is that you will lose sight of the purpose served by a rationale. The components, after all, are mentioned in order to help you develop a clear, cogent, and compelling justification for your curriculum. The questions that follow will help you refocus on the forest now that you have noted all the trees.

QUESTIONS FOR DISCUSSION: COURSE RATIONALE

After reading another person's rationale, use the following questions as a basis for group discussion:

1. Are you convinced by the rationale's formulation of the problem that a curriculum change is worth the bother?
2. Do you have a clear enough idea of what makes this particular curriculum different from current practice?
3. Do you have a clear enough sense of what the curriculum based on this rationale will look like? Each person in the group could try to describe a curriculum based on this rationale. Did the rationale mislead in any significant ways? Do people have misconceptions that the rationale needs to address?
4. Are you convinced that the approach is reasonable? Are there any blind spots or flaws? Does the approach appear to get to the heart of the problem?

Course Planning Step 3.2.   Revise your list of ILOs from chapter 2 in view of your course rationale.

REFERENCES

Ambert, A., & Menendez, S. E. (1985). *Bilingual education: A sourcebook.* New York: Garland.

Banks, J. A. (1988). *Multiethnic education: Theory and practice* (2nd ed.). Boston: Allyn & Bacon.

Bloom, A. (1987). *The closing of the American mind.* New York: Simon & Schuster.

Goodlad, J. I. (1966). *School, curriculum and individual.* Waltham, MA: Blaisdell.

Goodlad, J. I. (1979). *What schools are for.* Phi Delta Kappan Educational Foundation.

Goodlad, J. I. (1984). *A place called school: Prospects for the future.* New York: McGraw-Hill.

Grobman, H. (1970). *Developmental curriculum projects: Decision points and processes.* Itasca, IL: F. E. Peacock.

Gwynn, J. M., & Chase, J. B. (1969). *Curriculum principles and social trends* (4th ed.). New York: Macmillan.

Hirsch, E. D., Jr. (1987). *Cultural literacy: What every American needs to know.* Boston: Houghton Mifflin.

Johnson, M. (1967). Definitions and models in curriculum theory. *Educational Theory, 17*(2), 127–139.

Johnson, M. (1972). *Stating educational goals: Some issues and a proposal.* (A background paper prepared for the New York State Commission on the Quality, Cost and Financing of Elementary and Secondary Education.) Albany, NY: State University of New York. Mimeographed.

Johnson, M. (1977). *Intentionality in education: A conceptual model of curricular and instructional planning and evaluation.* Albany, NY: Center for Curriculum Research and Services.

Lamm, C. (1974). *Writing from experience.* Unpublished design for a course produced as a term project. Cornell University, Ithaca, NY.

Pai, Y. (1990). *Cultural foundations of education.* Columbus, OH: Merrill.

Powell, A. G., Farrar, E., & Cohen, D. H. (1986). *The shopping mall high school: Winners and losers in the educational marketplace.* Boston: Houghton Mifflin.

Ravitch, D., & Finn, C. E., Jr. (1987). *What do our 17 year olds know? A report on the first national assessment of history and literature.* New York: Harper & Row.

Smith, B. O., Stanley, W. O., & Shores, J. H. (1957). *Fundamentals of curriculum development.* New York: Harcourt, Brace, Jovanovich.

Tanner, D., & Tanner, L. N. (1980). *Curriculum development: Theory into practice* (2nd ed.). New York: Macmillan.

Tyler, R. W. (1950). *Basic principles of curriculum and instruction.* Chicago: University of Chicago Press.

Tyler, R. W. (1975). Specific problems in curriculum development. In J. Schaffarzick and D. Hampson (Eds.), *Strategies for curriculum development* (pp. 17–34). Berkeley: McCutchan.

Vickers, G. (1968). *Value systems and social process.* NY: Basic Books.

Walker, D. (1990). *Fundamentals of curriculum.* New York: Harcourt, Brace, Jovanovich.

Walker, D., & Soltis, J. F. (1992). *Curriculum and aims* (2nd ed.). New York: Teachers College Press.

Zais, R. S. (1976). *Curriculum: Principles and foundations.* New York: Harper & Row.

CHAPTER 4

Refining Intended Learning Outcomes

After completing this chapter, you should be able to:

1. Categorize ILOs into four classes: cognitions, cognitive skills, psychomotor-perceptual skills, and affects.
2. Write clear ILO statements for a course.
3. Check a set of categorized ILOs for balance.
4. Decide on the relative priority of each ILO in a set.

Chapter 2 helped you develop a set of intended learning outcomes initially categorized as skills and understandings, with little attention given to ILO format. This chapter presents guidelines for refining statements of ILOs based on your previous work. Your ILOs will become more useful for you, the course planner, and for others associated with the course. The result will be a set of clearly stated ILOs categorized according to the type of learning involved. This refined set of ILOs will be coherent, comprehensive, and consistent with the products of the preceding chapters. The ILOs will be important in later steps of course planning—in organizing the course into units, in selecting general teaching strategies, and in planning an evaluation strategy.

ILO STATEMENTS: FORM AND FUNCTION*

If you were to ask different groups of educators how ILOs should be stated, you would probably get several different answers. Educators with backgrounds in programmed instruction, educational measurement, or vocational education might list characteristics such as the following:

---

* This discussion is based on Posner and Strike (1975).

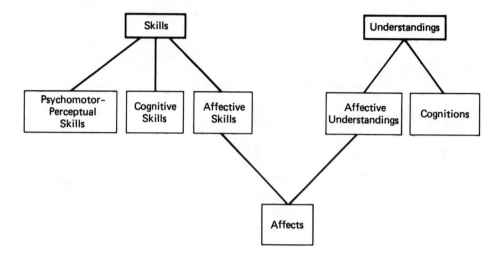

1. A subject: the learner
2. A verb: behavior, or behavior product
3. Given conditions: the situation in which the behavior occurs
4. Standards: of quality or quantity
   Example: The learner will solve nine out of ten equations containing two
   unknowns. The equations must be solved within 20 minutes.
   (Schutz, Baker, & Gerlach, 1971)

1. The overall behavior act
2. The important conditions under which the behavior is to occur (givens,
   restrictions, or both)
3. The criterion of acceptable performance
   Example: Given a human skeleton, the student must be able to correctly
   label at least 40 of the following bones; there will be no
   penalty for guessing. (List of bones inserted here.) (Mager,
   1962)

1. The situation faced by the pupil
2. The learned capability
3. The object of the performance
4. An action verb
5. Tools and other constraints: how must the performance be carried out
   Example: Given instructions to interpret the meaning of Hamlet's
   soliloquy in simple terms, generate an alternative
   communication of the soliloquy by writing sentences of simple
   content. (Gagné & Briggs, 1979)

Differences among these writers are apparent both in terminology and in the
precise number of elements considered important. But, they agree on at least one

point: A well-stated objective must specify the observable behavior that a student would exhibit if the objective was achieved. Because of this emphasis on behavior, we call objectives satisfying this requirement *behavioral objectives* (*performance objectives* is an equivalent phrase).

If, however, you were to ask your question on stating ILOs of educators with a primary interest in the humanities, particularly in the arts or with an allegiance to existentialism and phenomenology, you might get a hostile response to the idea of using a set of predetermined intended learning outcomes as a basis for planning instruction (see Macdonald, 1965).

Viewed in the context of this broad range of positions, much of the current debate on ILO statements suffers from a fallacy of too few options. It is as though one must be an advocate of either behavioral objectives or antiobjectives. We hope to point the way to an approach that is more sound educationally than either of these two extremes and more consistent with prevailing value systems of teachers. The position we take is that ILOs can be invaluable in curriculum development, so long as we allow the form of ILO statements to fit the subject matter and the specific function we wish the statements to serve.

There appear to be three primary functions that ILOs should serve: (1) they should guide instruction and instructional planning; (2) they should communicate to others (for example, students and the public) what we are using precious time, money, and facilities for; and (3) they should serve as a basis for developing indicators or evidence of success.

Instruction and Instructional Planning

Many educators claim (and we tend to agree) that instructional planning should be based primarily, though not exclusively, on what we want students to learn. They say other criteria, such as interest and personal involvement, are important, but if our teaching is not designed to lead to desirable learning outcomes, we are wasting our students' time and the valuable resources of the community. What do you think about this claim? What would constitute an argument against this claim? Clearly, the view of curriculum would have to be different from the one presented in chapter 1. (See, for example, Peters, 1977; Frankena, 1977; Schwab, 1978; and Walker, 1990, for discussions about whether or not there is a need for educational goals and objectives.) If you want instructional planning to be based on what students should learn, ILO statements should clearly specify the kind of learning outcomes involved so that appropriate instructional strategies can be designed to accomplish them. In addition, teachers should think about this during instruction, thus influencing their actions and responses in the classroom. As we will see in chapter 7, the type of learning intended for students influences the kinds of instructional strategies preferred.

Communication

It is reasonable to claim that students and other interested parties have a right to know what we hope to achieve when we ask them to cooperate with us and commit themselves to a presumably valuable educational program. It is even likely that if students understand a program's direction, they will learn more easily. To serve this function of communication, ILO statements should express the planner's intents as unambiguously as possible. Further, these statements should express these intents clearly to someone who is not already knowledgable in your subject matter. As we will see later in this chapter, clarity is no simple matter. Clarity usually turns out to be more an ideal than an attainable goal. In many cases what is perfectly clear to one person is not to someone else.

Planning Evaluation

It is not enough for us to want students to learn important ideas and skills; we must also find out whether or not they are achieving these desirable learning outcomes. If we find a discrepancy between what we intend and what students achieve, then we have a basis for course revision. But we do not want the evaluation tail to wag the educational dog. We do not want to teach in a way that atomizes and perhaps trivializes our ILOs by requiring them to indicate not only what we want learned, but also what sample behaviors we will accept as evidence that we have been successful. In order to help us plan an evaluation, an ILO statement must be stated only with enough clarity for us to generate from each ILO a set of observable behavioral indicators. Each behavioral indicator points to a piece of evidence that can be used to determine whether an ILO is, or is not, being achieved.

However, there is a serious danger in establishing a set of behavioral indicators of learning. Research indicates that students take seriously work for which they will be held accountable. Some teachers who use behavioral objectives claim to be seeking understanding or other significant outcomes but need indicators on a lesson-by-lesson basis in order to determine whether or not the students are "getting it." The problem here is that students quickly discern what teachers are looking for, that is, what "counts." Then the students merely adopt an approach to learning that enables them to perform as expected without attempting to achieve understanding of the subject matter. Students will not strive to undertand unless teachers are prepared to hold students accountable for understanding. Perhaps you recall doing well on a test even though you did not really understand the material covered.

ILOs versus Behavioral Objectives

Any behavioral indicator is only evidence of learning (and tentative evidence at that) and should not be confused with the ILO to which it corresponds. In contrast to advocates of behavioral objectives, we believe that an ILO typically need not, and probably should not, be stated in terms of observable behaviors because many ILOs are understandings or unobservable skills. Here we are distinguishing between ILO statements and statements derived from ILOs for data collection. (See Figure 4.1.) These latter statements are more properly termed behavioral evidence or indicators, and their function is to guide our observations. These statements, in contrast to ILOs, must be stated in terms of observable behavior. Therefore, a "behavioral objective" represents a lumping together of two distinct concepts in curriculum, ILOs or learning objectives (that is, what we want learned) and behavioral evidence (that is, how we will tell if the desired learning has occurred).

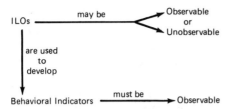

FIGURE 4.1 The relationship between ILOs and behavioral indicators.

From this discussion it should be obvious that there are no hard-and-fast rules for stating ILOs irrespective of audience, subject matter, and the particular approach to the subject matter. What can be claimed is that, by indicating the kind of learning involved and by using words that are not ambiguous, an ILO statement should be expressed clearly. Clarity does not typically require stating behaviors in observable, highly specific terms. If you restrict your options in stating ILOs, for example, by insisting that verbs must all describe observable behaviors, these restrictions will have a serious impact on your curriculum. You may well limit the kinds of ILOs that you will be able to express, thereby narrowing your curriculum or, worse yet, emphasizing trivial aspects of the subject matter while avoiding profound matters. You will also likely need large numbers of ILOs to express your intents.

Remember, course planning is not a strictly linear process but consists of constant revisions and improvements of earlier ideas as our thinking progresses. A final set of clear ILO statements cannot be written once and for all by simply working through this chapter. Instead, you will find that your course ILOs will be improved by a series of successive approximations. Chapter 2 resulted in your first approximation of ILO statements. The present chapter should help you through a second and better approximation. Subsequent chapters dealing with instructional and evaluation planning will result in more revision. When and if your course is ever taught, still further revision will be required. A cyclical process of course planning is the one most likely to lead to an educationally sound course design.

With this rationale for our approach in mind, let us proceed to refining the ILOs you developed in chapter 2.

CATEGORIZING ILOS

The first step in refining ILOs is categorizing them further according to the kind of learning involved. This additional categorization will have a significant impact on general teaching strategies (chapter 7) and evaluation (chapter 8) because each category entails special considerations for instructional planning and evaluation. Moreover, by classifying ILOs into these categories, gaps and redundancies will become evident, and revising, deleting, and generating new ILOs will become necessary. These are all aspects of the refining process.

Categorization is an instrumental step in course planning. You may not always categorize ILOs when you plan a course. But the categories we use in this chapter will compel you to think more clearly about what you want learned in your course. It is these conceptual tools that we hope you learn in this chapter.

For the purposes of course planning, four categories of ILOs appear useful;* they represent a refinement of the understanding/skill categories discussed in chapter 2. The "Skill" category is subdivided into "Psychomotor-perceptual skills" (roughly speaking, physical skills), "Cognitive skills" (mental skills), and "Affective skills." Similarly, the "Understanding" category is subdivided into "Cognitions" (conceptual knowledge) and "Affective understandings." Affective understandings and affective skills are then grouped together under the umbrella term "Affects." The conceptual map at the beginning of this chapter provides a graphic summary of the relationship between this four-category system and the two-category system used in chapter 2.

Categorizing Understandings

The ILOs classified as understandings in chapter 2 are now further categorized as either cognitions or affects.

An important kind of learning in most schools and colleges consists of the ideas (that is, facts, concepts, generalizations) that teachers hope students will learn as a result of schooling. We label this type of knowledge or understanding *cognition*.

Cognitions, in contrast to skills, have no directly observable referent. (Nevertheless, as we will see in chapter 8, observable behaviors such as explaining, listing, comparing, naming, discussing, and the like will have to be used as indirect indicators that cognitions have been achieved.)

Remember that your categorization should include all possible cognitions. Cognitions may be in the form of statements, lists of terms, or conceptual maps like those in chapter 2.

The following are examples of cognitions:**

1. The student should realize that almost all written and oral language affects individual bias to some degree.

---

* The categorization scheme proposed here is similar to categories of learning types or learning outcomes proposed by others. One set of categories familiar to many educators is that proposed by Bloom (1956), and Krathwohl, Bloom, and Masia (1964), among others, in their "taxonomies." Our psychomotor-perceptual category resembles the psychomotor domain described by Harrow (1972). Our affective category very roughly corresponds to the affective domain of Krathwohl et al. (1964). The cognitive skills in our scheme correspond to levels 2 through 6 of the Bloom (1956) cognitive domain. Our category of cognitions is a substantial expansion of level 1 of the cognitive domain (Bloom, 1956). Level 1 refers to memory of information, while our cognitions encompass the entire range of knowledge acquisition from memory to "deeper" levels of understanding. Gagné (1977) also describes categories of learning types. His "attitudes," "motor skills," "intellectual skills," and "verbal information" roughly correspond to our "affects," "psychomotor-perceptual skills," "cognitive skills," and "cognitions." Gagné's "cognitive strategies" represent a blend of our "cognitions and cognitive skills."

** A word about examples. Throughout this chapter you will find exercises and examples consisting of ILO statements. These ILOs are meant to elaborate the points made in the discussion. At this point in *Course Design*, the ILOs with which you are working are those you developed in chapter 2. These ILO statements are rough and were formulated without a great deal of concern as to their wording. For this reason, many of the ILOs used in the examples are worded so that they are similar to the kinds of ILOs with which you will be working. These ILOs, therefore, are not necessarily exemplars of clearly stated ILOs.

2. The student should know that proper timing can affect media coverage and attention.
3. The student should understand that a proper diet is one that contains all the essential nutrients.
4. Set theory.
5. Associative property of addition.
6. Bill of Rights.
7. Minimalist art.

Affect is an umbrella term that could cover a wide range of outcomes. Here we will take a narrow view and treat affects in a manner appropriate for course ILOs. It is likely that underlying most affects is understanding or knowledge, and thus, one major subtype of affective ILO is affective understanding. Affective understandings are distinct from cognitions largely in the knowledge or content area with which they deal. Affective content focuses on the self or the interaction of self with others. ILOs of this type may be expressed with verbs such as *understand, know that,* or others commonly used to indicate cognitions. Whenever the *object* of these verbs reflects self-knowledge, however, they are more appropriately categorized as affects rather than as cognitions. ILOs embodying self as content include developing aspects of a positive self-concept, understanding how behaviors are self-serving, awareness of feelings and attitudes, and knowledge that one is a capable learner. ILOs embodying the interaction of self with others include knowledge or understanding of the factors motivating others' behavior, knowledge that questioning a teacher's authority often leads to conflict, and understanding how to interact with others to achieve certain goals.

The other major subtype of affective ILO is affective skill. Affective skill involves being able to behave in ways that reflect certain attitudes. Counselors have to be able to listen and respond with empathy. Teachers and parents must act with patience when working with children. Members of a school committee must listen tolerantly to complaints by citizens. There are many situations when we must behave in a manner that can be characterized by an affective skill. These skills can often be taught and may, therefore, form a portion of the ILOs for a course.

Some people include aspects of personality as affective ILOs. We disagree. We believe that aspects of personality refer to those traits or attributes that describe the kind of person someone should become, not what the person should learn. Attributes are distinguished from affective skill and understanding in that they are *general* characterizations of people, rather than specific teachable skills that can be applied at the student's discretion or specific teachable knowledge of some affective content. For example, being honest in an interview situation is more specific and more teachable than being an honest person. The same could be said about being able to listen empathically as opposed to being an empathic person. In these two examples, the first items could be considered affective skills and the second might be viewed as attributes.

There are several reasons for not including attributes as ILOs. First, as we already pointed out, attributes can be modeled by a teacher, but they cannot be taught directly in the same sense that other ILOs can. Instead, students become more studious, honest, empathic, and the like as they develop intellectually and emotionally. Intellectual and emotional development involves both physiological maturation and the personal integration of things learned from teaches, parents, siblings, peers, and others. Even if we ignore the feasibility problems in teaching attributes, there may be serious ethical reasons for not considering attributes as ILOs.

We recommend that any attributes important to the course be incorporated into the rationale as educational goals. In this way their relationship to planning and teaching is more clearly defined. In addition, ethical and value issues are explicitly discussed in a rationale. While this approach doesn't eliminate the issues involved in teaching attributes, it does confront these issues more openly and directly, since a justification for these goals will be stated and thus will be readily available to debate.

The categorization of an ILO as affective has important implications because planning for affects raises issues and presents problems unique to this domain of learning.

The following are examples of affective ILOs:

1. The student should realize that commercial messages affect perceptions and judgments.
2. The student should be able to listen to others, and to respond with empathy and without altering the content of the message.
3. The student should be able to avoid ethnic and racial stereotyping.
4. The student should be able to convey enthusiasm when talking.
5. The student should be able to treat children firmly and with warmth.

Notice that many of these ILOs can be achieved, in part, through cognitive learning. For example, "realizing that commercials have affected perceptions" can be taught by showing students a variety of real-life situations where their perceptions have been shaped by commercial messages.

Affective and cognitive ILOs may be conceptually distinct but, frequently, teaching one type of ILO also entails teaching other types. This interrelatedness of cognitive and affective (and, we might add, psychomotor-perceptual) aspects of learning is not surprising when we remember that education involves teaching wholly integrated individuals whose thoughts and feelings accompany almost everything they do.

Categorizing Skills

The ILOs classified as skills in chapter 2 are now further categorized as either cognitive skills or psychomotor-perceptual skills.*

Cognitive skills demonstrate the ability to use or apply cognitions. Learning ideas without acquiring corresponding competencies does not necessarily enable the

---

* For the sake of simplicity, our previous discussion assumed that *all* your affective ILOs were originally categorized as understandings. We then showed how these ILOs consist of affective understanding and/or affective skill ILOs. We will not discuss affective skill ILOs any further in this section, although, strictly speaking, they are skills.

student to *use* the ideas. That is, cognitions may be prerequisites for performing cognitive skills, but they are not always sufficient. Often it is also necessary to teach students how to *apply* their ideas when analyzing a situation, creating a communication, predicting the occurrence of an event, solving a problem, constructing a logical argument, or comparing similar ideas.

The following are examples of cognitive-skill ILOs:

1. The student should be able to recognize the outward signs of presupposition in English.
2. The student should be able to analyze the decisions made by editors in terms of the factors that influence those decisions.
3. The student should be able to develop a logical argument.
4. The student should be able to distinguish descriptive from judgmental statements.
5. The student should be able to analyze and solve work problems involving the use of algebra.
6. The student should be able to evaluate a potential apiary site.

As you will recall, the flowcharts you created in chapter 2 include either cognitive skills or psychomotor-perceptual skills.

Psychomotor-perceptual skills encompass skills, abilities, and/or movements that are more observable than any of the other categories. The following kinds of learning are usually included in this category: fundamental and reflexive movements (for example, running, jumping, balance, and posture), perception and perceptual discrimination (for example, physical orientation, bodily awareness, visual tracking, and sound differentiation), physical qualities (for example, endurance, speed, strength, and agility), and complex skilled movements (for example, typing, sawing wood, playing golf, and performing trampoline stunts).

The following are examples of psychomotor-perceptual ILOs:

1. The student should be able to dodge a moving ball.
2. The student should be able to measure the volume of water using a 100 milliliter burette within a tolerance of 1 milliliter.
3. The student should be able to bisect a line with a compass and a straight edge.
4. The student should be able to move across the floor with grace.
5. The student should be able to adjust a carburetor's needle valve.
6. The student should be able to discriminate aurally among the calls of common local bird species.
7. The student should be able to pronounce correctly the *r* in French.

Blends of ILO Categories

Categorization will be useful in later planning steps. Nevertheless, one should not consider learning outcomes as belonging to one of four discrete categories. More often than not, an ILO represents a "blend" of several categories, rather than belonging to a "pure" category. In fact, it is probably more useful to think of the categories as continuous rather than discrete.

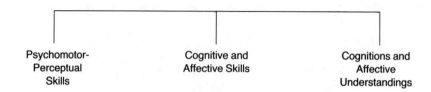

Psychomotor-
Perceptual
Skills

Cognitive and
Affective Skills

Cognitions and
Affective
Understandings

It is difficult to think about a psychomotor-perceptual skill without a cognitive component. The sort of knitting one can do while watching TV comes close to being purely physical, since it requires little, if any, conscious thought. However, dismantling a carburetor or operating a 35-mm camera both have significant cognitive components and thus represent a blend of psychomotor and cognitive skills. Plotting a graph for equations of the type $y = 1/x$ is largely a cognitive skill but with the psychomotor-perceptual component of actually doing the plotting.

It is also difficult to think about a cognitive skill existing without accompanying knowledge (that is, an accompanying cognition). A person can rehearse and memorize information, and thus acquire the cognitive skill of being able to recall the information without knowing or understanding the information in any real sense. However, a cognitive skill, such as recall, is usually accompanied by some degree of comprehension. Being able to solve long division problems involves knowing some procedure for doing it. Being able to analyze a novel requires substantial knowledge of the genre and literature in general. Cognitive skill ILOs almost always must be accompanied by cognitions to be meaningful. Cognitions can also be taught in a rather "pure" state. A person can be taught to know or understand something without also being taught to use the knowledge in the performance of some skill. While it is likely that once a person knows or understands something, this knowledge will be used in a variety of ways, the point is that none of these uses were intentionally taught.

Our purpose in having you categorize ILOs is not to force every ILO into a "pigeonhole" but to help you consider the kind of learning you are trying to accomplish in your course. Therefore, while you should try to decide if an ILO is properly categorized as a psychomotor-perceptual skill, cognitive skill, cognition, or affect, you need not base your decision on a criterion of "pure" membership. Since our categories are not mutually exclusive but instead continuous, you may want to categorize and label ILOs as being blends or mixtures of more than one category.

Course Planning Step 4.1.   Review the ILOs you have categorized as either skills or understandings. Understandings should now be categorized as cognitions or affective understandings. Skills should be categorized as psychomotor-perceptual skills, cognitive skills, or affective skills. If an ILO does not fit neatly into a category, do not hesitate to create an appropriate blend. If a psychomotor skill requires an accompanying cognitive component, write this component in. Similarly, if a cognitive skill requires an accompanying cognition, supply it. Remember, by categorizing ILOs you are making an important decision regarding the kind of learning you want your ILO statements to communicate.

GUIDELINES FOR CLARIFYING ILOS

You should be careful not to go overboard when stating ILOs. It is better to teach a few things well than to compile a long list of ILOs that may detract from a coherent course focus. It is likely that your conceptual map and accompanying statement, and your outline of the course content, taken together, provide an elegant and clear statement of cognitions. It may be superfluous to include a separate statement for each cognition. Similarly, a well-developed flowchart succinctly expresses a set of skills. In general, consider the overall goals of clarity, communication, and usefulness in working through the remainder of this chapter.

In the following guidelines for clarifying ILO statements, each category is discussed separately.

Expressing Cognitions

Cognitions involve the incorporation or storage of information in the brain. Describing the precise nature of this information storage—how information is acquired, remembered, and used—is a major task of the interdiscipline of "cognitive science." Most cognitive science descriptions of acquired information stress the interrelatedness, structure, and context of knowledge elements. Knowledge elements themselves vary and can include data about people (for example, their ages, occupations, traits), objects (for example, their size, color, shape), and events (for example, their sequence, time of occurrence), and a variety of more abstract information (for example, context and causes of events, purposes and lifestyles of people). Thus, acquired information varies in its structure and the quality and quantity of component knowledge elements. (See the discussion of conceptual mapping in chapter 2.) Numerous terms are used to characterize the structure and context of acquired knowledge elements. Examples include *concepts, facts, principles, propositions, generalizations,* and *theories.* Because these terms have no consistent and accepted usage, we will refer to these and similar cognitions by the everyday expression "ideas."

Ideas enable us to reduce the complexity of our environment through the use of abstractions. Abstractions make possible the grouping of objects, people, or events and thus enable us to respond to classes of things rather than to each and every thing that enters our awareness (Bruner, Goodnow, & Austin, 1956). When we acquire knowledge, we learn to make sense of our world, in contrast to the newborn child who perceives only "bloomin' buzzin' confusion." Ideas constitute our technical vocabulary and are our tools of thought; they are the units with which we think. The more fundamental and generative our ideas, the more potential we have for understanding basic processes (Bruner, 1960, 1966).

Acquiring knowledge enables us to analyze situations, solve problems, and discover relationships among events. While the acquisition of an idea may be necessary for the performance of such tasks, it is rarely sufficient. In addition to acquiring knowledge, we need to learn to use it; for the purposes of this book, such additional learning is considered cognitive skill rather than cognition. If acquiring an idea is supposed to result in certain capabilities, then those capabilities should also be made explicit as ILOs categorized as cognitive skills.

Ideas can be linked to form other ideas. For example, ideas about investment, ownership, and free market economy may be related to form an idea of capitalism. The space shuttle may become part of a person's idea of aircraft. Sometimes relationships between two or more ideas form statements of ideas that assert something. For example, the ideas of force (simply stated as a push or a pull) and acceleration (the rate of change in an object's velocity) can be combined to form an idea expressed as the following *assertion:* The acceleration of an object is directly related to the force exerted on it. Or the idea of bachelor may be used with the idea of "singleness" in the following two ideas that are assertions: All bachelors are single. All single persons are bachelors.

Note that the first statement is true and the second statement is false. Ideas that are assertions can be either true or false depending on the veracity of the relationships. This is not the case with all ideas. Many ideas such as aircraft, capitalism, and acceleration may be useful or useless, but they cannot be considered true or false.

Just as ideas differ in their structure, complexity, and truth value, they also frequently differ in the ways in which they are best taught. Some ideas are best taught through typical examples, through definitions (note the definitions of force and acceleration given above), and by showing the relationships between ideas (as in a map). Other ideas (particularly those that are assertions) are taught through argumentation, experimentation, or, more generally, through convincing presentations of reasonable evidence (as in a geometric proof or a set of empirically derived data).

Learning the meaning of an idea that is an assertion also entails learning the ideas inherent in it. For example, learning that force equals mass times acceleration consists of learning what force, mass, and acceleration mean and learning the ideas of mathematical equality and multiplication. A teacher cannot reasonably expect students to learn the meaning of an assertion if the students do not know the component ideas.

Just as assertions can be considered as the relation of one set of ideas to another, assertions can also be linked together, making the structure of the acquired information increasingly interrelated. At some level, this information begins to characterize our general thought in a certain area. We refer to ideas structured in this way as a *conception.* The origin of species can be considered from either an evolutionist or a creationist conception. In either case a conception will influence how new information is interpreted and what new information is important. A pond observed by a biologist and by an elementary school child could lead to very different interpretations and even different observations. A child may have a conception of a pond as a place where frogs and other interesting creatures live. An artist may see a pond in terms of the interplay of light and shadow in the subtle shadings of reflection and shoreline vegetation. A biologist's conception could be dominated by energy transfer and ecological ideas. As a result, the biologist may observe the particular network of related organisms in a pond environment, the artist may observe a perspective and location for a landscape, and the child may observe the hiding place of a large bullfrog.

Any set of terms for describing acquired knowledge is actually a set of rough labels referring to the acquired knowledge's depth, structure, extent, and complexity. Expressing cognitions clearly is difficult; we recommend several ways of expressing cognitions in order to achieve clarity. One way is to construct a conceptual map for the entire course, as well as for each unit. The maps should contain all the major ideas to be learned in the course. Relationships among ideas that correspond to assertions can be numbered. Two examples of the use of conceptual maps with lists of numbered assertions follow.

Our Federal Government, Sixth Grade Unit

1. The purpose of the federal government is to serve and protect its citizens.
2. The Constitution of the United States describes the rights of citizens and the structure and functions of the government.
3. The government has three branches—executive, legislative, and judicial.
4. The legislative branch enacts laws, the executive branch enforces laws, and the judicial branch interprets the Constitution.
5. The three branches are balanced, each checks the others' power, so that no single branch becomes too powerful.
6. Citizens influence government by electing representatives to the legislature and by participating in the election of the president (executive).

(See Figure 4.2.)

Energy, Eighth Grade Unit

Definitions

Energy   The capacity to do work; the property of a system that diminishes when work is done to another system.

Work   A transference of energy equal to the product of force times the distance through which the force acts.

Fossil fuel   Combustible matter composed of organic compounds from the remains of living organisms, usually plants.

Solar power   Technology that uses the sun's energy directly to do work.

Assertions

1. The earth's energy comes from two major sources—either from substances on earth (nuclear energy) or from the sun.
2. The sun's energy is used by plants directly. Others use the sun's energy indirectly by using plants or a plant product as fuel.
3. Living things use energy for growth and the maintenance of life. People use energy to do work.

Figure 4.3 is a map of a junior high school science unit about how and from where earth derives its energy, and how this energy is used. (The map is incomplete.) Each

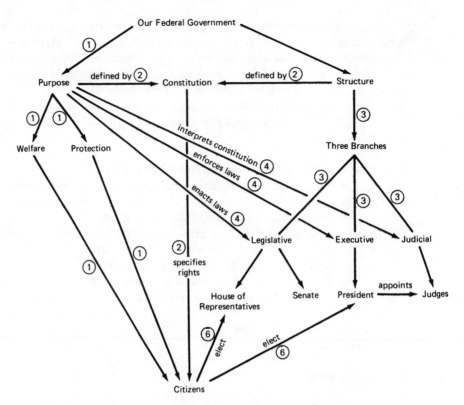

FIGURE 4.2 Conceptual map for "Our Federal Government."

term that signifies an important idea is listed and accompanied by a careful, clear, and concise definition. (If formal definition is not possible, the meanings of the terms can be explored using examples to help clarify them.) Ideas that are assertions desired as course ILOs are also represented on the conceptual map. Other examples can be found in the sample course designs presented in appendixes A, B, C, and D.

A *conception*, as stated earlier, is more than the sum total of the ideas which compose it. A conception constitutes a way of looking at the world. It roughly corresponds to a person's theory or belief system regarding some set of phenomena (for example, a conservationist's view of offshore oil exploration). Entire conceptual maps, or, in some cases, major aspects of the maps, will serve as representations of conceptions. Characterization of one's thinking by a conception is, in part, a result of acquiring considerable knowledge. If such a conception is a desired result of the course, it should be reflected in the map. In addition, the conception might be described in the rationale as an educational goal.

One way of further clarifying what we mean by "learning a cognition" is to consider where the learner stands in relation to the knowledge. There are several properties that describe this relationship. One property is memory; knowledge can be retained in the mind. Another property is comprehension; one can grasp the linguistic

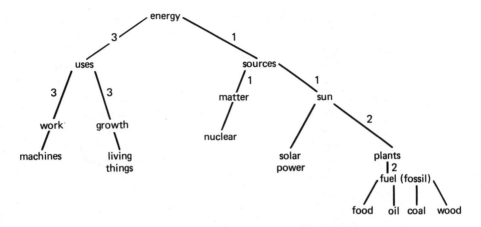

FIGURE 4.3 Conceptual map for "Earth and Its Energy."

and literal meaning of a statement expressing an idea. A third property is undestanding and justified belief. Understanding involves going beyond literal or linguistic comprehension and grasping ways in which ideas are related to other ideas. Understanding ideas that are assertions involves justified belief. By justified belief we mean acceptance of an assertion as true based on good reasons. Each of these properties implies a different kind of learning and suggests a distinct instructional strategy and evaluation technique. Any particular cognition might embody one or more of these three properties. Note that being able to use knowledge to solve problems, interpret data or situations, generate questions, and critique a work of art are cognitive-skill ILOs. Notice too that such ILOs are good illustrations of cognitive skills that must be accompanied by cognitions.

It is often wise to supplement a course's cognitions with explanations of their meaning, stipulating which of the three properties applies to each cognition. It is crucial for the planner not to shy away from ILOs just because clarity is difficult to achieve. Such a tendency can only harm the course by limiting its scope and perhaps rendering it trivial.

Course Planning Step 4.2.   Using maps, a list of definitions of major terms, a list of assertions, and statements with supplementary explanations (when needed), express your course's cognitions.

Expressing Affects

Expressing affects in a manner that clearly communicates their meaning to others is not a simple matter. In part the difficulty arises from the fact that many verbs used in stating affects (particularly verbs for affective understanding, such as *realize, be aware of,* and *appreciate*) have broad and overlapping meanings. Furthermore, the referent for the verb in a particular affective ILO (for example, "the opinions of others") may be clear in your mind even though there are many different ways to use that referent in a clearly stated affective ILO. For example, "to listen tolerantly to the expression of others' opinions that differ from the student's own," "to be able to evaluate one's ability to attend to views that differ from one's own, and "to be able to seek out the opinions of others as a means of personal growth and development" are all different ILOs that have essentially the same referent (the opinion of others). Therefore, the key ingredients of a clearly expressed affective ILO are (a) a carefully chosen verb describing the affect, (b) the identification of the referent (or object) of the verb, and (c) a thorough description of the specific context for the affect. Your rationale or introduction is an ideal place to set the context so that affective ILOs communicate clearly.

How might you improve the clarity of the following ILO by incorporating each of the three ingredients mentioned above?

The students should appreciate others' opinions.

One interpretation of this rather ambiguous ILO is as follows:

The student listens attentively (the verb) to views of others that are different from his or her own (the referent or object of the verb), particularly during discussions on controversial issues (the specific context).

The following illustrate other clearly expressed affective ILOs:

1. The student should understand how he or she responds to a literary work—what in the work and what in himself or herself leads to that response.
2. The student should be able to criticize another student's fiction writing objectively and constructively.
3. The student should view the claims made in TV advertisements with skepticism.
4. The student should know what he or she likes in commercial architecture and why.

Course Planning Step 4.3.   Using the guidelines discussed above, review your affective ILOs. Rewrite any affects that need clarification.

Expressing Cognitive Skills

Cognitive skills can often be expressed clearly in a single sentence. The range of verbs that can communicate the kind of behavior intended in a cognitive-skill ILO is broad. The following verbs are useful in describing the behavioral aspect of cognitive skills: *define, acquire, identify, recognize, translate, give in own words, illustrate, prepare, represent, interpret, reorder, differentiate, distinguish, draw, explain, demonstrate, estimate, infer, conclude, predict, determine, extend, interpolate, extrapolate, fill in, apply, generalize, relate, choose, separate, organize, use, employ, transfer, restruc-*

ture, classify, distingiush, detect, identify, clarify, discriminate, assert, categorize, deduce, analyze, simplify, devise, write, tell, produce, constitute, transmit, originate, modify, document, propose, plan, design, specify, develop, combine, organize, synthesize, compute, formulate, judge, argue, validate, assess, decide, compare contrast, standardize, appraise. *

Some verbs represent "higher order" or more complex cognitive skills than others (see Bloom, 1956). For example, "the ability *to distinguish* a valid from a faulty research design" is not as complex a cognitive skill as "the ability *to design* a valid research study for a particular problem." Likewise, "the ability *to organize* ideas and write an effective piece of expository prose" is a more complex cognitive skill than "the ability *to explain* a piece of expository prose in your own words." It is important in stating cognitive-skill ILOs to write them at a level of complexity appropriate for the situation.

Earlier in this chapter we noted that cognitive skills are often complex blends of cognition and skill. In chapter 2 we discussed cognitive task analysis of skills that results in a flowchart of subskills and component understandings (that is, cognitions). Just as conceptual maps form an important part of clearly stated cognitions, flowcharts form an important part of clearly stated cognitive skills. Statements of "higher order" or complex cognitive skills should be accompanied by a flowchart or list that represents major components of the skill. Keep in mind that you must determine the depth or level of detail that best serves to clearly state your cognitive-skill ILO. The following examples illustrate complex cognitive skills stated with the help of a flowchart or list.

List
1. The student should be able to design a simple experiment given a hypothesis.
   a. Identify the variables of the hypothesis.
      (1) Determine which variables are presumed causes (independent) and which are effects (dependent).
   b. Operationalize the variables in measurable terms.
   c. Understand the idea of control and the need to vary variables one at a time (in a way that each variable's influence can be independently determined—thus one at a time or orthogonally).
   d. Form the set of all possible combinations of variables.
   e. Analyze the measured effect of independent variables on dependent variables in order to reach a decision about hypothesis.

Flowchart
2. The student is able to write a well-constructed narrative. (See Figure 4.4.)

---

* The guidelines for stating cognitive skills and psychomotor-perceptual skills list some verbs that are descriptive of behaviors often sought in these types of ILOs. You might want to use a thesaurus when searching for a verb that accurately communicates your intention. The appropriateness of any verb used in an ILO depends on that particular ILO. There is nothing inherently "good" about a particular verb.

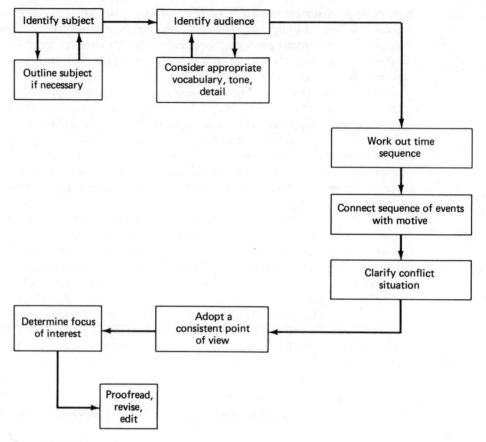

FIGURE 4.4   Procedure for writing a narrative.

Although the following cognitive-skill ILOs consist of subskills and understandings, they are clear enough to guide further planning and thus do not have to be accompanied by a flowchart or list:

1. The student should be able to specify the information needed to calculate the trajectory of an object.
2. The student should be able to draw a Venn diagram illustrating a simple problem of set membership.
3. The student should be to classify common foods into their appropriate nutritional group.
4. The student should be able to detect underlying racism or sexism present in commercial messages and advertisements.

Course Planning Step 4.4.   Considering the guidelines for stating cognitive skills, review your ILOs. Make sure that all ILOs intended as cognitive skills communicate their meaning clearly. Rewrite any ILOs that are unclear and include flowcharts or lists for the most complex cognitive skills.

Expressing Psychomotor-Perceptual Skills

Psychomotor-perceptual skills also can often be stated in a single sentence. Any verb that accurately describes the intended behavior can be used in stating psychomotor-perceptual skills. The following verbs are often used in ILOs of psychomotor-perceptual skill: *run, jump, walk, repair, dismantle, construct, type, write, flex, stretch, pull, push, grip, handle, hear, discern, detect, follow, pronounce.*

The examples illustrate some clearly stated ILOs of psychomotor-perceptual skill:

1. The student should be able to calibrate a triple-beam balance visually.
2. The student should be able to mount a pack and frame weighing 75 pounds correctly on the back.
3. The student should be able to focus correctly a microscope at 400×.
4. The student should be able to band a crate safely and securely.
5. The student should be able to apply wood stain so as to enhance the wood's grain optimally.

Course Planning Step 4.5.   Considering the guidelines for stating psychomotor-perceptual skills, review your ILOs. Make sure that all ILOs intended to be psychomotor-perceptual skills communicate their meaning clearly. Rewrite any ILOs that are unclear. Add flowcharts as necessary.

Clarity: Some Examples

The preceding steps for expressing ILOs are all aimed at achieving clarity. A clear ILO accurately indicates the kind of overt or covert behavior being sought and the context for that behavior. Clear ILOs also identify the knowledge a learner is supposed to acquire in a way that makes the structure of that knowledge explicit. A clear ILO statement is neither so vague that it cannot guide planning nor so specific that it is trivial. Some ILOs can be expressed with sufficient clarity in a single statement. On the other hand, some ILOs require maps, charts, definitions of terms, or explanatory paragraphs in order to achieve clarity. This is particularly true for complex cognitive skills and cognitions. However, there is no hard-and-fast rule. Clarity is the goal toward which to work. The following examples may help to illustrate these points:

1. *The student should know the ten trees most frequently found in the northern hardwood forest zone.* The object or content portion of this ILO (that is, "the ten trees most frequently found in the northern hardwood forest zone") is clear. But the verb *know* is not clear. "Know" in this instance could mean "be able to recognize" (a cognitive skill), "remember the names" (a cognition), or "understand why these trees are

the most numerous" (a cognition), among other things. Of these possibilities, only the last one, "understand why they are most numerous," would require an accompanying map. In any event, for this ILO to be clearly stated, "know" must be elaborated so that it is more descriptive of the desired behavior.

2. *The student should comprehend the expression "due process of law."* This ILO is a cognition. The verb *comprehend* is aimed at grasping the meaning of the expression and is clear. A map identifying the ideas that constitute "due process" should accompany this and other ILOs for this course. Since the content and the nature of the intended learning are clear, a teacher could plan instructional activities and evaluative measures for this ILO.

3. *The student should be able to explain the practicality of fad diets.* The use of "fad" suggests that such diets are *not* practical, but the ILO requires the student to explain their practicality. If this statement is to express a cognitive skill, it might be clearly stated as "the student is able to evaluate fad diets for their practicality in terms of the body's nutritional requirements." If the ILO is to express a cognition, it could state that "the student should understand the nutritional deficiencies of most fad diets." If the student is to evaluate fad diets, a flowchart describing how one proceeds to do this would be helpful. If this is a cognition, the ideas needed to understand nutritional deficiencies should be mapped.

4. *The student should be able to relate economics, sociology, politics, and geography to history.* As a cognitive skill, "ability to relate" is not an adequate description of desired behavior, and the content portion of this ILO is too general. If a cognitive skill is desired, the ILO might be expressed as "the student should be able to synthesize economic, political, sociological, and geographical factors in an analysis of a historical event." This is a very complex cognitive skill, one that assumes a great deal of knowledge on the part of the student. To state all this presumed knowledge is beyond the requirements of a clearly stated ILO.

5. *The student should be able to load a 35-mm camera correctly.* This ILO is a clearly stated psychomotor-perceptual skill. The behavior and the context are clear. A teacher should have little difficulty in understanding precisely what is intended here.

6. *The student should be able to fix a broken bone.* The psychomotor-perceptual skill might better be expressed as "the student should be able to fashion a temporary splint for a simple fracture of an arm or leg."

7. *The student should appreciate backpacking.* For this affective understanding, *appreciate* is not a clear verb. If an affect is desired, the ILO might better be stated as "the student views backpacking as an experience having deep personal meaning." As a cognition, the ILO could state that "the student understands why individuals take up backpacking as a recreational activity."

PRIORITY OF ILOs

Your list of ILOs may be short (5–10) or lengthy (more than 50). The list may include ILO statements with supplementary explanations (when needed), lists of concepts and assertions, and flowcharts or lists for skills. The list may be a conglomerate of crucial learnings and relatively trivial learnings. If the list is long, it may be wise to eliminate some less important items. Everything cannot be taught. Often we accomplish more (in depth) by attempting to cover less (in breadth). Now is the time to consider priorities.

By indicating ILOs of highest priority, the set of ILOs as a whole communicates its meaning more clearly. Guidance for later phases of course planning (instructional planning and evaluation) is provided by specifying which ILOs are of greatest importance to the course and thus should receive greatest emphasis. Priority should be assigned in terms of the course as a whole rather than on the basis of each category of ILO. Your course may be balanced in terms of category or have a cognitive, affective, or psychomotor emphasis. Whatever the emphasis, high-priority ILOs are those cognitions, affects, cognitive skills, and psychomotor-perceptual skills that a student cannot leave the course without learning.

The following guidelines should assist in selecting the ILOs of highest priority in your course:

1. The basic question to consider in selecting high-priority ILOs is: If only a limited number of ILOs can be achieved by the students in your course, which would they be? ILOs thus identified are high-priority ILOs.
2. Consider the goals expressed by your course rationale. Which learnings are absolutely essential to achieving those goals?
3. Consider your ILOs in light of your central question(s). Which ILOs must be achieved to enable a student to answer or deal with the central question(s)?
4. Consider your ILOs in light of your conceptual map and flowchart. What ideas occupy central or high positions on your map? What relationships among which ideas are crucial to understanding the content?
5. Are some ILOs prerequisites for a number of other ILOs, so that they must be mastered early in the course?
6. What would a learner have to achieve for you to consider that learner as having successfully completed your course?

Course Planning Step 4.6.   Identify ILOs in your course that are of highest priority based on a reexamination of (a) your course rationale, (b) your central questions, (c) your conceptual map, and (d) your flowchart(s). Place an asterisk next to each high-priority ILO on your list of categorized ILOs. Leave unmarked those ILOs that are important but not of *highest* priority. Now eliminate from your list any ILOs that you consider trivial.

OVERALL BALANCE OF ILOS

The final step in refining ILOs is to examine them in their entirety, focusing on their balance as a whole. Each ILO should be clearly stated by this point.

Balance entails completeness and nonrepetitiveness of ILOs as well as consistency with the course rationale. The following questions may be helpful when considering course balance:

1. Do the ILOs fit the rationale? Reread the course rationale, and examine the set of ILOs. Are learnings in conflict with the rationale? Are additional learnings necessary to make the course fit the rationale more closely? Does the rationale now need revision?
2. Are there redundancies? This requires looking for ILOs that are essentially restatements of other ILOs. These can be literal repeats or ILOs stated so that they encompass other ILOs.
3. Are there gaps? This requires looking for ILOs that are not included. This may occur in the form of content or behaviors that are omitted.
4. Is there a predominant category? This requires looking at the four categories of ILOs. Are one or more categories missing? Does one category seem overloaded? For example, if someone is to define, describe, explain, and identify something, aren't there also some ideas that person should grasp? If someone is to value a procedure, should the individual understand or be able to do it?
5. Are high-level cognitive skills supported by appropriate cognitions? Conversely, are cognitions accompanied by learnings that make use of the ideas?

You have great freedom in determining the balance of the course. There may be valid reasons for gaps, redundancies, or the predominance of a particular category of ILOs. *These considerations are intended only to assist you in creating the balance you desire.*

Course Planning Step 4.7.   Examine your ILOs as a whole, looking for overall balance. This requires eliminating redundancies and filling in gaps. Check the rationale for consistency and make any necessary revisions.

SUMMARY

The combination of proper category, indication of relative priority, clearly described behavior and content, and supplementary explanations or elaborations when needed should give you a set of ILOs that is clear, coherent, and comprehensive. A person reading your intended learning outcomes should have little difficulty understanding what is supposed to be learned in your course. These ILOs will be used in instructional planning, which, among other things, consists in designing the units of your course.

The ILOs should be appropriate to serve this function. That is, each ILO should be teachable and learnable rather than a goal that can be achieved only indirectly (that is, through other learnings). This chapter ends for the time being the curricular aspects of course planning. You have now clearly formulated the "what" and "why" of your course. What remains are instructional considerations (the "how") and evaluation ("Was it successful?"). Naturally, you will return to your ILOs and rationale as further planning lends new insights to your previous work.

QUESTIONS FOR DISCUSSION: INTENDED LEARNING OUTCOMES

1. Are the ILOs clear enough for each of the following:
   a. Instructional planning. Are there too many or too few ILOs to be helpful to someone attempting to plan units and lessons for the curriculum? Do the ILOs provide sufficient direction for this planning?
   b. Communication. Do they communicate clearly the important skills and understandings learners are to acquire?
   c. Evaluation planning. Do the ILOs provide enough direction for someone wishing to evaluate the curriculum? Remember, your ILOs need not suggest specific evaluation techniques. There may be many possible evaluation approaches appropriate for a particular ILO. The danger in worrying too much about evaluation at this point is that you might not try to teach something that is difficult to evaluate.
2. Are the ILOs consistent with the rationale? If not, which element (i.e., the rationale or the ILOs) needs to be adjusted?
3. Critique the ILOs on the basis of their validity, importance, and feasibility.
   a. A good test of validity is to give your ILOs to subject matter experts to determine if they agree that each ILO represents something that is true, up to date, and/or consistent with accepted practice. For example, you might ask if the facts you are proposing to teach are true, whether the theories are the most current ones available, and whether the skills are accepted by experts as the state of the art.
   b. A good test of importance is to ask experts if they think that you are proposing to teach any trivial ILOs, whether the high-priority ILOs are the most important for people to learn, and whether there are any significant ILOs that you have omitted.
   c. A good test of feasibility is to ask teachers if any of your ILOs are too ambitious or cannot be effectively taught to people at this particular age or with this particular background. Also, you might inquire about the length of time it is likely to take the learners to master each of the ILOs.

Do not abandon your proposed ILOs because someone has questioned their validity, importance, or feasibility. You might be able to show that the critic is wrong. But do consider the criticism.

REFERENCES

Bloom, B. S. (Ed.) (1956). *Taxonomy of educational objectives, Handbook I: Cognitive domain.* New York: David McKay.

Bruner, J. S. (1960). *The process of education.* New York: Vintage.

Bruner, J. S. (1966). *Toward a theory of instruction.* Cambridge, MA: Harvard University Press.

Bruner, J. S., Goodnow, J. J., & Austin, G. A. (1956). *A study of thinking.* New York: John Wiley.

Frankena, W. K. (1977). Educational values and goals: Some dispositions to be fostered. In A. A. Bellack & H. M. Kliebard (Eds.), *Curriculum and evaluation.* Berkeley, CA: McCutchan.

Gagné, R. M. (1977). *The conditions of learning* (3rd ed). New York: Holt, Rinehart, & Winston.

Gagné, R. M., & Briggs, L. J. (1979). *Principles of instructional design* (2nd ed). New York: Holt, Rinehart, & Winston.

Harrow, A. J. A. (1972). *Taxonomy of the psychomotor domain: A guide for developing behavioral objectives.* New York: David McKay.

Krathwohl, D. R., Bloom, B. S., & Masia, B. B. (1964). *Taxonomy of educational objectives. Handbook II: Affective domain.* New York: David McKay.

Macdonald, J. B. (1965). Myths about instruction. *Educational Leadership, 22*(8), 613–614.

Mager, R. F. (1962). *Preparing instructional objectives.* Palo Alto, CA: Fearon.

Peters, R. (1977). Must an educator have an aim? In A. A. Bellack and H. M. Kliebard (Eds.), *Curriculum and evaluation.* Berkeley, CA: McCutchan.

Posner, G. J., & Strike, K. A. (1975). Ideology versus technology: The bias of behavioral objectives, *Educational technology, 15*(5), 28–34.

Schutz, R. E., Baker, R. L., & Gerlach, V. S. (1971). *Stating educational objectives.* New York: Van Nostrand Reinhold.

Schwab, J. J. (1978). The practical: A langugage for curriculum. In I. Westbury & N. J. Wilkof (Eds.), *Science, curriculum, and liberal education: Selected essays, Joseph Schwab.* Chicago: University of Chicago Press.

Walker, D. (1990). *Fundamentals of curriculum.* New York: Harcourt Brace Jovanovich.

CHAPTER 5

Forming Units of the Course

After completing this chapter, you should be able to:

1. Cluster a set of ILOs into coherent units after considering each of the five bases for clustering. This ability assumes an understanding of each of the five bases and how they can be used for clustering ILOs.

2. Design instructional foci for each of a course's units. This ability entails an understanding of four criteria: appropriateness for ILOs, appropriateness for learners' abilities, motivation, and feasibility.

To this point we have been concerned with developing a set of refined and carefully expressed intended learning outcomes and with explicating educational goals in a course rationale. The intended learning outcomes express what is to be learned. The educational goals and the whole rationale justify these ILOs.

With this chapter, we enter the instructional planning phase of course design. Instructional planning consists in planning a series of events around a particular activity, stimulus, or vehicle for communicating ideas. These events and the focus around which they are planned are designed to lead to the learning of something desirable (that is, the ILOs). Instructional planning can occur at various levels of specificity, ranging from individual lessons to groups of lessons to groups of groups of lessons. Planning around a focus and toward an objective can be done at a highly specific level (that is, lesson planning) and at a general level (that is, unit planning). This chapter deals with the task of forming units for the course, each unit specifying one or more "instructional foci" around which the instructional events will be organized and one or more ILOs toward which the events will be directed. The subsequent chapters continue the process of instructional planning by showing how

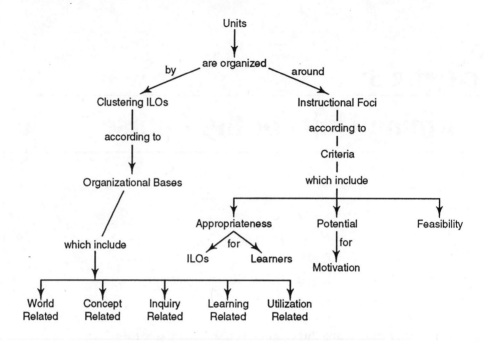

to sequence and group the units into a unit outline and how to specify the instructional events that are to take place within each unit.

Forming the course's units can be approached in two distinct ways. We can cluster the ILOs into coherent groups, with each group then becoming a unit. Alternatively, we can design units around an instructional activity (for example, a field trip), stimulus (for example, a case study), vehicle for communicating ideas (for example, a sonnet), or around groups of activities, stimuli, and vehicles for communicating such as themes and problems. Each activity, stimulus, or vehicle for communicating that serves as a means of learning a set of ILOs we will call an *instructional focus*. Whether we form units around clustered ILOs or instructional foci, we are breaking up the course into "chunks"; each chunk represents a coherent portion of the course designed to achieve a specified set of ILOs. Since neither approach is appropriate for all courses, we present both approaches to forming units. Then you, as the course planner, can decide which approach (or combination of approaches) is most appropriate for your particular course.

Elementary teachers rarely plan courses. As we have said in chapter 1, the *unit* is a more appropriate curriculum "chunk" for elementary planning. The next two chapters of *Course Design* deal with course organization and the arrangement of units in particular. If you are planning a unit instead of a course, you will have to make some adjustments so that the guidelines presented are appropriate for your level of planning. The principles of course organization will remain the same but their application will have to be modified. We have incorporated suggestions for these changes at the end of this chapter. Elementary teachers or others planning units should read through that section before doing any further work.

Forming internally coherent units is one major step in producing a coherent course design. This built-in coherence increases the likelihood that students will see the interrelationships of course elements and thus see how the elements fit together into a whole.

CLUSTERING ILOs INTO UNITS

The clustering of ILOs into units is a process of creating units from the list of ILOs previously developed. But before presenting guidelines for clustering ILOs, we must deal with some preliminary questions.

Units

How big is a unit? No precise answer, such as "between five and ten ILOs," can be given to this question. Nevertheless, considerations of coherence and scope may help you decide on the unit size for your course.

First, a unit should be a coherent whole. That is, the ILOs composing the unit should make some sense together. Upon completion of a unit the student should know or be able to do some things that are related to each other. Each unit should be given a title. This serves as one check on the coherence of each unit.

Second, each unit should be manageable in scope. Students should be able to view each unit as a coherent set of learnings that relate to one another. Each unit should not be so large as to inhibit discussing it as a whole. For example, a unit on the Civil War is probably more manageable than a unit on American History, 1850–1900. Similarly, a unit on Central Tendency in Statistics is more manageable than a unit on Descriptive Statistics.

Should ILOs from various categories be together in a unit? This is a difficult question to answer unequivocally. It probably makes sense to mix various categories of ILOs (that is, cognitions, cognitive skills, affects, psychomotor-perceptual skills) together in a unit. This is particularly true when the ILOs support one another. But a unit may, at times, consist of just one type of ILO. This can occur when basic ideas or skills need to be provided or a set of ideas or skills is so important that it must stand alone for emphasis.

Can an ILO be included in more than one unit? Certainly, particularly high-priority ILOs. How many units should you have? As many as you need to cover or include all the ILOs, with repeated ILOs if necessary for emphasis.

As in earlier course planning steps, the guidelines presented here should assist you in making decisions but not make decisions for you. Which ILOs should be clustered to form a unit may sometimes appear obvious and at other times appear almost arbitrary. We recommend that you go through the guidelines and consider the options you have for clustering before deciding which ILOs will compose each of your units.

Bases for Clustering ILOs

There are five major organizational bases for ILOs. ILOs can be organized according to (1) the way the world is (*world-related*), (2) the way ideas are organized (*concept-related*), (3) the way knowledge is generated (*inquiry-related*), (4) the way pupils learn (*learning-related*), and (5) the way learnings are to be utilized in life (*utilization-related*). These five main bases for organizing ILOs are used in this chapter to help you think about clustering ILOs into units. These same bases are used again in the next chapter to help you organize the units into an appropriate sequence.

The world-related basis for clustering groups ILOs in a manner consistent with the temporal, spatial, and physical properties of things as they exist in the world. Some world-related dimensions include: chronology (should ILOs be grouped because they occur or occurred simultaneously or because they all represent causes or effects?); physical complexity (should ILOs be grouped because they deal with objects, processes, or entities alike in their physical characteristics?); and location (should ILOs be grouped because they entail content that is arranged together spatially in the world?). The world-related basis is particularly applicable for ILOs dealing with events, objects, or processes that have identifiable properties.

Following are two examples of ILOs clustered on a world-related basis:

Unit: The Pond (location)
Identifies pond-dwelling insects.

Identifies pond-dwelling fish.

Compares types of plant life common in ponds.

Understands the contribution of various forms of pond life to ecological balance.

Unit: Low Tide (chronology)
Understands the effect of the moon on tides.

Understands how some fish are trapped at low tide.

Remembers names of plant and animal life observable at low tide.

The concept-related basis for clustering is a consideration of the conceptual properties of ILOs. Some concept-related dimensions include: logical prerequisites (should ILOs be grouped because the ideas must be learned and understood before later ideas can be understood?); conceptual similarity or relatedness (should ILOs be grouped because the ideas involved are related in some respect?). Note that the concept-related basis is particularly applicable to cognitions.

When considering clustering ILOs on a concept-related basis, the conceptual maps developed in chapter 2 should prove helpful. Examination of the conceptual map should enable you to identify related or similar concepts. Some maps may also help you identify ideas that are logically prerequisite to other ideas.

Following are two examples of ILOs clustered on a concept-related basis:

Unit: The Circle (prerequisites)

Understands the notion of diameter.

Understands the notion of radius.

Understands the notion of circumference.

Remembers the value of pi.

Can relate the diameter to the circumference of a circle.

Can apply the formula for the area of a circle to various problems.

Unit: Respiratory Systems (conceptual similarity)

Understands the mechanics of how people breathe.

Understands the process by which fish extract oxygen from water.

Understands respiration in reptiles.

Understands how seagoing mammals breathe.

The inquiry-related basis for clustering is a consideration of how knowledge is produced. Using this basis for grouping ILOs, the question to consider is: Should ILOs be grouped together because they represent similar phases of inquiry (that is, the process of generating, discovering, or verifying knowledge)?

Following is an example of ILOs clustered on an inquiry-related basis:

Unit: Facts about Light that Require Explanation

Knows that light travels in straight lines.

Knows that light can be reflected.

Knows that light can be absorbed.

Knows that light can be transformed into heat.

Knows that light can be diffracted.

Knows that light can be refracted.

The learning-related basis for clustering is a consideration of how students will learn the ILOs. Some learning-related dimensions include: familiarity (should ILOs be grouped because the learners are familiar with them or should familiarity vary within the clusters?); interest (should ILOs be grouped because they are of equal interest to the students or should relatively more interesting ILOs be grouped with relatively less interesting ones?); difficulty (should ILOs be grouped because the ease or difficulty with which they can be learned is similar or should the groups have a mix of difficulty level?). Another dimension of the learning-related basis is empirical prerequisites. An empirical prerequisite as used in reference to ILOs is something a student must learn to do before learning a subsequent ILO; that is to say, skill B cannot be learned unless the student has already mastered skill A. This dimension is particularly appropriate in the areas of psychomotor and cognitive skills. Your flowchart(s) will be particularly relevant here. In general, the learning-related basis is appropriate for any course because how students learn is an important consideration in planning.

Following are two examples of ILOs clustered on a learning-related basis:

Unit: English Classes (ease of identification)
Can identify nouns.

Can identify the singular/plural distinction and formation.

Can identify irregular nouns.

Can identify verbs.

Can identify inflectional endings of verbs.

Can identify irregular verbs.

Unit: Beginning Skating (empirical prerequisite and difficulty level)
Ability to start.

Ability to balance standing still and gliding.

Ability to stride.

Ability to stop.

Ability to regain one's feet.

Ability to push off.

Ability to maintain posture.

The utilization-related basis for clustering is a consideration of how the ILOs are to be used in the future by the learner. If there are skills that are part of a procedure and hence will be performed together in the future, you may want them to be grouped into a unit. Here again your flowcharts may be useful. Certain facts or theories may be expected to be used together in solving personal or societal problems, so this is a consideration for clustering. The utilization-related basis for clustering is probably most appropriate in occupational, recreational, or problem-oriented courses because the future use of the ILOs is specific and even predictable, and this future use of the learnings is probably a prime, if not the only, reason for the course.

Following is an example of ILOs clustered on a utilization-related basis:

Unit: Water Pollution (societal problem)
Understands how industry contributes to pollution.

Understands how municipalities contribute to pollution.

Understands how private citizens contribute to pollution.

Clustering Guidelines

1. When clustering, do not hesitate to include a particular ILO in more than one unit. This may be necessary to emphasize a high-priority ILO or because more than one unit's topic suggests its inclusion.

2. Undoubtedly the five bases for clustering vary in their appropriateness for particular courses. There may be other bases for clustering ILOs. Moreover, any set of ILOs composing a course can be clustered in many ways. What is important here is flexibility; you should at least consider the many alternatives available to you.

3. Consider your course rationale in making clustering decisions: think about what you have said about your approach to the subject matter, about your conception of the individual learner and the learning process, and about how you see that individual interacting with society. Course planning decisions are interdependent; what you decided about the course's approach should influence present decisions.

4. Keep in mind that any one consideration for clustering is probably inadequate and that the ILOs composing a unit are probably best clustered on several bases simultaneously. Don't hesitate to use a novel approach to unit organization.

Course Planning Step 5.1.   Cluster the ILOs of your course into units. You may find it convenient to use code numbers from your list of ILOs so that you do not have to write them over (for example *CS1* refers to the first of your cognitive skills in your list from chapter 4).

If you experience difficulty in completing Step 5.1 or if you find that the clustering of ILOs seems an inappropriate approach to forming units for your particular course, you may want to try forming units around instructional foci. This alternative approach to forming units is particularly appropriate for those courses in which nearly all the ILOs cut across all or most units. Naturally, if most ILOs apply to many units, clustering the ILOs into units presents serious problems. In such cases, some focal points other than ILOs would have to be designed to produce a set of coherent units. The section that follows presents such an approach. You should read this section whether or not you use this approach to forming units; eventually you will have to select instructional focal points in order to plan a teaching strategy for each of your units.

FORMING UNITS AROUND INSTRUCTIONAL FOCI

Clustering ILOs into units is a useful approach in constructing units for most courses. Nevertheless, many planners (particularly those mainly concerned with affective ILOs) have difficulty thinking about units without first considering their teaching strategies.

Instead of forming units around clusters of ILOs, units can be designed around themes and problems; around instructional activities such as projects, debates, field trips, papers, and experiments; around stimuli for thinking such as case studies and photographs; or around vehicles for communicating what we know or feel, such as books or poems. Such themes, problems, activities, stimuli, and vehicles for communicating are *instructional foci;* they serve as focal points for learning and lend coherence to a set of ILOs.

Chapter 7 shows how an instructional focus forms the "heart" of a teaching strategy (that is, what teachers and students *do* with the instructional focus). But the point here is that instructional foci may be useful for you to think about as an approach to course organization.

Instructional Foci

The concept of an instructional focus for learning has been most clearly explicated by John Goodlad (1963). Notice that he uses the term *organizing center,* which we will consider equivalent to our term, *instructional focus.*

> The organizing center is a focal point for teaching and learning. It is instructional flesh on curricular bones. The organizing center for learning occupies a segment of time and of space, being intended for identifiable learners in a specific instructional setting. It may consist of a picture to look at, a book to read, an idea to contemplate, an issue to resolve, a place to visit. The organizing center may be useful for a few minutes, hours, days, or even weeks. It may be intended for one person or for hundreds. (p. 94)

Instructional foci (or organizing centers) are not aims or ends in themselves but are instrumental in nature. For example, "understanding the wave properties of light" could not be considered an instructional focus, while "experiments with shallow, glass-bottomed tanks of water ('ripple tanks')" might well be an instructional focus through which the properties of waves might be observed and understood. In a similar manner, "appreciating the beauty of late Beethoven quartets" couldn't be an instructional focus, though it is a potential ILO; but "the March University concert" is a good candidate for an instructional focus.

Much attention has been given to "ends," in terms of specified ILOs. Now we turn to the "means" by which these ends are to be accomplished. Several words of caution are appropriate here. First, it is sometimes difficult to distinguish clearly between means and ends. For example, if one activity in a course is to " type several original business letters," this could clearly be expressed as an ILO, "the student has the ability to type grammatical and correct original business letters" or as an instructional focus, "original business letters." It could even be seen as an evaluative device to determine whether or not the above ILO has been accomplished. The temptation in such a situation is to shrug and plead indifference. After all, as long as the student really does type several original business letters, does it matter what we call it? The answer to this is that it isn't just "what we call it," but how we see, understand, and plan the educational process.

Instructional foci (as the term implies) serve as focal points for course-related experiences; ILOs provide direction for those learning experiences. Together they give the structuring of learning experiences coherence and rationality. Thus, while it may appear difficult to determine what is a means and what is an end, it is important to decide on means and ends and to consider the consequences of these decisions for the course as a whole.

In his discussion Goodlad (1963) specifies several criteria for good instructional foci. First, instructional foci should encourage students to practice the type of behavior desired. In our terms this would suggest that the instructional focus should put the student in a position to use the psychomotor or perceptual skills to be taught, to use cognitive skills in making genuine choices, and to come to an understanding of content. Next, the instructional focus should encourage the practice of several behaviors simultaneously. This is not only for the sake of economy and efficiency, but is also completely consistent with the formation of unit-sized course chunks. It is the function of the instructional focus to help students achieve a coherent set of ILOs within a particular unit.

Goodlad (1963) goes on to specify other criteria. The good instructional focus should support and complement learnings in different areas of instruction. It should be planned with both past and future learning outcomes considered and should be designed so that all levels of student accomplishment, from the highest to the lowest, are reached, and so that a variety of interest and learning styles are accommodated. A good instructional focus has an educational significance of its own. It has intrinsic merit and contributes to a worthwhile learning experience. Whenever possible, literature should be good literature, art and film of recognized worth, and texts of high quality. Finally, Goodlad suggests, a good instructional focus "leads beyond itself to other times, other places, other ideas" (p. 100).

One example of an instructional focus that might be used for a course is a field trip to a local historical museum. This might have been chosen to accomplish ILOs such as the following:

The student has a sense of history about the community.

The student recognizes the change in lifestyle accompanying technological change.

The student recognizes certain artifacts as characteristics of the Revolutionary period.

Many of the same ILOs might be appropriate to several other instructional foci, a certain book, for example, or a film. The course would have many more ILOs, and not all would be accomplished by or even related to the field trip to the local historical museum. For example:

The student knows the major causes of the American Revolution.

The student can remember tactics in the major battles of the Revolution.

The student recalls the names of the major military leaders of the Revolution.

It is hard to see how a trip to a local historical museum could be instrumental in accomplishing the above outcomes.

In thinking about instructional foci like this field trip, we might think of unexpected but nonetheless valuable things that could be gained. Perhaps something unusual in the museum will catch the interest of a student strongly enough so that independent research is done on material related to the course. Such an unexpected spinoff is characteristic of good instructional foci. While these things cannot be written into the plan of a course (you certainly can't plan the unexpected!), no course should be so inflexibly formed that it can neither admit nor capitalize on surprises.

Another instructional focus might be a case study of prejudice in a northern suburb. Discussions of the case study might relate to ILOs concerned with the student respecting his or her own opinions, valuing the opinions of others, and having a high regard for logical and accurate discussion. An instructional focus of this sort, although addressed directly to a body of content (bias, justice, tolerance of others, equality under the law, etc.), can be an indirect means for accomplishing affective understandings.

Selecting Potential Instructional Foci

What instructional foci you select for each of your units and how you use them will be crucial for your course. Therefore, this step in course planning should receive a great deal of serious thought. First you will be asked to develop a set of potential instructional foci that are interesting, appropriate for your audience, and appropriate for your ILOs. If you already have formed units by clustering ILOs, then the discussion should be placed in the context of selecting instructional foci for units with specified ILOs. If you are still in the process of forming units, then you should consider this discussion in the context of the course as a whole.

In order to stimulate your thinking on instructional foci, the following general considerations may be useful:

1. **a.** How do you want your audience to perceive the unit or units?
   b. What instructional foci will provide for interaction with students that will be exciting? fun? challenging? comfortable?
2. **a.** What emotional climate is desired?
   b. What instructional foci will contribute to group cooperation? competition? self-fulfillment?
3. What energy levels should be developed?
   a. Do you want to provide for variety by shifting from an intense to a more relaxed setting?
   b. Should the pace be fast or slow, or should it vary?
   c. When during the course do you need an interest "grabber"? For example, energy typically drops about two-thirds of the way through a course. Is that the time to try to provide an "engaging experience"? How about something special in the beginning to get the students into the course and one at the end to leave them on an "up" tempo?

Course Planning Step 5.2.   With these general considerations, together with your ILOs, jot down a list of potential foci for each of your units (if you already have formed units) or for your course as a whole (if you are presently in the process of forming units around instructional foci).

The process of sorting through your *potential* instructional foci and selecting the ones *most appropriate* for each unit is best done by considering your ILOs. Some instructional foci increase the probability for instructional events that foster the achievement of key ILOs. Others do not make such events probable but do make them possible. Still other instructional foci, however interesting, make such events improbable and perhaps impossible.

Selecting the Most Appropriate Foci

In deciding which instructional foci are most appropriate for your units, you should consider four major criteria: appropriateness for the ILOs, appropriateness for the learners' abilities, potential for motivation, and feasibility. The appropriateness for the ILOs will depend on the degree to which an instructional focus provides an opportunity for learners to practice the intended learnings (for ILOs that are skills) or for learners to interact with good examples of the ideas to be learned (for ILOs that are understandings). The appropriateness for the learners' abilities will concern the background understandings and skills necessary for competent use of an instructional focus. The capacity an instructional focus has for motivation will depend on how well it challenges the learners and stimulates their interests. The feasibility of an instructional focus will depend on the availability of resources, their ease of use, and the cost involved.

We cannot prescribe how to make your decisions about what instructional foci to select. Nevertheless, we suggest that you consider your ILOs and then rate each potential instructional focus as 1, 2, or 3 (high to low) on each criterion.

Several examples that illustrate the selection of the most appropriate instructional foci follow. Each of these examples illustrates a different design problem through an actual student-developed project. The first three illustrate the process of selecting instructional foci for as yet unformed units. Examples 5.4 and 5.5 illustrate the process of selecting instructional foci for units already formed. As such, these examples should be examined carefully by all planners after they have formed their units by whatever approach has proved most useful.

Example 5.1.   In a course entitled "German, Level III,"* the ILOs could not be clustered into units. Instead, the planner decided to organize units around themes. Each theme would serve as a vehicle for learning most of the course ILOs. Each unit in turn could be taught through a number of more specific instructional foci. The themes can be considered instructional foci (or categories of specific instructional foci) because they serve as focal points for teaching a set of ILOs. They introduce content into the course that is not represented in ILOs but is used only as a device for accomplishing ILOs. In other words, each theme represents a category of *instrumental content* (that is, content used as a vehicle for learning) rather than a category of *curricular content* (that is, content that is to be learned). For convenience we will call this sort of design element a *thematic instructional focus.*

Within each unit, methods and materials must be selected. Within-unit instructional foci are still necessary. Since Examples 5.4 and 5.5 illustrate the process of

---

* We are indebted for this material to Raquel Thomison, Cornell University, 1977.

TABLE 5.1. Chart for German, level III.

Total Score	Possible Unit Title	Criteria for Unit Topics*				
		ILOS	*Ability*	*Motivation*	*Feasibility*	*Comments*
6	Politics	1	2	2	3	Complicated subject matter: topic could be discussed in unit on the DDR
4†	Religion	1	1+	1	2	Important unit on Christmas; appropriate materials might be difficult
6	Industry	1	2	2	2	Stimulating articles difficult to find
4†	Family	1	1	2	1	Partial repetition from Level II
3†	Women	1	1	1	1	Timely topic
3†	Youth	1	1	1+	1	Excellent for motivation
3†	School	1	1	1	1	Good opportunity to compare school experience
5	University	2	2	2	1	Less appropriate than topic on school
6	Science	3	1	2	2	Surveyed in German, Level II
4†	Occupations	1	1	2	1	Good materials available
6	Modern History	2	1	1	2	Too broad
6	German/Austrian Cooking	2	2	1	3	Difficult to find materials; topic included in other units
3†	Free Time	1	1	1+	1	Opportunities for cultural comparison
3†	Social Life	1	1	1+	1	Opportunities for cultural comparison
4†	Sprache	1	1	2	1	Unifies topics
3†	DDR (East Germany)	2	1	1+	1	Timely topic
5	Description of German/Austrian Cities	3	1	1	2	Highlights covered in Level II; is a detailed approach warranted?

* Scale: 1 = Good, 2 = Fair, 3 = Poor.
† Indicates a thematic instructional focus rated high enough to be used as a unit.

selecting instructional foci for units already formed, we will discuss here only the process of selecting thematic instructional foci (that is, units) for this course.

After some research, the planner was able to list potential themes for her course. See the results in Table 5.1.

Example 5.2. In forming units around instructional foci (IF) the important decision is often not which foci to use (if they are all equally appropriate for the ILOs and learners' abilities, and are equally stimulating and feasible) but how to organize them into coherent units. The situation is typically faced when each focus requires only a brief amount of time.

For example, one planner* designed a course to make "readers aware of how

---

* We are grateful to Margaret Berger for the following excerpts from her project at Cornell University, 1974.

authors consciously or unconsciously influence the readers' feelings, moral attitudes, and social values." This course attempted to help pupils "read with discrimination and care in order to understand just what it is a writer is protraying as 'good' or 'bad,' how those values relate to accepted societal values, and how the author's values affect the reader."

This planner decided on the following instructional foci:

1. Comic books
2. Folk songs
3. Advertisements
4. Newspaper articles, columns, and editorials
5. Nursery rhymes
6. Fairy tales
7. Short stories
8. Children's stories
9. Magazine articles
10. Popular songs
11. Novels
12. Religious songs
13. Protest poetry
14. Plays
15. Ethnic poetry
16. English and American "accepted" poetry

Then she organized these foci into the following units:

Unit 1: Obvious Propaganda Techniques
IF: advertisements

Unit 2: Newspapers and Other Written Media
IFs: newspaper articles, columns, and editorials
        magazine articles

Unit 3: Young People's Literature
IFs: comic books
        children's stories
        nursery rhymes
        fairy tales

Unit 4: Prose, Fiction
IFs: novels
        short stories

Unit 5: Poetry
IFs: popular songs
        folk songs

religious songs
ethnic poetry
protest poetry
English and American "accepted" poetry

Unit 6: Drama
IFs: plays

Example 5.3.   Often in designing units for a course, the decision we face is what *kind* of instructional focus will be the *primary* one around which to form our units. For example, one planner* developing a course on nineteenth-century British literature stated the following ILOs (among others):

1. Students will be able to recognize their own feelings, thoughts, and values as they encounter them in their reading of great works of fiction and nonfiction.
2. Students will be able to analyze and organize these familiar feelings, thoughts, and values as they encounter them in great works.
3. Students will be receptive to, and will comprehend, feelings, thoughts, and values that are unfamiliar to them as they encounter them in great works.

Clearly, this planner is attempting to bring together two sources of content, one from the literature and one from within the student. Since these ILOs could not be clustered into units, this planner considered various ways of forming units around instructional foci. For example, the planner could have organized units around themes such as the following:

1. The child in society
2. Women in society
3. The individual in society
4. Class consciousness
5. Humans and their thoughts
6. Writers and their art

Or the planner could have organized the units around genres:

1. Prose fiction: Dickens (*Oliver Twist*), Brontë (*Jane Eyre*), Carroll (*Alice in Wonderland*), Butler (*The Way of All Flesh*), Hardy (*Jude the Obscure*), Conrad (*The Secret Sharer*)
2. Poetry: The Romantics (Wordsworth, Byron, Keats), Tennyson, Browning
3. Nonfiction: Carlyle (portraits of his contemporaries), Arnold and Mills (essays), Keats (letters)
4. Secondary sources: texts, histories, biographies

---

* We are indebted for his ideas on this course to Chris Connelly, Cornell University, 1974.

Or units could have been organized around activities:

1. Hypothetical problem situations
2. Discussions
3. Lectures
4. Laboratory groups dramatizing passages
5. Tutoring sessions

Instead of choosing only one of these three designs, the planner could combine all three designs. For example, the planner could organize units around themes, then around genres within each unit, and then employ the five activities whenever appropriate. This is only one of several possible solutions to the problem. Which solution is the best depends on which aspect of the course (that is, themes, genres, activities) the planner wishes to emphasize.

These three examples show that there are many ways of forming units around instructional foci because there are many kinds of instructional foci. There is no single approach appropriate for all courses. All we can recommend is to consider as many alternatives as you can think of and analyze the strengths and weaknesses of each.

Examples 5.4 and 5.5 illustrate the selection of instructional foci for units already formed.

Example 5.4.*

Unit: Ecosystems
1. The student grasps the concept of an ecosystem and its four subdivisions. (Grasping the concept here involves knowledge of what constitutes an ecosystem and what does not, as well as a knowledge of what phenomena are explained by ecosystem.)
2. The student understands the interrelationships of the component parts of ecosystem subdivisions. ("Understand" here includes the belief that these subdivisions are related, the knowledge of what counts as evidence for this belief, and an awareness that the subdivisions act as one system.)
3. The student is able to trace the flow of energy through a food chain.
4. The student is able to define habitat and niche and will know how each relates to the other. ("Know how" here involves recognition of what counts as evidence of the relationship between habitat and niche.)

Potential Instructional Foci
Basic Ecology, Buchsbaum

field trip to wetland and climax forest

terraria

SRA film series

---

* The inclusion of ILOs is intended to give you a better feel for the sample unit. The ILOs are not meant to represent a complete unit.

outside reading, in-class reports

lecture with visuals

These potential foci were then placed on a chart (see Table 5.2) and rated on the criteria.

Example 5.5.

Unit: Manipulations through Language

1. The student will know that language is a powerful manipulative tool. ("Know that" in this ILO refers to the student believing in the power of language and understanding why language is powerful.)
2. The student will be able to recognize words and phrases that often convey misleading meanings.
3. The student will be able to identify what impression an author wants to make on a reader.

Potential Instructional Foci

teacher presentation

newspapers and magazines

commercials (produced by students)

commercials (TV)

These potential foci were then charted (see Table 5.3) and rated on the criteria.

Course Planning Step 5.3. From your list of potential instructional foci, select those that are (a) most appropriate for the ILOs, (b) most appropriate for the learners' abilities, (c) most likely to provide motivation, and (d) most feasible. When considering appropriateness for ILOs, pay particular attention to high-priority ILOs. If you are selecting instructional foci for units already formed, limit yourself to two foci

TABLE 5.2. Selecting instructional foci (IF): Ecosystems.*

| Potential IF | Criteria† | | | |
	ILOS	Ability	Motivation	Feasibility
Basic Ecology	1 (high)	2	2	1
field trip	1	2	1	3 (low)
terraria	2	1	1	2
SRA film	2	2	2	2
reading	2	1	3	1
lecture	1	1	3	1

* Using this chart as an aid in evaluating potential instructional foci, the following instructional foci have been selected for this unit: *Basic Ecology* as text; terraria.
† Scale: 1 = Good, 2 = Fair, 3 = Poor

TABLE 5.3.   Selecting instructional foci (IF): Language manipulations.*

Potential IF	Criteria†			
	ILOS	*Ability*	*Motivation*	*Feasibility*
Teacher presentation	2	2	3	1
Newspapers and magazines	2	1	2	1
Writing commercials	2	2	1–2	2
Viewing commercials	1	2	1–2	3

* Using this chart as an aid in evaluating potential instructional foci, the following instructional focus for this unit
   has been selected: newspaper and magazines.
† Scale: 1 = Good, 2 = Fair, 3 = Poor.

per unit. If you are selecting instructional foci as an approach to forming units, then each instructional focus or coherent group of foci you choose will constitute a unit.

Course Planning Step 5.4.   If you are designing each of your units around an instructional focus, list the ILOs appropriate for each unit. That is, key ILOs to each of your units based on what each instructional focus or group of foci (that is, unit) is supposed to accomplish.

TITLING THE UNITS

Providing the title for a unit is very similar to the elementary school exercise of choosing the best heading for a paragraph or title for a story. In the context of course design, titling a unit serves as a check on the coherence of a unit. If a group of ILOs together with a small group of instructional foci cannot be titled, it may be wise to examine them for coherence and make any necessary changes.

Course Planning Step 5.5.   Title each of the units of your course.

ORGANIZATION AND SEQUENCE FOR ELEMENTARY UNIT PLANNING

One of the most important benefits of unit planning is that teachers have a "bigger picture" on which to base their decisions and actions. Unit plans form the bridge between the curriculum and daily lesson plans. Lesson plans should not reflect day-to-day planning but should be part of a long-term planning effort. Having thought about the unit as a whole, teachers can plan and teach with greater flexibility. Pace is more easily adjusted, "teachable moments" are more readily recognized and taken advantage of, misconceptions are more apparent, and enrichment can be better conceived. Perhaps most importantly, the themes or ideas underlying a unit can be appropriately emphasized in every lesson.

Most elementary teachers plan units rather than courses. These units have neither the length nor the scope to make clustering ILOs a useful approach to organization. Elementary instruction typically employs a wider variety of instructional foci and learning activities than secondary instruction does. Compared to secondary and postsecondary teachers, elementary teachers must deal with shorter student attention spans, students who cannot reason formally, and, often, students with fewer areas of common knowledge in their backgrounds. This usually necessitates a more active instructional mode with different foci of shorter duration.

The units are typically organized into subunits. Elementary teachers use a variety of formats to express subunits. (See Meyen, 1981, and Dick & Carey, 1990, for examples.) Most include an introduction that briefly describes the emphasis or focus of the subunit and where it fits in the overall unit sequence. Following this section many teachers list or refer to the intended learnings related to the particular subunit. Typically material or instructional foci are also listed. Last comes a brief description of the general teaching strategy. It is from this description that the specific lesson plans are derived. Lesson plans may include questions, discussion starters, all forms of grouping or other instructional arrangements, the specifics of assignments and homework, decisions about timing, and more. As is true of other unit plan components, the subunits are revised and supplemented as they are taught. This is the place for teachers to record what worked particularly well, what needs improvement or replacement, and so forth.

Several examples of subunit plans follow. These plans include teaching strategies that you will read about in chapter 7. They are included here to give you some ideas about the shape your plan may take.

The Native American unit has a subunit format quite different from the River unit. The description and explanation of the sequence comes in a single introductory section. The ILOs for all the subunits are also listed before any instructional strategies are outlined. Excerpts from the introduction and the relevant ILOs are included. The instruction for this subunit consists largely of student research projects. Much of the teaching strategy outlines the necessary skills and procedures that students will need to benefit from this project.

The World Geography unit is designed to carry through the entire fourth grade year. At times the work on geography is the primary focus of the class's work in all content areas. At other times geography takes a "back burner" position to other aspects of the curriculum. After an introductory subunit, students are introduced to maps and taught some skills that they will use throughout the unit. Subunit 1 is the introduction to maps and consists of three distinct pieces, mapping the classroom, round earth versus flat maps, and types of maps. Each piece is worked out in considerable detail. In fact, this is a unit that has been taught once and the teaching strategies presented here reflect the kinds of additions and revisions that come with experience.

Native American Culture

The close connection of the Native American's culture to their environment is the underlying concept in this unit. This concept will be built up gradually throughout the unit. The goal is to have a clear understanding of Indian cultural values with respect to nature so that the conflict between the white culture and the Indian cultures can be understood in part in terms of the differences in their cultural values. The beginning point to develop this concept is to understand the basic relationship to the environment that all cultures share. Students need to understand the concept of a culture in general along with understanding that a culture adapts to its environment. All cultures meet basic needs by using the resources of the environment and so all people share a relationship to nature, since they must meet their basic needs.

The unit moves to a study of three cultural areas. Applying this framework of culture developed through the introductory activities, students study the environments across North America and the ways that Indian cultures evolved to meet their needs in these environments. In this part of the unit, they will be learning specific information about the Native American cultural areas. In this way, students will be able to understand values shared by Native Americans while also learning about their diversity. Understanding the Native American attitude toward nature, students have a way of bringing together the information about the different Indian cultures. Without this conceptual background to pull together information, the study of Indian cultures would be only a catalogue of different shelters, clothing, food gathering techniques, and folk tales.

The last part of the unit is about the history of the clash between the Europeans and Indian tribes. The difference between how the two cultures viewed man's relationship to nature will be contrasted. It is not the aim of this unit to include a thorough chronology of the history of European and U.S. interaction with the Native Americans. Instead historical events were selected to typify the issues central to the conflict between the Native Americans and European/U.S. settlers. This material uses storytelling and drama to present the conflict between the European and Indian cultures. Listening to stories read aloud is engaging to fourth graders and drama is highly motivating.

Europe and the United States developed increasingly sophisticated ways to control the environment. They were so successful at using natural resources for energy and for manufacturing that after a while they lost sight of their basic connection to nature. This difference is what accounts for much of the misunderstanding and conflict between the white and Indian cultures.

Activities that involve students experientially with the topic are important for creating a concrete understanding of what Native American cultures were like. The field trip led by a Native American woman at the Skan center in Shelburne, in a beautiful rural countryside, is a central activity for the unit. Students spend time in a teepee and have the opportunity to experience a little of what it would be like to live in this way. As a group, students discuss how the space would affect how people related to each other. They also listen to stories, sing songs, and handle Indian tools.

In order for students to appreciate the culture and values of Native Americans, they need learning activities that help them understand the Indian perspective. Literature about Native Americans allows students to "live" this perspective. Discussing the underlying themes in Native American myths and stories should be incorporated throughout the unit. There is a danger in studying another culture of having a "museum" perspective, viewing the information about Indian tribes as artifacts to be categorized. Although being able to classify information is a skill that is important for this unit, these activities should be balanced by activities that bring this information to life.

At the Campus School, the art program corresponds to the social studies unit being taught in the classroom. For this reason, I did not include very many activities involving Indian crafts. These activities add interest and motivation to the unit. I have included some art activities to supplement the unit in the second appendix.

A goal of a social studies unit in general is learning skills for getting information from nonfiction sources and organizing this information. At this age, taking notes is a relatively new experience. The act of writing is still fairly time consuming and difficult for many students. Through the use of outline maps, or webbing, students will classify information around categories. The students will be reading short pieces and using sources of information such as photographs, speeches, stories, art objects, and slides (there is an extensive source of Native American art at the Smith College art library). It is important to have reading selections at different reading levels, if possible, or the selections could be taped for students to listen to while reading the text. The process of organizing information from a text will be modeled with the class.

The content outline includes a broader range of material than has been included in the unit plans. This information has been included in the outline to show the scope of the topic and other possible topics to include in this unit. For example, the unit could have focused more on ancient Indian cultures to show the evolution of cultures over a long period of time. Another alternative focus would be the Indian tribes of New England.

Although the final area of the unit—current issues for Native Americans—is not developed in this unit plan, it should be included for a thorough coverage of the topic and for closure.

ILOs for Subunit 2: Native American Cultural Areas

Know that a Native American cultural area is a geographical area in which the environment is fairly similar and the tribes within the area have similar cultures.

Be able to organize and classify information into an outline map.

Describe the environment and know the main tribe names of the cultural areas (Northeast, Southwest, and Plains).

Know information about the culture: food, shelter, clothing, art, and tools.

Know information concerning the lifestyle and community structure (government, decision making, organizations).

Know information about religion and ceremonies of Native American cultural areas.

Describe similarities and differences between the different cultural areas.

Describe the shared values and religious views of Native Americans regarding nature and the environment.

Be able to restate information and ideas in a text into the student's own language.

Be able to use the concept of a culture (i.e., aspects of a culture) to identify and to classify information from texts and other sources.

Teaching Strategy for Subunit 2: Native American Cultural Areas
Introduce procedure for studying culture areas. Begin with the Northeast, since this is the first group to come in contact with the Europeans and it is the area the students live in.

As a class, study the Northeast cultural area together.

Model the procedure for organizing information into an outline map and displaying this information so it clearly communicates to others.

Procedure
1. Introduce outline web

    Review categories of a culture. Write each aspect and subcategories on cards. Explain the idea that we want to show how these ideas are related and fit together. Cards include: culture, Northeast, food, shelter, clothing, basic needs, community structure, religion, and so on. Discuss where to place the cards, starting with just a few. Introduce the idea that you can show ideas are related with connecting lines and by writing a phrase to show how they are connected. Students arrange the cards on poster paper and draw lines to show relationships.

    With some cultural aspects, like community structure, ask what these mean in their own words. How would you find out about this? What would you look for? For example, lifestyle would include whether a tribe was nomadic, settled, or warlike.

2. Introduce note taking

    Each student has a short section on the Northeast cultural area. The students understand that their purpose for reading is to add information about the Northeast Native American tribes to the class cultural area map. To introduce the note-taking procedure, the teacher reads aloud part of the passage and the students underline when they hear a part that gives information about the culture that they can add to the map. The steps for turning the information read into an outline map are (1) put information into own words; (2) determine what kind of information it is, or what category; (3) add the information to the map.

3. Discuss ways to illustrate the information and whether some information would be easier to understand with a picture, such as a shelter. In small groups, students illustrate information on the map using art materials and natural materials (leaves, grass, twigs) and add to the map.

    In addition to reading texts for information, have other sources available—pictures, art objects, tools, slides, stories, and music. To learn about religion and values, use stories and statements by Indian leaders expressing these views (see the resource list). Make a listening center in the room for music, stories, and games using a small tent. Stories, music, and so on could be taped and students could have a text to look at while they are listening. The tent could be decorated by the class to resemble a Southwest kiva (used for ceremonies and meetings).

4. Practice reading the map by asking students to describe aspects of the culture and how aspects are related.

5. After this procedure is clear and the research and outline map of the Northeast cultural area is complete, the class is divided into working pairs to work on one of two cultural areas, the Plains or the Southwest. The advantage of having many students working on the same information independently is that they can compare different ways to organize information.

The task is divided into steps that the teacher checks before the students go on: (1) read overview and answer questions (questions to help focus students on the aspects of culture categories, suggesting ways information is related; (2) add information to their map from the section they read; (3) use further materials (pictures, tapes, maps, etc.); (4) find ways to illustrate items on map for final draft using pictures or collages.

Using information on their finished map, students make a diorama, or three-dimensional model, of their cultural area as a way of putting together information about the culture.

World Geography: Subunit I—An Introduction to Maps

The conventions, types, and sources of maps, as well as applications of map skills, will be explored in this introduction. Since this area of study encounters a wide range of skills and information with a multitude of possibilities, I have divided it into a number of sections or activities, each of which builds upon the others. Since map skills and understandings are an integral part of a study of geography, it is appropriate to begin the unit with a fairly in-depth look at maps.

A. Mapping the Classroom

This section of the introduction to maps introduces students to a number of essential terms and skills necessary for success in this course. Students will have the opportunity to create their own maps.

Intended learning outcomes: 2, 6a, 6c, 6d, 6h, 6j

Terms to be presented: directionality, perspective, grid, proportion, scale, cartographer, key

Instructional foci: paper, pencils, grid (string and tape), chalkboard, fine line markers, colored pencils

Teaching strategy: The end product of this series of lessons will be a map of the classroom from a bird's-eye perspective that includes a key and is fairly in proportion. Before instructing students to create such a map, it will be necessary for the teacher to introduce or review a number of concepts and skills. To begin, students will be oriented to the concept of directionality (north, south, east, west). Directionality is discussed and signs with each of the directions are hung on the appropriate wall in the classroom for all students to see.

Next, the idea of a bird's-eye perspective is explored. The teacher will begin by asking if students have ever heard the term *bird's-eye view* and ask if they can explain what it means. The teacher will ask students to imagine themselves flying (northward, for example) above the playground and to explain what they would see. A diagram can be drawn on the chalkboard. The teacher can use the diagram as a teaching point to introduce the need for the depiction of correct proportions and the possibility of including a key. Here, too, the teacher should explain that it is from the bird's-eye perspective that most maps are drawn, and that accurate proportion and the representation of the objects or places seen below are problems with which mapmakers (cartographers) struggle. The teacher should assure students that these are ideas that will be explored in greater detail in the days to come.

The students will then be introduced to the idea of a grid and its purpose in facilitating true proportions. The teacher can explain and provide examples that demonstrate the idea that grids can be used to create an accurately proportioned shrunken or enlarged representation of a given picture or field. The teacher, using tape and string, will set up a grid on the classroom floor. Students will then be informed that they will be using this grid to draw a map of the classroom. The teacher will provide each student with a grid on a sheet of paper. This grid has the same number of squares as the grid on the classroom floor. The teacher should explain that this grid is drawn from a bird's-eye perspective as if looking down on the classroom from the ceiling. (The teacher may choose to allow students to draw their own grid, but it may require a considerable amount of time. Perhaps this would be a more appropriate task for older students.)

The teacher will then point out that the two grids are identical except in size. The concept of scale should be introduced here. Students will be asked to label north, south, east, and west on their own grids. (The teacher can model with a grid taped to the chalkboard.) Once this is completed, the teacher will involve the students in a short game. The teacher repeatedly stands in a box on the floor and asks students to point to the corresponding box on their own grids. Students are then asked to find the box in which they would find their own desk. The teacher could then ask students to work in pairs to locate where various objects in the room (teacher's desk, book shelf, sink, pencil sharpener, clock, etc.) would be found. Here, the teacher should point out the problem students might encounter when drawing the clock or other objects on the wall—they may be positioned above other objects. In addition, he or she should point out the difficulty students might have including the representation of all the desks and chairs. The teacher should emphasize that a key is the solution to these problems. The purpose and ways that keys work should be reviewed.

The teacher will then give instructions as to how the students should go about creating the map of the classroom and set specific expectations for the maps. For example:

1. From a bird's-eye perspective, in pencil and on the grid, students should draw a map that includes everything in the classroom. When this is complete, the map must be checked with the teacher before students move on.
2. Fine line markers should be used to go over all lines except for the grid.

3. The grid should be erased.
4. Students should make a box for the key.
5. Colored pencils should be used for coloring the map.
6. Students should fill in the key.
7. The end product should be as simple as possible so as to be easily read, and it should be pleasing to the eye.

The teacher will then divide the class and send a pair of students into each box to draw the contents of that box on the grid provided. A predetermined signal will initiate a change in box. The teacher should assure students that details can be completed at a later time if necessary.

SUGGESTED TIME: Three to five lessons (45–60 minutes each)

B. Round Earth vs. Flat Map

In this section of the introduction to maps, students will be exposed to the representation of a spherical earth on a flat field and the difficulties that arise from such a representation. Students will be introduced to a number of projections while the issue of distortion is explored.

INTENDED LEARNING OUTCOMES: 2, 6c, 6d, 6e, 6g, 6h, 6j

TERMS TO BE PRESENTED: distortion, equator, Tropic of Cancer, Tropic of Capricorn, latitude, prime meridian, longitude, projection, degrees

INSTRUCTIONAL FOCI: a globe, a variety of projections (Mercator, Peter's, Interrupted, Robinson's, etc.), an orange

TEACHING STRATEGY: The teacher will attempt to elicit from students responses that prove the spherical nature of the earth by stating "I think the earth is really flat." If these are not generated by the students, the teacher should initiate a discussion on the nature of a globe—that it is the same shape and proportion as the earth, only a different scale. The teacher should point out that a globe is the most realistic representation of the earth, but that globes are sometimes awkward to work with, going on to explain that this is the reason we have maps and that maps are really "flattened out" globes. In order to make this idea as concrete as possible, the teacher can peel an orange, without dividing the peel, and flatten the peel.

The idea of a grid of the earth can be described through the introduction of the equator, Tropics of Cancer and Capricorn, and lines of latitude as the horizontal lines of the grid, while the prime meridian and lines of longitude make up the vertical lines. It should be explained that these imaginary lines that are organized by degrees help us to locate points on the earth and show scale.

With the flattened orange peel in full view of all students, the teacher will display a variety of maps—Peter's projection, Interrupted projection, Mercator projection, and Robinson's projection. The teacher will introduce the term *projection* and discuss the fact that different maps have varying functions and political biases. The teacher will ask students to verbalize any differences they see in the maps displayed. If these are not brought up by the students, the teacher should initiate a discussion of distortion and point out that this is a problem of all maps. Students will be encouraged to find distortions. The teacher will expand on the problem of Greenland.

SUGGESTED TIME: One lesson (45—60 minutes)

C. Types of Maps

A study of maps would be incomplete without an examination of different types of maps, each with its own purpose. Although students will primarily be working with political maps throughout the year, other types of maps will be encountered as well. Students will be asked to recognize the different types introduced here and to be able to use the conventions to extract information from each.

INTENDED LEARNING OUTCOMES: 2, 6a, 6b, 6f

TERMS TO BE PRESENTED: projection, political map, physical map, thematic map

INSTRUCTIONAL FOCI: chalkboard, overhead transparencies, teacher-made dittos, political map, physical map, thematic map, road map

TEACHING STRATEGY: The teacher will hang four different types of maps on the chalkboard: a political map, a physical map, a thematic map, and a road map. If available, all four of the maps should represent the same geographical area. Maps of New England would be ideal, since students would already be familiar with the area.

Before introducing each type of map, the teacher will ask students to comment on some of the differences and/or similarities they notice among the maps. Students will be encouraged to go to the board and point out anything they see as relevant. A list of specific characteristics of each map will be generated and written on the board next to each. The purpose of each map should be explored in detail and the name of each type introduced. The teacher will need to instruct students on how to read the various maps and how to extract information from each. Overhead transparencies and/or dittos of each map type should be used to reinforce and test students' understanding.

The teacher should go on to explain that political maps will be the most widely used maps in this study of geography. Also, he or she should explain that physical and thematic maps will be encountered on a number of occasions, and students should be familiar with the conventions of each. Road maps, on the other hand, will not be used during the year and were used in this lesson only as a point of comparison.

A follow-up exercise is included in Subunit II—An Introduction to Atlases.

SUGGESTED TIME: One lesson (45–60 minutes)

SUGGESTIONS FOR ELEMENTARY UNIT PLANNING

We suggest that elementary teachers proceed through chapters 5, 6, and 7 as follows:

1. Review all the planning you have done so far. Return to your list of initial ideas. Gather and browse through any resources containing activities, materials, and other instructional ideas related to your unit. Compile *all* the instructional ideas that you find appealing. Instructional ideas include a great many things. Some examples are library research projects, teacher demonstrations, reading and discussing newspapers, debate, simulations, experimentation, teacher presentation, writing assignments, and building scale models. In short, any of the many tasks elementary students typically engage in qualify here.

2. ILOs should now be "keyed" to these instructional ideas. That is, decide which activities are likely to lead to which ILOs and indicate this.

3. Examine the list for coverage. Are all your high-priority ILOs included at least once? Add instructional ideas if necessary.

4. Eliminate some of the instructional ideas on your list. To do this, use the criteria suggested for selecting instructional foci. Decisions about appropriateness, feasibility, and motivation should, of course, consider the age and the development of the students. Priority of ILOs must be considered in making this section; be sure to specify any time constraints with which you must work. You should now have a list of ideas that you intend to use in teaching your unit.

5. Chapter 6 discusses the sequence of course units. As we noted with secondary teachers, elementary teachers have more alternative instructional sequences than they usually realize. You should read chapter 6 now and then make a sequence of the instructional ideas you have developed. Many suggestions in chapter 6 should prove helpful; your instructional ideas will probably fall together into groups and these groups can then be put into a sequence.

6. Chapter 7 deals with the development of general teaching strategies. You should find the chapter's guidelines helpful. We suggest that you consider teaching strategies for each of your clusters of instructional ideas.

QUESTIONS FOR DISCUSSION: FORMING UNITS

1. Which do you feel are your best instructional foci? Why? What does this choice indicate about your own personal criteria for choosing foci?

2. What does your choice of approach in forming units indicate about your course?

3. Have you decided on the sequence of your units or is this decision still open?
4. What approach to forming units was followed in *Course Design*? What are the book's "units"?
5. Does any instructional focus predominate in this book?

REFERENCES

Dick, W., & Carey, L. (1990). *The systematic design of instruction* (3rd ed). Glenview, IL: Scott, Foresman.

Goodlad, J. I. (1963). *Planning and organizing for teaching*. Washington, DC: National Education Association.

Meyen, E. L. (1981). *Developing instructional units* (3rd ed). Dubuque, IA: Wm. C. Brown.

CHAPTER 6

Organizing the Course's Units

After completing this chapter, you should be able to:

1. Know that there are alternative ways of sequencing content.
2. Think about alternatives when faced with the task of sequencing content.
3. Group and sequence a given set of units into a coherent outline.

In part, instructional planning consists of organizing instructional content into a coherent, feasible design for teaching. The previous chapter dealt with one part of this process, that is, forming unit-sized chunks of content for the course. The present chapter continues organizing the course by showing how to sequence and group these units into a course design that is coherent, not only within each unit, but also across units. The coherence of the course as a whole is the major concern of this chapter.

We discuss, first, the ways in which content can be organized for instructional purposes. More specifically, we consider the question, What are the alternative principles by which instructional content can be sequenced? These principles are then applied to the task of sequencing your course's units.

ALTERNATIVE SEQUENCING PRINCIPLES*

The sequencing principles presented here are essentially the same principles you met in the previous chapter as "bases for organizing ILOs." Therefore, the first part of this

---

* This section is adapted from Posner and Strike (1976).

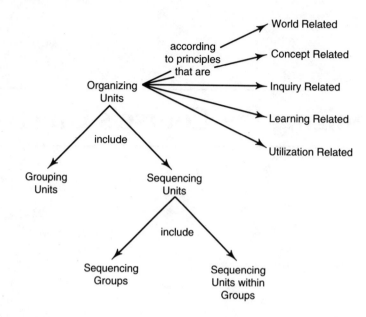

chapter reiterates and expands on familiar ideas in order to apply these ideas to the problems of sequencing units rather than clustering ILOs.

The five major bases or principles for organizing units can be summarized by the five questions that follow. Each question represents a category of sequencing principles.

1. What relationships exist among people, objects, or events of the world and in what ways can units be sequenced so that their sequence is consistent with the *world*? Subcategories include relationships based on space, time, and physical attributes.
2. What are the *conceptual* properties of the knowledge to be taught and in what ways can units be sequenced so that their sequence is logically consistent with the organization of the ideas? Subcategories include relationships based on class relations, propositional relations, sophistication level, and logical prerequisites.
3. How does knowledge come about and in what ways can units be sequenced so that their sequence is consistent with this process of *inquiry*? Subcategories include relationships based on the logic and the empirics of inquiry.
4. How does the student learn and in what ways can the units be sequenced so that their sequence is consistent with the learning process? Subcategories include relationships based on empirical prerequisites, familiarity, difficulty, interest, internalization, and development.
5. How will the student utilize the knowledge and skills learned and in what ways can the units be sequenced so that their sequence is consistent with

the *utilization* process? Subcategories include relationships based on procedural order and anticipated frequency of utilization.

Many decisions regarding the sequencing of units are not based on any of these five major categories of sequencing principles; instead, they are based on factors relating to the implementation of programs in specific situations. Such factors as materials and the facilities available, time schedules, weather and climate, location of the school, transportation needs, and teachers' interests or competencies are likely to be powerful determinants of sequencing. These factors have been referred to as "frame factors" (Dahllof & Lundgren, 1970) and may be considered a sixth basis for organization, *implementation-related*. Principles that are implementation related, however critical they may be in organizing programs, are dependent not on relationships among units of content (the focus of this chapter) but on the administrative, physical, personnel, societal, and time frames of the particular teaching situation. As such, this type of situation-dependent sequencing principle has not been included in the present scheme.

Sequencing Principles: Types and Subtypes

The five major types of sequencing principles are discussed here in greater detail. In addition, several subtypes are described for each major type. (The scheme is presumed to be comprehensive for major types but not for subtypes.) This categorization can be considered a sort of "shopping list" from which to choose sequencing principles for your course. Although the principles are presented in relatively "pure" form, consider how you might combine several of them to create the most feasible and rational approach possible.

1. *World-related sequences* are those sequences in which there is consistency between the ordering of units, on the one hand, and empirical relationships between events, people, and objects as they exist or occur in the world, on the other hand. World-related subtypes include spatial relations, temporal relations, and physical attributes, to name just a few. An exemplar of this type is the typical sequencing of history content based on the chronological sequence of events (that is, the subtype Time).

   a. *Space.* Sequences based on spatial relations are those in which the units are ordered in accord with the physical arrangement or position of the phenomena of interest. Sequencing principles of this subtype include closest-to-farthest, bottom-to-top, east-to-west, and so forth. *Examples:* Teach the positions of the offensive line, the halfbacks, and the quarterback in that order. Teach the parts of a plant from the root to the stem to the leaves and flower, in that order. Teach about the states according to geographical location.

   b. *Time.* Often the content (most typically history content) is sequenced chronologically from the earliest to the most recent events. *Examples:* Teach the major ideas of Marx before teaching about the nature of the

Russian Revolution. Teach the names of the states in order of admission to the Union.

c. *Physical attributes.* World-related sequences may be based on physical characteristics of the phenomena of interest such as size, age, shape, number of sides (for example, in geometry), brightness (for example, in astronomy), empirical complexity (for example, in comparative anatomy), and countless other physical (and chemical) characteristics. This subtype is most commonly employed in the natural sciences because these disciplines are concerned with properties of things in the natural world. *Examples:* Teach the names of the states in size order (size). Teach the anatomy of an amphibian, then a shark, then a cat (empirical complexity). Teach the structure of a primitive society before teaching about a complex industrial society (empirical complexity).

2. *Concept-related sequences* are assumed to reflect the organization of the conceptual world. That is, a sequence in which units (each unit organized around a major idea) are structured in a manner consistent with the way the ideas themselves relate to one another is termed a concept-related sequence. The conceptual maps developed in chapter 2 are particularly useful in guiding concept-related sequences. A traditional course embodying concept-related sequences is geometry when taught deductively (see the subtype 2*b*, Propositional Relations). Many courses developed in the 1960s placed a high priority on the organization of ideas (for example, BSCS biology, ESCP earth science, PSSC physics, CHEM Study chemistry). These courses are described by the term *the structure of disciplines* (Atkia and House, 1981; Elam, 1964; Ford & Pugno, 1964; Goodlad & Su, 1992; Kliebard, 1965; Schwab, 1962). This term describes an approach in which the "fundamental" ideas of a discipline (that is, those ideas that subsume many others) are used as the central themes for purposes of grouping and sequencing content (Bruner, 1960). One argument for this approach is that since the "knowledge explosion," the student can no longer learn everything. Therefore, analysis of each discipline is needed to determine those fundamental ideas that form the structure of the discipline (Bruner, 1960). By learning this structure, the student can learn the essence of the discipline in the most economical manner, without having to learn every one of the many facts subsumed by each "basic" idea.

a. *Class relations.* A class concept is a concept that groups a set of things or events together as instances of the same kind of thing because they share common properties. Sequences embodying this subtype include teaching the characteristics of the class before teaching about the members of the class (Ausubel, Novak, & Hanesian, 1978), or vice versa (Bruner, Goodnow, & Austin, 1956). In either case, the order of teaching the members of the class is less important than teaching them in conjunction with or separately from the class concept. *Examples:* Teach about mammals before teaching about specific animals in that group. Define "discrimination" before examining racial and sex discrimination. Investigate various forms of democratic governments through case study before attempting to define "democracy." Compare sound and light before teaching about wave motion.

b. *Propositional relations.* A proposition is a statement that asserts something. Sequences of this sort include teaching evidence prior to the proposition that the evidence supports or teaching a theory prior to the facts that the theory explains. *Examples:* Teach an overview of the theory of natural selection before studying the adaptation of Darwin's finches (theory-instance). Teach the principle of "equal protection under law" before studying the 1954 Supreme Court decision on civil rights. Teach the volume of a gas at several temperatures and pressures before teaching Boyle's Law (evidence-conclusion). Teach about chemical compounds before teaching about biological organisms (reduction).

c. *Sophistication.* Ideas can differ in their level of precision ("acceleration" is less precise than v/t), conceptual complexity (the number of ideas subsumed by another idea), abstractness (the distance from particular things or facts; usually the opposite of concrete), and level of refinement (adding qualifications to an idea refines it). Sophistication embodies all these aspects. The concept of sophistication here is similar to Bruner's (1960) in his discussion of the "spiral" curriculum that returns periodically to ideas at higher and higher levels of sophistication. *Examples:* Teach real numbers before teaching about imaginary numbers (abstractness). Teach the idea of stimulus before the idea of conditioning (conceptual complexity). Teach Newton's laws before Einstein's refinement of those laws.

d. *Logical prerequisite.* An idea is a logical prerequisite to another concept or proposition when it is logically necessary to understand the first idea in order to understand the second. (See Phillips & Kelly, 1975, for the distinction between logical and empirical prerequisites.) *Examples:* Teach what "velocity" means before teaching that "acceleration" is the change in velocity. Teach the concept of set before the concept of number.

3. *Inquiry-related sequences* are those that derive from the nature of the process of generating, discovering, or verifying knowledge. Such sequences reflect the nature of the logic or methodology of a given area of thought (Parker & Rubin, 1966; Schwab, 1964). Dewey's attempt to structure teaching according to his analysis of the scientific method (1916, chaps. 11, 12) is a major example of an inquiry-related approach to sequence.

a. *Logic of inquiry.* Logic may be narrowly defined as the science of valid argument, or more broadly defined as the analysis of the norms of adequate inquiry. Sequencing principles rooted in logic reflect views of valid inference. For example, two different logics (epistemologies) yield different sequencing principles concerning discovery learning. A view that considers discovery to be a matter of generalizing over numerous instances (that is, induction) provides instances of a generalization prior to attempting to have the student discover the generalizations (Glaser, 1966). A view that considers discovery to be a matter of testing bold conjectures seeks to elicit hypotheses and then turns to a process of evidence collection (Bruner, 1960; Popper, 1959). (See Shulman, 1970, for a comparison of these two approaches to discovery learning.) *Examples:* Explain how Galileo arrived at the hypothesis that the change in velocity per unit of time for a freely falling object is a constant; then have the students find that the acceleration of any object allowed to fall freely is 9.8 m/sec, so long as air resistance is not a factor (hypothesis generation–evidence collection). Discover ways to light a bulb with a battery, then generalize a rule (induction).

b. *Empirics of inquiry.* Some features of proper inquiry are rooted in descriptions of how successful scientists actually proceed or in the social or psychological conditions of fruitful inquiry. Let us suppose, for example, that successful scientists were found to study a problem area before working on specific problems. This might lead to sequencing content in such a way that it emphasizes the need for a general survey of an area prior to the consideration of special problems. *Examples:* Teach what other researchers have discovered about reinforcement schedules before teaching students to frame hypotheses about optimum reinforcement schedules. Teach how to write grant proposals before teaching how to collect data.

4. *Learning-related sequences* draw primarily on knowledge about the psychology of learning as a basis for curriculum development and instructional planning. Most psychologists, although they might disagree about the particular instructional approach to be used, argue that the nature of the subject matter is not as relevant to course organization as are empirical claims about the way people learn (see, for example, Gagné, 1970; Ausubel, 1964). Exemplar sequences of this type can be found in AAAS's *Science—A Process Approach,* which is sequenced on the basis of empirical prerequisite relationships, and ESS science, which is sequenced on the basis of interest.

a. *Empirical prerequisite.* If it can be determined empirically that the learning of one skill facilitates the learning of a subsequent skill, the first skill can be termed an empirical prerequisite of the second (Gagné, 1970).* *Examples:* Teach discrimination between initial consonants; then teach the use of word-attack skills; then teach reading. In basketball, teach passing skills before teaching the fast break. In English, teach alphabetizing words before dictionary skills.

---

* Refer to Posner and Strike (1976) and Phillips and Kelly (1975) for the distinction between logical and empirical prerequisites.

b. *Familiarity.* An individual's past experiences are often the basis of sequencing. Familiarity refers to the frequency with which an individual has encountered an idea, object, or event, that is, how commonplace it is to the individual. Seldom-seen phenomena or phenomena that an individual has heard about only occasionally are considered remote from that person's experiential past. Sequences of this subtype order units from the most familiar to the most remote (Dewey, 1938). *Examples:* Teach about American schools before teaching about Swedish schools. Teach the various occupations in the local community before teaching about careers in other communities and in other nations.

c. *Difficulty.* Factors affecting difficulty as conceived here include the following: how fine a discrimination is required, how fast a procedure must be carried out, and the mental capacity required for learning (for example, memorizing five names is typically more difficult than memorizing two names). Sequences of this subtype would teach the less difficult content before the more difficult (see Suppes, 1967). *Examples:* Teach long vowel sounds before short ones. Teach weaving slowly, then teach the pupil to speed up. Teach the spelling of short words before longer words. Teach rhymes before blank verse.

d. *Interest.* Instructional foci that stimulate or arouse interest are commonly those with which the student has had some limited experience (that is, not totally unknown to the individual) but which remain a challenge, retain the potential for surprise, or can arouse curiosity. The most commonly prescribed sequence of this subtype is to begin with those elements that are more likely to evoke student interest. The "activity" and the "children's interest core curriculum" (Smith, Stanley, & Shores, 1957) serve as illustrations of this subtype. *Examples:* Teach students how to pick a lock before teaching them how a lock works (Mager & Beach, 1967). Teach students how to dig out a local cellar hole before teaching archeology.

e. *Development.* The work of Piaget and Kohlberg has served as a focus for much current dialogue on the sequencing and structure of subject matter (see, for example, Sullivan, 1967; Strauss, 1972). Much of this dialogue centers on the importance of organizing instruction in a way that reflects the manner in which people develop psychologically. Developmental psychologists such as Piaget and Kohlberg contend that ILOs are best learned when the learner is developmentally "ready" to learn them. That is, "the ideal order of studies is one in which each experience is introduced at the most propitious time in the person's development" (Phenix, 1964). *Examples:* Teach students to base their concepts of morality on authority, then on democratically accepted law, and finally on individual principles of conscience (Kohlberg, 1963).

f. *Internalization.* When the educational intent of a sequence is to have the student internalize a belief or value, units can be ordered in a manner that reflects an increasing degree of internalization (Krathwohl, Bloom, &

Masia, 1964). *Examples:* Teach students to listen willingly to Marxian ideas, then teach them to interpret events in terms of a Marxian ideology, then teach them to view the world based on a Marxian value system. Teach students to recognize certain behaviors in others, then in themselves.

5. *Utilization-related sequences.* Knowledge and skills can be utilized in social, personal, and career contexts. These three contexts can serve as bases for organizing units. Organizing units around personal and social needs has been advocated by some leading proponents of the "core curriculum" (Giles, McCutchen, & Zechiel, 1942). After needs are identified by "experts" (for example, psychologists, sociologists, anthropologists), units are organized around them. The "adolescent-needs core," the "social-functions core," the "social-problems core" (Smith, Stanley, & Shores, 1957), and the "life activities curriculum" (Saylor & Alexander, 1966) are representative of this approach. Another utilization-related approach to organizing units employs vocational and career-based topics. Saylor and Alexander describe how

> units of study are organized on the basis of the knowledge and skills needed to perform an occupation or to carry out the duties required in a job. The mode of organization is determined by an analysis of what the workers do in a particular job and what responsibilities they fulfill as a part of the job. (1966, pp. 179–180)

The personal, social, and career contexts are appropriate primarily as categories of clustering principles, for clustering ILOs into units, and for grouping units. Within each utilization context, units can be sequenced in a way that reflects procedures for solving problems or fulfilling responsibilities, or according to the utilization potential for a given content element.

a. *Procedure.* In training programs, when a procedure or process is being taught and the units represent steps in the process, it is often appropriate for the sequence to reflect the order in which steps will be followed in carrying out the procedure. Your flowcharts for skill ILOs might be particularly useful here. One important type of procedure that is often taught is that used in confronting personal or societal problems (for example, career decision making or air pollution) (Smith, Stanley, & Shores, 1957). When units are developed to enable the pupil to solve these types of life-related problems, the units may be sequenced in an order consistent with the individual's utilization of knowledge for this purpose. *Examples:* Teach the effects of air and water pollution (that is, establish a phenomenon as a "problem"), then teach the causes (that is, analyze the problem), and then teach how to eliminate or correct the factors that cause pollution (that is, suggest solutions). In landscape architecture, teach students how to analyze a site; then how to choose landscape structures and construction materials; then how to fit trees, shrubs, and flowers to the plan; then how to design the public and living areas.

b. *Anticipated frequency of utilization.* Some course designs begin with the most important content, where "most important" means that which the student is likely to encounter most often. That is, the likelihood of encounters the student will have with various phenomena is predicted, and the order of the phenomena taught is based on the anticipated frequency of utilization in the student's future experiences. *Examples:* Teach compound interest before stock transactions. Teach how to change a TV tube before teaching how to change a resistor (Mager & Beach, 1967).

Use of the Categorization Scheme

One use of the categorization scheme is to provide a "shopping list" of sequencing principles. Awareness of this categorization system increases the probability that you will sequence units in a particular way because the chosen sequence is the most appropriate for your purposes, as state in your rationale, not because you have never thought of any alternative sequences. That is, the use of the scheme will presumably lead to greater flexibility as you organize the units of your course. For further reading of this topic Goodlad and Su (1992) is a good starting point.

QUESTIONS FOR DISCUSSION: PRINCIPLES
OF UNIT ORGANIZATION

1. In what subject-matter areas is unit organization most important? Why?
2. Are there courses of study that will include divergent, practically unrelated units in which organization will serve little or no purpose?
3. What are the criteria for choosing one principle of unit organization over another? How do these reflect educational philosophy?
4. Think of one of the best courses you have taken. Do you recall how the units were organized? Did that make a contribution to the quality of that course?
5. Think of one of the worst courses you have taken. Do you recall how the units were organized? Did that affect the quality of the course?
6. What would be the effect if, due to unexpected questions in class, the instructor teaching your course were to teach a unit out of sequence? Would this significantly weaken your course?
7. To what extent should the student be consciously aware of the unit organization?
8. Do you see any possible dangers in leaving the student uninformed about the organization of a course?
9. Can you think of other principles for organizing units other than those mentioned in this chapter?
10. What principle(s) were followed in the organization of chapters in *Course Design?*

ORGANIZING THE UNITS

Often courses are organized in a "traditional" manner; for example, history content is traditionally sequenced chronologically, with each unit representing a historical period. The preponderance of traditionally organized courses probably reflects, in part, the failure of planners to consider alternative course organizations adequately. For example, a history course could be organized around such ideas as industrialization, nationalism, and revolution rather than being organized chronologically.

Each organization can result in distinct kinds of learnings being achieved. Pupils in a history course organized chronologically would presumably gain a good sense of what events came before what other events; pupils in a conceptually organized course would likely learn the ideas the course was organized around. (Chapter 8 discusses these side effects more thoroughly.) Course organization can be an important factor in implementing a course's rationale. For this reason, a course's organization should be planned so that it is consistent with the rationale.

The overriding goal of this section is to organize the course's units in the most teachable and reasonable manner possible, as well as in the manner most consistent with the course's rationale. This goal will be accomplished by considering alternative patterns of organization.

Organized units are units in the order in which they will be presented to students taking the course. This organization is expressed in the form of a unit outline. There are three levels of unit organization: (1) the grouping of units, (2) the sequencing of groups, and (3) the sequencing of units within groups.

Grouping units consists in clustering units together in a meaningful fashion. This is analogous to clustering ILOs into units except that it is done on a more macro-level, that is, units themselves are clustered. Sequencing groups consists in ordering the grouped units in the way they will be taught. Sequencing units means ordering the units within a group in the way they will be taught. The lists that follow should help clarify what we mean by levels of grouping and sequencing of units. In these lists, the *ILOs* for a course in general math have been *clustered* into the following *units:*

the set of whole numbers

measurement

the system of decimal fractions

the metric system

subtraction and division of whole numbers

finite decimal operations

addition and multiplication of whole numbers

set theory

whole numbers—bases other than ten

the number line

real numbers

These *units* could be *grouped* as follows:

Measuring
the metric system

measurement

Whole numbers
subtraction and division of whole numbers

the set of whole numbers

addition and multiplication of whole numbers

Decimals
finite decimal operations

real numbers

the system of decimal fractions

Sets
set theory

the number line

whole numbers—bases other than ten

The *groups* could then be *sequenced* as follows:

whole numbers

sets

decimals

measuring

Within these *groups* the *unit sequence* may be as follows:

Whole numbers
the set of whole numbers

addition and multiplication of whole numbers

subtraction and division of whole numbers

Sets
set theory

whole numbers—bases other then ten

the number line

Decimals
the system of decimal fractions
finite decimal operations
real numbers

Measuring
measurement
the metric system

The example illustrates an organized course in which ILOs have been clustered into units, the units have been organized into groups, the groups are sequenced, and the units within each group are sequenced. There are really two major decisions to make. One is deciding at what levels you wish to organize your course; the other is the choice of actual organizational principles for those chosen levels. We will not attempt to prescribe which decision you should make first. For some planners, depending on the course, choosing levels of organization may be the appropriate first decision. In other instances, the planner must begin planning at one level, and wait to see if other organizational principles suggest themselves as the planning proceeds.

ALTERNATIVE ORGANIZATIONS: SOME EXAMPLES

To illustrate what is meant by alternative approaches to organization in the context of course design, let us examine some examples of unit outlines for various courses that have each been organized two different ways. You will probably receive maximum benefit from the discussion following the examples by closely examining the examples and then comparing them carefully.

Example 6.1.

American History I
1. Exploration of North America
2. Early Settlement of North America
3. Europe and the New World
4. British Dominance of Eastern North America
5. Colonial Life
6. Relationship between Colonies and Great Britain
7. American Revolution
8. Foundations of American Government
9. Westward Expansion of North America

American History II
Settlement of North America
1. Exploration of North America
2. Early Settlement of North America
3. Westward Expansion of North America

Colonial Society
4. Colonial Life
5. Foundations of American Government

Issues in Colonial North America
6. Europe and the New World
7. British Dominance of Eastern North America
8. Relationship of Colonies to Great Britain
9. American Revolution

The nine units of American History I are organized in chronological sequence. That is, the events in unit 1 temporally precede those in unit 2, the events in unit 2 precede those in unit 3, and so on. American History II is an example of a conceptual organization. That is, the units are grouped around three historical ideas: settlement, society, and issues. The units within the groups can be considered chronologically sequenced. An American history course that has as a goal providing students with an appreciation or understanding of causal factors in history or a sense of the timing of various events would probably best be sequenced chronologically. Course emphasis, on the other hand, could be on underlying issues, major themes in history, or the ability to think about history in a conceptual way, in which case a conceptual sequence would be most suitable.

Example 6.2.

Geology I
Observable Features of the Earth
  1. Gross Features of the Earth
  2. Rivers and Valleys
  3. Atmosphere, Weather, Climate
  4. Minerals and Rocks
  5. Snow and Ice
  6. Elements and Compounds

Forces Acting on the Earth's Form
  7. Rock Weathering and Soil
  8. Ground Water
  9. Valley Glaciers
  10. Continental Glaciers
  11. Wind as an Agent of Gradation
  12. Gradation by Mass Movement of Surface Materials

Geology II
Units of Earth's Geologic System
1. Elements and Compounds
2. Minerals and Rocks
3. Atmosphere, Weather, Climate
4. Snow and Ice

Forces Shaping the Earth
5. Rock Weathering and Soil
6. Valley Glaciers
7. Continental Glaciers
8. Wind as an Agent of Gradation
9. Graduation by Mass Movement of Surface Materials

Physical Features of the Earth
10. Gross Features of the Earth
11. Ground Water
12. Rivers and Valleys

Geology I contains units sequenced within groups according to the assumed familiarity of the content of the learners. The units progress roughly from those most familiar to the learner to those least familiar. Note that sequencing on the basis of familiarity requires information about the audience because different audiences may find different topics more or less familiar. The groups are formed on the basis of common properties: features and forces. Geology II contains units grouped in a conceptual organization. The units are formed around three geological ideas: basic units, forces, and physical features. The groups are, in turn, logically sequenced from raw materials, to forces acting on them, to the resulting geological features. The two sequences reflect very different though not incompatible concerns on the part of the course designer. Geology I is sequenced in a manner designed to facilitate learning based on the assumption that the content is difficult because of the students' unfamiliarity with it. Geology II emphasizes a concern for the students being able to grasp geological ideas and to relate physical features to their shaping forces. The difference between Geology I and II is one of emphasis.

Example 6.3.

The Media I
Media Functions
1. Role of the Media in Shaping Society
2. Current Activities of Broadcast and Print Media
3. Differences Between Various Media
4. Advertising

Historical Context
5. Development of U.S. Media
6. International Media Systems
7. The Future of the Media

Influences on the Media
8. External Influences on the Media
9. Legal Constraints on the Media

Accessibility
10. Public Access to the Media

The Media II
1. Advertising
2. Public Access to the Media
3. Role of the Media in Shaping Society
4. Current Activities of Broadcast and Print Media
5. The Future of the Media
6. External Influences on the Media
7. International Media Systems
8. Differences Between Various Media
9. Development of U.S. Media
10. Legal Constraints on the Media

The Media I and II represent part of a high school senior English course. The Media I has a conceptual organization of units. That is, the units are grouped around the concepts of function, historical context, influence, and accessibility. The units in The Media II are ordered on the basis of interest. That is, the sequence progresses from those units thought to be of greatest interest to the learner to those units thought to be of least interest. The Media II reflects a greater concern, on the part of the planner, with the motivation of learners. That is, an emphasis on understanding conceptual relations (stressed in The Media I) is sacrificed for an emphasis that is likely to get the students interested in the course.

Exercise 6.1.   Now try suggesting alternative organizations. For each set of units below, decide on two possible types of organizations that could be employed and organize the units in each of the two selected patterns. You will probably find that additional units must be added to effect your chosen patterns. Feel free to add these units. The units presented in the exercises are listed in random order. Your task is to create a sensible pattern or flow of units.

Exercise A: Basic Ecology
Biomes of the World

The Community

Ecological Succession

Periodic Changes in Communities

The Living Environment

What Is Ecology?

The Distribution of Plants and Animals

Climatic Gradients in Plants and Animals

The Physical Environment

Exercise B: Introduction to Sociology
Culture

Groups

Social Organization

Collective Behavior

Socialization

Social Stratification

Major Social Institutions

Urbanism and Industrialism

Exercise C: American History I
The Jacksonian Era

The Road to Revolution

The Origin of the Thirteen Colonies

The Confederation and the Constitution

The War of 1812

The Winning of Independence

The Development of the Thirteen Colonies

People Moving West

Jefferson in Power

To this point the outlines presented have been examples of relatively pure types. A "pure" type refers to the use of just one basis or principle of organization at a particular level. Often it is impossible or undesirable to produce a pattern that represents a pure type of organization. For example, we might want our course organization to reflect the way the world is, the way people learn, and the way they will utilize learnings in life. In such cases we attempt to produce a unit organization that reflects an optimal blend of principles. A "blend" refers to an organization of content that embodies more than one principle or basis.

Example 6.4.

Economics and History I
1. Basic Economic Concepts
2. The Depression (an in-depth view)

3. The New Deal (policies and politics)
4. The Development of the U.S. Economy
5. The Economy Today
6. Economic Futurism (the next 50 years)

Economics and History II
1. The Economy Today
2. Basic Economic Concepts
3. The Development of the U.S. Economy
4. The Depression (an in-depth view)
5. The New Deal (policies and politics)
6. Economic Futurism (the next 50 years)

Economics and History is an advanced high school course. Economics and History I begins with basic ideas; takes a micro-look at a period of economic upheaval in the United States; then takes a macro-look at past, present, and future economic conditions. The organization of units represents a blend of logical prerequisites (that is, basic economic ideas), level of abstraction (since a "micro-look" at the Depression is more concrete than a "macro-look" at the New Deal), and chronology (that is, past, present, and future). Economics and History II begins with the present, moves to basic ideas, then to a macro-to-micro view, and finally ends with a look at the future. The organization of units represents a blend of learning theory (since the unit starts with something familiar, that is, the present), conceptual structure (that is, the basic ideas), and chronology (that is, past to future). The major difference between these two units is that Economics and History II is sequenced so as to interest and presumably motivate students. Economics and History I reflects the planner's concern for providing basic economic ideas at the very outset of the course.

Example 6.5.

Juvenile Delinquent Behavior I
1. The Prevalence of Juvenile Delinquency
2. Types of Juvenile Delinquent Acts
3. Types of Juvenile Delinquents
4. Primary Causes of Juvenile Delinquency
5. The Prediction of Delinquency
6. The Prevention of Delinquency
7. The Treatment of Delinquency

Juvenile Delinquent Behavior II
1. Primary Causes of Juvenile Delinquency
2. The Prediction of Delinquency
3. Types of Juvenile Delinquents
4. Types of Juvenile Delinquent Acts
5. The Prevalence of Juvenile Delinquency
6. The Treatment of Delinquency
7. The Prevention of Delinquency

Juvenile Delinquent Behavior I begins with an overview describing the prevalence of delinquency. Ideas are then presented (that is, types of acts, types of delinquents, primary causes), and methods of prediction, prevention, and treatment are included. Thus Juvenile Delinquent Behavior I represents a blending of learning-, concept-, and utilization-related bases. Juvenile Delinquent Behavior II intersperses methods of prevention, prediction, and treatment of delinquency with a logical development of ideas (that is, causes, types of delinquents, types of acts, prevalence). Thus Juvenile Delinquent Behavior II represents a blend of utilization- and concept-related sequencing principles. These two organizations are similar in emphasis. Juvenile Delinquent Behavior II integrates theory and practice to a greater extent than Juvenile Delinquent Behavior I. Delinquency II is directed more toward people who might actually counsel youth, whereas Delinquency I emphasizes an understanding of theory and of treatment instead of an understanding of how theory and practice are related.

This discussion of blending should be viewed as a representative rather than a comprehensive cataloging of options. Once understood, these alternatives should serve merely as a basis for thinking about unit organization flexibly, not as a structure into which thinking must be forced.

Exercise 6.2.   Organize the set of units below into a pattern that embodies two or more organizational principles or bases. Again, feel free to add any units you may need.

Introductory Business Math
Interest and Compound Interest

Stocks and Bonds

Fundamental Mathematical Processes

Payrolls and Taxes

Fractions: Decimal and Common

Financial Statements

Percentage in Business

The organizational alternatives in both pure and blended forms should provide you with a number of options when organizing units. You should keep in mind the goals of teachability, reasonability, and consistency with the course rationale.

Again, flexibility is of primary importance when organizing your units. Carefully consider the various alternatives available before deciding on an organization.

Also try to approach course organization imaginatively. For example, one course planner used an approach that included "floating units," those units that can be inserted at any time in the course. A floating unit provides a breather at various times during the duration of a course, although course-related learnings are involved.

The makeup of each unit (that is, the particular cluster of ILOs) determines to some extent where that unit falls in a course. You may, at this time, want to reform some of your units in order to organize the course in a way that appears most appropriate to you.

Course Planning Step 6.1.   Organize the units of your course into a unit outline. This step involves a combination of grouping and sequencing your units as explained by the various options. If in the process of organizing your units you find that the units themselves need to be reformed, don't hesitate to do this. Also, take another look at your rationale, making sure it is consistent with the unit outline. Now is a good time to revise your list of ILOs, adding new ones as needed or eliminating some if you find that they do not fit into any of your units.

Remember, course design is not a linear process. You will constantly need to go back to previous work, revising, adding, and deleting as you progress.

QUESTIONS FOR DISCUSSION: THE UNIT OUTLINE

1. Is your organization of the units consistent with the course rationale? What does the course rationale imply (if anything) about the organization of the course?
2. Is the curriculum coherent? Around what does it cohere? Content? ILOs? Projects? Problems? Media? Other foci?
3. What does the organization of the curriculum contribute to the curriculum as a whole? For example, does it highlight the conceptual nature of the subject matter (as in a history course organized around conceptual themes)? Does it emphasize the utility of the subject matter (as in a course guiding the learner toward the completion of some product, such as *Course Design* attempts to do)?
4. In the process of organizing your unit outline, were any new ILOs suggested? If so, specify them.
5. Suppose that considerations of time forced you to abbreviate your course by one-fifth. How would you do this? Would you shorten units, delete one or more units, combine units, or none of these?
6. Suppose you were able to add 20 percent more instructional time to your course. What would you do? Would you expand some units (which?), add new units, split some units into two, or would you do something else?
7. Is there a midpoint "break" in your course? Should you have a "review" unit any place in your unit outline?
8. Sometimes a unit may serve more than one purpose. Could any of your units be retitled to indicate their other purpose? Which ones?
9. How are your high-priority ILOs distributed across your units? If they are distributed unevenly, does this accurately reflect the relative priority for each unit? Are any units crucial? Are any units trivial or of little consequence?
10. You may have rejected several alternative organizations. What grounds can you give for rejecting them?

ANSWERS TO EXERCISES

Answers to Exercise 6.1

The organizations or "answers" given here represent possible orderings of the units provided in the exercise. "Correctness" of your answer rests on whether or not your organization is justifiable as being both teachable and reasonable.

A.
1. What Is Ecology?
2. The Physical Environment
3. The Living Environment
4. The Community
5. Periodic Changes in Communities
6. Ecological Succession
7. The Distribution of Plants and Animals
8. Climatic Gradients in Plants and Animals
9. Biomes of the World

This is a concept-related sequence. Each chapter or unit is logically prerequisite to each succeeding chapter. The ideas presented in one unit are necessary to understand ideas presented in later units. Another possible ordering of units is illustrated below. This organization is also concept-related, but the units are grouped into categories.

A (alternative):
Introduction
1. What Is Ecology?

Adaptation of Living Things
2. The Distribution of Plants and Animals
3. Climatic Gradients in Plants and Animals
4. Biomes of the World

An Ecosystem
5. The Physical Environment
6. The Living Environment
7. The Community

Changes in Ecosystems
8. Periodic Changes in Communities
9. Ecological Succession

B:
1. Groups
2. Social Organization
3. Collective Behavior
4. Socialization
5. Social Stratification
6. Major Social Institutions
7. Urbanism and Industrialism
8. Culture

This ordering of units is illustrative of a sequence based on conceptual sophistication. The units progress from least to most sophisticated.

> *C:*
> 1. The Origin of the Thirteen Colonies
> 2. The Development of the Thirteen Colonies
> 3. The Road to Revolution
> 4. The Winning of Independence
> 5. The Confederation and the Constitution
> 6. Jefferson in Power
> 7. The War of 1812
> 8. The Jacksonian Era
> 9. People Moving West

The units of this sequence are presented in chronological order.

Answers to Exercise 6.2

> 1. Fundamental Mathematical Processes
> 2. Fractions: Decimal and Common
> 3. Percentage in Business
> 4. Interest and Compound Interest
> 5. Payrolls and Taxes
> 6. Financial Statements
> 7. Stocks and Bonds

This sequence is a blend of two major types. Units 1, 2, and 3 are logically prerequisite to each other and logically prerequisite to the other units. That is, fundamental mathematical processes are needed in order to learn fractions. Likewise, the operations of the first three units are needed in order to calculate interest. Units 4 through 7 are sequenced on the basis of how frequently they are used. That is, problems and situations involving interest arise more frequently than problems or situations involving financial statements.

REFERENCES

Atkin, J. M., & House, Z. R. (1981). The federal role in curriculum development, 1950–1980. *Educational Evaluation and Policy Analysis, 3,* 5–36.

Ausubel, D. P. (1964). Some psychological aspects of the structure of knowledge. In S. Elam (Ed.), *Education and the structure of knowledge* (pp. 220–262). Chicago: Rand McNally.

Ausubel, D. P., Novak, J. D., & Hanesian, H. (1978). *Educational psychology: A cognitive view.* New York: Holt, Rinehart, & Winston.

Bruner, J. S. (1960). *The process of education.* New York: Vintage Books.

Bruner, J. S. (1976). *Toward a theory of instruction.* New York: Norton.

Bruner, J. S., Goodnow, J. J., & Austin, G. A. (1956). *A study of thinking.* New York: John Wiley.

Dahllof, U., & Lundgren, U. (1970). *Macro and micro approaches combined for curriculum process analysis: A Swedish educational field project.* Paper presented at the annual convention of the American Educational Research Association, Minneapolis, MN.

Dewey, J. (1916). *Democracy and education.* New York: Macmillan.

Dewey, J. (1938). *Experience and education.* New York: Macmillan.

Elam, S. (Ed.). (1964). *Education and the structure of knowledge.* Chicago: Rand McNally.

Ford, G. W., & Pugno, L. (Eds.). (1964). *The structure of knowledge and the curriculum.* Chicago: Rand McNally.

Gagné, R. M. (1970). *The conditions of learning* (2nd ed.). New York: Holt, Rinehart, & Winston.

Giles, H. H., McCutchen, S. P., & Zechiel, A. N. (1942). *Exploring the curriculum.* New York: Harper & Row.

Glaser, R. (1966). Variables in discovery learning. In L. S. Schulman & E. R. Keislar (Eds.), *Learning by discovery: A critical appraisal* (pp. 13–26). Chicago: Rand McNally.

Goodlad, J. I., & Su, Z. (1992). Organization of the curriculum. In P. W. Jackson, (Ed.), *Handbook of research on curriculum* (pp. 327–344). New York: Macmillan.

Kliebard, H. M. (1965). Structure of the disciplines as an educational slogan. *Teachers College Record, 66,* 598–603.

Kohlberg, L. (1963). The development of children's orientation toward a moral order: I. Sequence in the development of moral thought. *Vita Humana, 6,* 11–33.

Krathwohl, D. R., Bloom, B. S., & Masia, B. B. (1964). *Taxonomy of educational objectives. Handbook II: Affective domain.* New York: David McKay.

Mager, R. F., & Beach, K. M. (1967). *Developing vocational instruction.* Palo Alto, CA: Fearon.

Parker, J. C., & Rubin, L. J. (1966). *Process as content.* Chicago: Rand McNally.

Phenix, P. H. (1964). *Realms of meaning.* New York: McGraw-Hill.

Phillips, D. C., & Kelly, M. E. (1975). Hierarchical theories of development in education and psychology. *Harvard Educational Review, 45,* 351–375.

Popper, K. R. (1959). *The logic of scientific discovery.* London: Hutchins.

Posner, G. J., & Strike, K. A. (1976). A categorization scheme for principles of sequencing content. *Review of Educational Research, 46,* 665–690.

Saylor, J. G., & Alexander, W. M. (1966). *Curriculum planning for modern schools.* New York: Holt, Rinehart, & Winston.

Schwab, J. J. (1962). The concept of the structure of a discipline. *Educational Record, 43,* 197–209.

Schwab, J. J. (1964). Structure of the disciplines: Meanings and significances. In G. W. Ford & L. Pugno (Eds.), *The structure of knowledge and the curriculum* (pp. 1–30). Chicago: Rand McNally.

Shulman, L. S. (1970). Psychology and mathematics education. In E. G. Begle (Ed.), *Mathematics education. The sixty-ninth yearbook of the National Society for the Study of Education.* Chicago: University of Chicago Press.

Smith, B. O., Stanley, W. O., & Shores, J. H. (1957). *Fundamentals of curriculum development* (rev. ed.). New York: Harcourt Brace Jovanovich.

Sullivan, E. V. (1967). *Piaget and the school curriculum: A critical appraisal* (Bulletin No. 2). Toronto: Ontario Institute for Studies in Education.

Suppes, P. (1967). Some theoretical models for mathematics learning. *Journal of Research and Development in Education, 1,* 5–22.

CHAPTER 7

Developing General Teaching Strategies

After completing this chapter, you should be able to:

Elaborate instructional foci into general teaching strategies for course units.

Instruction, in our framework, is made up of all the teacher's purposeful activities aimed at producing, stimulating, or facilitating learning by students. Instruction deals with how and what methods, materials, strategies, tasks, and incentives can be employed to encourage learning. Instructional planning is a task carried out by teachers. Teachers may set the stage for learning but they share that stage with students, and once instruction begins it is students who occupy the center of the stage.

Learning is an active process and, therefore, requires that students engage in some activity. As Walker succinctly states:

> The most important principle of classroom activity design is that **the students' actions determine what will be learned**. . . . The kernel of an educational activity, then, is what the student is to do. (Walker, 1990, pp. 366–367)

The activity need not be overt and physical; it can be listening, reading, and thinking. In fact, except perhaps for simple motor skills, it is mental activity that is most important. Teachers should try to design instructional tasks, activities, and environments that will engage learners in the appropriate kinds of processing, thinking, or mental activity. Appropriateness is gauged by the kind of learning being sought. Different kinds of thought are needed for different types of learning outcomes. Instruction is well planned to the extent it succeeds in fostering appropriate thinking.

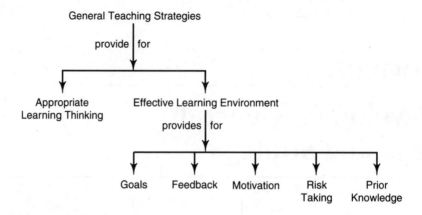

EFFECTIVE LEARNING ENVIRONMENTS

Effective instruction exists in many forms and varieties. A comprehensive treatment of instruction and instructional planning is beyond the scope of this book. This chapter presents some general guidelines and examples to get you started thinking about and designing appropriate instructional strategies for your course. The guidelines begin with points to consider in creating an optimal environment or atmosphere for learning. Such environments include (but are not limited to) provisions for the following:

1. Goals
2. Feedback
3. Motivation
4. Risk taking
5. Prior knowledge

Goals

Stop to think about some of your significant educational experiences. It is likely that you or your teacher began with a goal or purpose. That goal may have been like a destination you were trying to reach, such as achieving a certain degree of skill in debating, playing the piano, or playing tennis. Or your goal may have been developing an understanding of a particular topic, or an idea, such as the gross national product. While still a novice, you probably had only a vague idea of what there was to be learned in a particular area. In fact, your initial goal might be described more as a direction than a destination. Students can begin to learn and teachers can begin to teach once they have some initial direction. As they progress, they will undoubtedly modify and clarify their goals. In addition, they will probably arrive at some initially unanticipated points. Their accomplishments will often result in a readjustment of their plans and a resetting of their goals.

It is important that students' conceptions of learning go beyond the narrow view that they are simply acquiring a discrete piece of knowledge or skill. When school-work is seen as made up of independent elements of knowledge and skill, students will master the elements without being able to use the knowledge broadly or flexibly. They will not be able to transfer what they have learned to other contexts and situations. What they will have acquired is "inert knowledge" (Whitehead, 1916). Students' views of what they are trying to achieve should include a clear perspective on the use and usefulness of the knowledge or skill being taught.

Feedback

Most successful educational experiences also require feedback. Feedback means getting information about progress toward one's goal. Good instruction includes such feedback. Besides guiding students personally and directly, teachers can set up situations that inherently provide students with feedback. Playing tennis against an opponent, clocking speed on a stopwatch, answering textbook questions while reading difficult material, working collaboratively with other students, engaging in a conversation about a new topic, and solving problems while studying new material all provide feedback for students. Feedback does not mean that the teacher judges the student's performance. Instead, feedback helps students in monitoring their own progress and in deciding for themselves how best to expend their energies.

Motivation

For a host of reasons, people typically learn well what they want to learn. Although students can get a good grade in a boring course or in a subject in which they have little interest, significant learning is not likely when students are unmotivated (see Borich, 1992).

Motivation is a complex topic. Many factors contribute to the motivation of students, and all students are different. Interest, curiosity, competition, social reasons, parental pressure, the need to achieve, health, money, power, and fear are a few motivating factors. These act in complex combinations as well as alone.

Although there is much debate about the topic, motivation is best thought of as internal. That is, the attitudes, energy, concentration, and excitement that make up student motivation can be brought about only by the students themselves. Teachers don't motivate students, strictly speaking. Teachers' responsibility is to design environments that are likely to engage students so that students motivate themselves to learn. Among the most powerful instructional factors that teachers can employ is making instruction interesting and relevant to students' lives. At the same time teachers can design environments where student effort pays off in terms of successful learning. Teachers can draw attention to the fact that effort is important. Whether teachers' actions result in student motivation is always a question. Not all students will find the same material interesting or relevant. Teachers cannot afford to worry about motivating every student every single day. Motivation is best thought of as a long-term undertaking, not a day-to-day search for instructional gimmicks.

Risk Taking

Significant learning often occurs in a setting where it is safe to try. Learning always has beginning stages. Skill and understanding, depending on their complexity, can require much time and effort before any level of competence or mastery is attained. Learning, particularly in a group setting, can be a very threatening, high-risk venture. Yet students learn better when they take reasonable chances and do not restrict their output—when they make errors and learn from their mistakes. Instruction is improved by creating a learning environment in which students will take reasonable risks, where there is no danger of ridicule, and where errors are instructive, not embarrassing.

When thinking about evaluating or critiquing student work, teachers might consider rewarding certain kinds of mistakes. Mistakes that suggest students are trying new skills or approaches, formulating new ideas, putting old ideas together in novel ways, or otherwise taking intellectual risks could be rewarded. This would go a long way toward creating a supportive learning environment.

Prior Knowledge

Learning is a profoundly relative process. What students learn depends enormously on what they already know. The more one knows and is able to do, the more and more easily one can learn new material. Meaningful learning occurs when new and existing knowledge are related. Instruction, to be successful, depends on having students build on their existing knowledge. When students lack any point of reference, learning is relegated to rote memorization of information or procedures. This kind of learning is typically short lived and not very useful. Thus good instruction provides opportunities for teachers to gain some understanding of their students' current knowledge states. Having a conception of what students know helps teachers plan instruction that builds bridges between new and existing knowledge and, when necessary, provide opportunities for students to acquire background knowledge.

We raise these initial points in order to place instruction and instructional planning in perspective. Planning and carrying out instruction involves more than creating strategies directly aimed at achieving intended learnings. Instruction is not an independent, day-to-day collection of activities or tasks. We have met teachers who think instructional planning is writing objectives and designing activities the night before they are to be used. This is far too reductionist a view of instructional planning. Students do not learn in nice, neat daily bites; this is especially true if our intentions include cognitions. The details of daily plans may be formulated in this way but these daily plans ought to come from a general teaching strategy that takes a broader and more integrated view of the curriculum. Instruction also involves providing an effective and humane instructional context in which these activities take place. Keeping these initial points in mind can help create an effective learning environment.

ACADEMIC TASKS

Research in cognitive science suggests that a crucial determinant of learning is students' thinking or cognitive processing, and this processing is directly influenced by the kind of tasks in which students actually engage. Teachers think of schoolwork as the material they present and the work they assign. Sometimes, however, there is a difference between schoolwork as teachers plan it and the academic tasks and commensurate thinking in which students ultimately are engaged (Doyle, 1983).

This potential discrepancy means that teachers ought to think about not only what they will assign and present but the qualities of student thought or engagement that they are seeking to engender. Doing so requires teachers to consider performances or products the students will formulate (for example, book reports, essays, comments during discussion, arithmetic worksheets), the operations used in this formulation (for example, memorizing, following correct steps, reading and synthesizing), and the resources students are provided for their work (for example, directions, books and other materials, knowledge they are presumed to have). Appearing to do the work is not enough—teachers need to hold students accountable for the desired quality of thought or engagement. Student accountability is conveyed through tests and other formal methods of evaluation and also through the questions teachers ask, the feedback teachers give, and all the other cues teachers provide that indicate and emphasize desired learnings. Whenever possible, learners should have a clear idea of the kind of learning for which they are accountable.

Being clear about intended learning outcomes does not mean one should simplify them. Ambiguity is a concomitant feature of academic work and the classroom accountability structure (Doyle, 1983). Some learning is relatively unambiguous. This is the case for cognitive skills, especially simple skills. For example, holding students accountable for multiplying decimals or recalling a set of definitions is unambiguous. Students know quite clearly what they will be asked to do. In fact, accountability and learning activities are often identical. However, accountability can require considerable ambiguity. This is typically the case for understanding and higher-level learning in general. If, for example, students are to understand "balance of trade," we do not want to tell them explicitly how they will be held accountable. We may ask them to explain balance of trade in their own words, provide examples of unfavorable and favorable balances, or describe an imaginary nation and ask for predictions about its trade balance. The learning activities that lead to understanding "balance of trade" also will be varied. They may be similar to accountability tasks, but should not be identical. If teachers describe accountability tasks or performances unambiguously, students are likely to learn only what the teacher has told them they will have to "do."

Students do not like ambiguity. They direct significant effort at reducing the ambiguity of tasks and expectations. Most teachers are familiar with questions students ask about how long assignments must be, whether material will be included on tests, and what the nature of tests or other performances will be. Teachers can help students realize that comprehension, understanding, and other high-level outcomes (i.e., cognitions), while difficult, are worth working to achieve. Over time students will realize that understandings require learning strategies that go beyond memorization or narrowly focusing on the acquisition of a specific performance. Learning activities will require that students encounter and use content in many different ways. Accountability tasks will be ambiguous because they require novelty that goes beyond the learning tasks.

For example, a teacher may want to present material about the relationship of gas volume to pressure and temperature. If the intended learning involves comprehension of this relationship, students will have to understand how pressure and temperature affect molecular behavior. They will need to know or learn a model that allows them to picture molecules and understand the effects of changing energy states on molecules. Students should be engaged in tasks requiring inferences about how changing these variables affects molecular structure. Experiments that allow students to "play" with these relationships and begin to develop their own formulae expressing the relationships are desirable academic tasks. Too frequently, however, our tasks and accountability system emphasize solving problems that require the simple application of formulae (for example, $PV = nRT$). Students learn how to substitute numbers into a formula rather than gain the higher level of understanding originally intended. Teachers' questions, such as what happens to tire pressure when traveling at high speeds, or how a racquetball feels after being hit many times, would help students realize that they are accountable for more than applying a formula.

TEACHING STRATEGIES

In this chapter you will design general teaching strategies (that is, the instructional events) for each of your course's units. These general teaching strategies are described in your course design at a level more general than daily lesson plans but more specific than a list of resource materials to be used. A teaching strategy is based on instructional foci (see chapter 5) and thus covers a unit or subunit-sized chunk of your course. An instructional focus (for example, a poem) identifies the "heart" of a strategy but does not describe the pattern of interaction among the students, material, and teacher. This interaction (that is, who does or says what, with or to whom) is described in the instructional strategy.

Even the most elegantly organized course, designed for the achievement of the most worthwhile learning, can fail if the teaching strategies employed are inappropriate or insufficient for the desired learnings (Greenwood & Parkay, 1989; Bellon, Bellon, & Blank, 1992). A good deal of attention and effort has already been given to the categorization of intended learning outcomes. One of the reasons cited for this work was the fact that different kinds of learnings require different kinds of instructional strategies (see Bell-Gredler, 1986). Let us examine several special considerations for designing teaching strategies aimed at skills, cognitions, and affects.

Teaching Skills

In teaching a cognitive or psychomotor-perceptual skill, practice is a crucial learning activity. Instruction for skills typically includes a presentation or initial teaching of the skill and then opportunities to practice. Skills are often broken down into simpler subskills for the purposes of presentation and practice. Complex skills should be subjected to a cognitive task analysis resulting in flowcharts or other specifications of substeps (see chapter 2.) Teachers can then decide what size chunks to teach. Skills need not be taught intact. That is, complex skills consisting of many substeps can be mastered incrementally. Students may learn the first several substeps before proceeding on to successive steps. Once the steps or substeps of a skill are presented, students need opportunities for practice. Instructional strategies that provide for practice need to consider goals, guidance, motivation, risk taking, and prior knowledge. All of these points are important but motivation is crucial, since too often practice becomes unchallenging, boring, repetitive seat work.

Two additional factors teachers might consider when designing skill instruction are difficulty and transfer. Opportunities to practice skills can vary from easy to hard. Maintaining a single or narrow level of difficulty in practice activities is misleading to both students and teachers. For example, if students are learning how to outline, they can be given multiple opportunities to outline. Initially material that is not too long or intricately structured can be outlined. Later practice could be based on longer, more complex material.

Transfer too is something teachers designing skill instruction can think about. Skill transfer tends to be quite specific. The more similar a situation or context is to that in which the skill was practiced, the more likely the skill will be employed properly. Unfortunately, knowing how to perform a skill does not guarantee that a person will know when to do so. If students are to know when to use skills and can use them in different contexts and in flexible ways, practice opportunities need to be varied. For example, students might outline a variety of material, for example, fiction, journalism, technical text, and historical writing. In addition, students can be given practice opportunities where they use more than one skill and are not explicitly directed to use the skill. Students, for instance, may need to gather information for a debate. Outlining would be an appropriate skill to use. However, instruction or guidance would come after students had an initial opportunity to use their outlining skills spontaneously. Teachers could point out aspects of the situation that cue the utility of this skill to students who did not use outlining.

Sometimes students attempt to learn a skill by memorizing the skill's specific steps or substeps; their practice often takes the form of mental rehearsal or repetition. Rehearsal often is not the most effective strategy for remembering a skill's steps. Students would benefit greatly from explicit instruction that taught them to use other strategies such as imagery, chunking, and various mnemonics. (See West, Farmer, & Wolff, 1991; Bransford & Stein, 1984; Halpern, 1989.) Memorization may be an appropriate strategy for the early stages of skill acquisition. However, a learning strategy that relies exclusively on memory is apt to result in rote learning. Teachers should guard against rote learning of skills by making clear the reasons for the steps and by showing how a skill relates to other skills or ideas.

Teaching Cognitions

In teaching cognitions, the principal instructional consideration is providing for elaboration. Elaboration requires that students have multiple and diverse opportunities for engaging new content. When comprehension or understanding is the goal of instruction, students must integrate new knowledge with existing knowledge. To accomplish this, students must think about and think with the new material in a variety of ways. Listening, note taking, explaining, analyzing, discussing, developing, critiquing, inventing, experimenting, comparing, arguing, defending, and justifying are a few of the kinds of engagement that lead to elaboration. Teachers can design instruction that provides such opportunities. Time constraints often necessitate compromise. Teachers cannot include all the possible forms of elaboration. However, they can select activities that suit their content and audience. Keep in mind that to the extent new ideas build on existing knowledge, students will have repeated chances to use their knowledge in a variety of ways.

Transfer and difficulty are important considerations when instruction focuses on elaboration. Transfer and varied difficulty are virtually built into the notion of elaboration. Nevertheless, they should not be taken for granted. Activities can be consciously designed to vary in difficulty and context. Clearly, teaching for cognitions is a slow process. The multiple learning activities required by an elaboration strategy take time. We believe that this is truly an instance where "less is more" (Sizer, 1984). The power, flexibility, and durability of meaningful learning are worth the time and over the long haul provide students with more lasting and worthwhile outcomes.

Teaching Affects

The teaching of affects is a difficult area for which to provide guidance. In addition to cognitive engagement, affective learning usually requires emotional involvement and often some degree of personal commitment. The range of how people cognitively react to a situation is great, but it is probably much less variable than their emotional reaction. Combine this with the fact that educators disagree as to what affects are (let alone agreeing on acceptable instructional practice), and you will understand the difficulty of suggesting strategies for affective learning. We cite some samples of general instructional practices currently used or advocate for teaching affects.

1. Involvement in the learning experience is crucial to affective teaching and learning. Emotional involvement differs in some ways from intellectual or cognitive involvement; it involves strong feelings, some degree of risk, and a relating of the experience to the learner's personal life. If the learner is expected to attach positive value to a thing or person (for example, liking, enjoyment, value, respect), the learning experience must allow for positive emotion. The obverse is true for an ILO aimed at negative values or feelings.

2. An atmosphere of freedom and trust facilitates the willingness of the learner to take risks. Learnings that require self-understanding, self-knowledge, or beliefs and values involve varying degrees of personal risk. For example, learning whether or not to sample new recipes is much less profound and involves much less risk for the learner than learning whether or not he or she is prejudiced. When personal risk is high, the learner must trust and feel comfortable with the environment.

3. The depth or level at which the affective strategies can be used depends largely on the group (their age, maturity, size, trust, and respect for one another) and how comfortable the teacher is in leading these exercises.

4. Affective intended learnings usually have specific referents for the learner, such as respecting others' opinions, valuing clear writing, and being aware of one's attitude toward minority groups. The techniques we present are intended to give some idea of what teachers can do to involve learners emotionally. The referent or subject matter depends on the particular course, the learners, the teachers, and the milieu.

5. Many affects are best learned through modeling; that is, the teacher (or fellow classmates) act in ways that embody the affect and learners attempt to imitate or model themselves after these "significant others." Clearly, modeling accounts for much of our significant informal educational experiences. Parents, for example, have long realized that their children ignore suggestions to do as the parents say, not as they do.

What follows are suggestions for teaching affects. They represent a compilation of techniques that have been found to facilitate affective learning. These techniques include ways to structure learning situations and kinds of activities that may be used. The techniques are illustrative of the type of classroom situation or activity appropriate for teaching affects.

The techniques are organized into five categories. Each category represents a useful framework for thinking about these and other affective teaching techniques. In planning to teach an affective ILO, a teacher would probably want to use techniques from a number of categories rather than from only one type of category.

There are always ways in which to structure interpersonal interactions that facilitate the giving or receiving of feedback. Feedback is a response or return of information from one person to another. The response may be to an act performed by a person or simply to the person's presence. The response may be descriptive of what was seen, sensed, felt, and thought, or the response may be judgmental, that is, placing a value on the object or actor. Feedback is best accomplished in small group situations in which people are with the same group members for several meetings. Each time the group meets, exercises and activities should aim at building trust. Two- and three-person groups, referred to in much of the affective literature as *dyads* and *triads*, are often employed to help establish this feeling of trust.

Techniques can be used to help students explore thoughts, feelings, and fantasies about themselves, others, or even places and things. The teacher often sets up the situation that people will explore either individually or as a group. This technique makes the experiencing or expressing of certain feelings or values easier, as the risks associated with simulation are typically less than those associated with reality.

Relatively straightforward technique can be used to help students pay attention to present physical and emotional sensations and to feelings and values. They are an aid in helping students explore feelings and discovering how and when they block out the present. The techniques may be as simple as having students begin sentences with the word *now*.

Techniques that involve students playing the role of another person or object can be used. Role playing is related to fantasy explorations except that role playing is more active; typically students act out a role in front of others. These techniques allow students to try out behaviors, feelings, and values not usually a part of their repertoire. In this way they can add to their own behavior repertoire, as well as identify more easily with the behaviors and the feelings of others. Becoming an object or playing the role of another person, describing these experiences, and generally using theater games are all role-playing techniques.

This category is a broad one, encompassing a great deal of the interpersonal interactions of the students. It includes kinds of communication often ignored by students, such as facial expressions, body language, and other nonverbal forms of communication. This category also includes situations in which the content of communication is specified. Describing "things I like to do" is such a situation.

These categories are neither exhaustive nor mutually exclusive. They illustrate the range of considerations necessary when planning for affective learning. You will find many ideas and examples of the situation and exercises described above in Borton (1970), Brown (1971), Gordon (1966), Hawley and Hawley (1972), Morris (1978), Raths, Harmin, and Simon (1966), Schmuck and Schmuck (1974), Stevens (1971), and Weinberg (1972).

APPROACHES TO INSTRUCTION

Many theories, approaches, and models of instruction have been devised and presented to teachers. Some of these are short-lived fads while others endure. Some are content specialized, such as process writing or whole language instruction. Some are more general, such as mastery learning and individually guided instruction. While we cannot present even a fraction of the available instructional approaches, we would like to call your attention to some that are current and seem promising in that they incorporate many features that are essential for effective instruction. These approaches to instruction are not exclusive; many of the features that make an approach effective are shared.

Below is an annotated bibliography. Reading these items will provide you with some helpful background about current instructional approaches. Readings are included, in part, because their own references are extensive. You will find complete citations for this bibliography in the chapter's reference section.

Baron, J. B., and Sternberg, R. J. (Eds.). (1987). *Teaching thinking skills: Theory and practice.*
   This collection is focused on incorporating thinking skills into classroom instruction. Teachers will find in these chapters many useful suggestions for engaging students in

problem solving and critical thinking as part of regular content-based instruction. Of particular note is the chapter by Robert H. Ennis in which he provides a comprehensive taxonomy of critical thinking skills. Critical thinking, thinking skills, and reasoning are used so commonly, often with a lack of clarity. Ennis's chapter is a tonic for teachers who have wondered just what critical thinking is but have been afraid to ask.

Charles, R. I., and Silver, E. A. (Eds.). (1988). *The teaching and assessing of mathematical problem solving.*
This is an edited volume sponsored by the National Council of Teachers of Mathematics. While especially applicable to teachers of mathematics, many of the articles discuss problem solving in ways that have general interest and application. Several chapters discuss the use of social and collaborative structures to create a classroom culture that supports learning, problem solving, and intellectual discourse. Other chapters focus on metacognitive aspects of instruction, that is, helping students become more self-regulating learners.

A special issue of *Educational Psychologist.* (Spring 1987).
This is a special issue devoted to school and classroom organization. Several contributions by Robert Slavin review and describe various approaches to grouping for instruction. Tracking, ability grouping, and hetero- and homogeneous grouping for instruction are important issues for teachers. This volume will help teachers think about these and other issues of instructional grouping.

Gardner, M., Greeno, J. G., Reif, F., Schoenfeld, A. H., diSessa, A., and Stage, E. (Eds.). (1990). *Toward a scientific practice of science education.*
A collection of articles about instruction in science. One section explores the social context of learning and how this can be taken advantage of and incorporated into instructional designs. An article by Brown and Campione explains explicit strategy instruction and reciprocal teaching. Teachers should be aware of both of these instructional strategies.

Halpern, D. F. (1989). *Thought and knowledge: An introduction to critical thinking* (2nd ed.).
A comprehensive and readable treatise on the key components of critical thinking. Compounds include deduction, induction, analysis of arguments, hypothesis testing, probability and uncertainty, decision making, and creativity. This is an excellent resource for teachers wishing to learn more about critical thinking. Each chapter presents a framework for thinking about and using an aspect of critical thinking. Chapters end with suggestions for applying the framework. These suggestions can be incorporated readily into instructional design.

Johnson, D. W., and Johnson, R. T. (1991). *Learning together and alone* (3rd ed.).
The latest edition of a popular book describing cooperative instructional environments. The authors' approach to group instruction is focused largely on motivational issues and is provided as an antidote for individualistic and competitive classroom environments.

Jones, B. F., and Idol, L. (Eds.). (1990). *Dimensions of thinking and cognitive instruction.*
This is an edited volume with chapters that span a wide range of instructional issues. The organizing theme is the integration of thinking and problem solving with traditional content and skill instruction. Chapters look at teaching in various content areas and at general issues of metacognition and creativity. A chapter by Bransford, Vye, Kinzer, and Risko explains the concept of anchored instruction, an instructional approach designed to foster transfer and make knowledge acquired in school more accessible to learners in "everyday" settings.

Liben, L. S. (Ed.). (1987). *Development and learning: Conflict or congruence?*
The theme of this volume is the relationship among development, instruction, and learning. The relative contributions of development and instruction have been the subject of considerable debate. This book will help teachers understand how instruction can be designed to take advantage of students' developmental levels. Any teacher who devalues the potential contributions of instruction or takes the opposite view, that a student's developmental level has little relevance to instructional planning, should read this book.

Resnick, L. B. (Ed.). (1989). *Knowing, learning, and instruction: Essays in honor of Robert Glaser.*

An edited volume in which most of the contributions focus on the problems of "inert knowledge," that is, knowledge that has little applicability for thinking about or solving problems in the "real" world. Of particular interest to instructional planners are the chapters by Brown and Palincsar and by Collins, Brown, and Newman. Brown and Palincsar describe reciprocal teaching, an approach for providing guidance and scaffolding to novice learners through the structured use of social supports. Collins et al. describe cognitive apprenticeship, a way to situate instruction in a more realistic and supportive context that serves to make learning more easily transferred and applied.

Resnick, L. B., and Klopfer, L. E. (Eds.). (1989). *Toward the thinking curriculum: Current cognitive research.*

This is an important and helpful volume for instructional planners. Each chapter is devoted to a different content area: reading, writing, mathematics, science, and problem solving. The chapters are well written and addressed to classroom teachers. Explicit instructional guidelines are presented. This volume is a high-priority read for teachers interested in the latest developments in instructional psychology.

Rosenshine, B., and Stevens, R. (1986). Teaching functions. In M. C. Wittrock (Ed.), *Handbook on research on teaching,* 3rd edition.

A review of research and explanation of an approach to teaching that has come to be known as "direct instruction," "effective teaching," "mastery teaching," and "explicit teaching," popularized by Madelaine Hunter. It emphasizes explicit objectives, clear explanations, opportunities for practice, and feedback on performance.

SOME EXAMPLES

The examples that follow illustrate several general teaching strategies based on each unit's ILOs and the points and guidelines presented in this chapter. A rationale or introduction for each unit or subunit describing what the unit is about, what it builds on, and what it leads to is also included. The examples are not models to emulate. They demonstrate the variety and individuality of general teaching strategies for different grade levels and subject areas as conceived by different teachers. As you look at the examples you should consider or discuss the following questions:

1. How does this strategy provide for an effective learning environment?
   a. Are the goals apt to be clear to the learners?
   b. Are opportunities for feedback provided? Does the feedback vary in its source and when it is available?
   c. Are students likely to be motivated? Is the material presented in an interesting, lively, and/or relevant fashion?
   d. Are students likely to take risks? Will they be rewarded for trying new behaviors or ideas?
   e. Are attempts made to ascertain what students already know? Is their prior knowledge incorporated into the unit's activities?
2. Do the academic tasks fit the kind of learning being sought? Are students, through assigned products and performances, likely to be held

accountable for the features that reflect the kind of learning being sought?

3. Do students have opportunities to practice skills at varying levels of difficulty? Are students given opportunities and encouraged to transfer skills to new contexts? Are skills presented in ways designed to make them meaningful?

4. When students are required to understand, comprehend, or otherwise acquire new ideas, are they required to think about and work with these ideas in a variety of ways? Do students have opportunities to apply ideas in contexts and situations that are not identical to those in which the ideas were presented?

5. When students are learning affects, are they encouraged to take a stand on issues, defend their beliefs, encounter opposing beliefs, and otherwise become emotionally involved in their learning?

EXAMPLE 7.1. SUBUNIT TWO—WONDERS OF THE FOREST COMMUNITY

This is the second subunit of a first grade science unit entitled Forests.

Introduction

Once the students have become familiar with the attributes of a variety of forests, they will begin focusing on nearby deciduous woods to examine closely the forest ecosystems.

Instructional Foci

1. Forest walks
2. Forest mural
3. Examination of rotting log
4. *A Day in the Woods, Wonders of the Forest, Forests and Jungles, Once There Was a Tree, An Oak Tree Dies and a Journey Begins, The Dead Tree,* and various other books

ILOs

Cognitions
1. Students will understand that forest communities are self-sustaining systems with basic features that allow energy and matter to flow through them.
2. Students will realize that animals depend on plants for their basic needs.
3. Students will understand that forest communities rely on the ability of plants to convert radiant energy into food.

4. Students will understand that plants have basic needs.
5. Students will understand that plants interact with their environment.
6. Students will understand that plants have properties that allow them to live, thrive, adapt, and meet their needs.
7. Students will realize that plants benefit from animals in meeting their needs.

Cognitive skills

1. Students will be able to represent the layers of the forest.
2. Students will be able to recognize several species of trees based on their varying properties.
3. Students will be able to describe ways in which plants affect their environment.
4. Students will be able to illustrate the members of a food chain.
5. Students will be able to identify the parts of a plant and their purpose.

General Teaching Strategies

This subunit begins with the teacher informing the students that they will be constructing a forest mural that depicts a nearby forest. They need to be as accurate as possible in their representation, so they will visit the forest and read books to promote accuracy. They will also be told that scientists who study the forest have identified several layers of the forest where different plant and animal activities take place. When they take their first walk to the nearby forest, they will try to recognize those layers. To help understand the meaning of forest layers, they will look at pictures of large cities with different layers of buildings. The names of the forest layers will be given before the students take their walk. They will draw the layers that they can see and try to attach the appropriate label to each layer. When they return to the classroom, they will share their observations and decisions along with the reasons for their decisions.

Over the next two weeks, students will construct a forest mural. They should represent the forest in its current season. They can decide which time of day they want to depict, in order to make decisions about which animals should be visible.

Throughout the mural-building process, students will use books listed in the bibliography as an added resource for information about the growth forms and species that they might include. The plant subunit, which is interspersed throughout the unit as a whole, will receive its primary emphasis during this subunit, relating the properties of green plants to properties of trees and forest plants.

The teacher will read *A Day in the Woods* to focus students on the abundance of animal life that finds shelter in the forest, as well as the interrelationships between plants, animals, and environment.

Wonders of the Forest will also be read to relate the attributes of the forest that were presented in the previous subunit to the forest ecosystem. Students will also read along and listen to *Forests and Jungles* on an accompanying tape to gain further information. The students will then make decisions as to how they want to represent the elements of the forest ecosystem on their mural.

The students will identify the various feeding relationships they have encountered in their reading. The teacher will list these relationships on chart paper. Then the students will work in small groups to see if they can discover any feeding patterns—animals eating plants or animals eating animals, which animals and plants were involved in the various relationships, which layers of the forests were involved, and so on. The students will use the names of the plants and animals they have identified to create food chains. They will sort the animals into plant eaters and meat eaters. After considering questions such as "Where do plants get their energy?" and "What happens to animals when they die?" they will represent the relationships between producers, consumers, and decomposers on food chains that they will create in small groups. They will then assume the roles of the plants and animals in their chains. The teacher will connect the children with a ball of string as their relationships to the rest of the group emerge. The final product will represent a more complex food web.

The students will take a trip to the forest to compare their mural to the type of forest they are representing. They will also examine a rotting log and its surrounding environment. They will observe and record the animal and plant life they see on, under, and around the log. They will examine the forest floor around the log and examine the changes in materials from the leaves on the top of the forest floor to the matter several inches down. They will consider the log as nonliving matter being returned to the environment.

EXAMPLE 7.2. SUBUNIT TWO—RIVERS

This is the second subunit of an upper elementary unit on Rivers.

Introduction

The first subunit ended by studying the major rivers of the world, geologically and geographically speaking. This unit begins by investigating the relationship between humankind and rivers, from the beginning. The relationship began long ago, in far off lands, making a transition from one subunit to the next relatively smooth. This unit looks at the development of civilization as it flourished on the banks of rivers around the world.

ILOS Emphasized

1. Students will know why rivers have such an impact on the development of civilization.
2. Students will comprehend the various steps in the development of civilization as influenced by rivers and their resources.
3. Students will recognize the historical importance of rivers as various resources to humans.
4. Students will recognize the various resources of rivers used historically by people.
5. Students will demonstrate the knowledge acquired from subunit one (specifically flood plains, soil deposits, and sediment) during discussions.
6. Students will describe in chronological order the development of human settlements along rivers.

7. Students will identify the various functions of travels along rivers.
8. Students will explain the reasons why humans first settled along rivers.
9. Students will identify the factors that lead a people to develop agricultural settlements.
10. Students will explain the development of towns and cities from those agricultural settlements.
11. Students will explain why it was beneficial throughout history for cities to be located along rivers.
12. Students will recognize the importance of rivers as a means of exploration and expansion during the settlement of North America.
13. Students will document the development of settlements in the Connecticut River Valley.

Instructional Foci

1. Pictures of historical settlements along rivers, ancient irrigation systems, historic forms of river transportation
2. Northfield Mountain Recreational and Environmental Center field trip—boat along river, slide show on Indian life in area
3. Library and historical society
4. Field trip to Old Deerfield Village
5. See annotated bibliography: items 1–5, 11, 20, 21, 26–31, 33, 39, 45, 47, and 48

Teaching Strategies

This subunit begins with a teacher presentation of the time when humans first discovered rivers as a resource. The presentation should be filled with questions directed at students and use different forms of presentation (visual, oral, written). "Let's list some of the biggest cities in the world" . . . point out that most of the cities on the list are built either along a river or on a body of water. Explain how the earliest agricultural settlements developed.

Through literature, students will further investigate this development. They will read about different forms of irrigation and how plant and animal life was domesticated.

In small groups, children will construct scale models of early agricultural settlements along the Hwang-Ho, Nile, Euphrates-Tigris, and Indus rivers. These models should incorporate the concepts covered in subunit one, meaning that students should be discussing the flood plains, land formations, and life cycle when constructing the models.

Students will keep a journal of a fictitious character who lives in an early settlement. In the entries, the student should demonstrate what that person's life is like during the time and place. It is imperative that the teacher make the goal of the journal clear: Students should demonstrate knowledge of that particular time period, what it might have been like to live along that river then.

Further readings and teacher presentations are needed to cover the concepts of how settlements evolved along rivers. The teacher can begin by asking, "What resources did people get from rivers back in ———?" Can you think of any examples of how these resources might have evolved to people using rivers in different ways?

The topic can shift back to North America, with a discussion of how early explorers traveled, considering that there were no roads, only dense woods. There are many biographies on famous explorers of North America who traveled along rivers. Divide the children into small groups (could be based on choice of book, teacher's choice, etc.) and assign them a book to read, with discussion periods. The group makes a final presentation to the rest of the class, with accompanying visuals (map of explorer's journey, mural of scene from the book). The presentation could also be a dramatization of the explorer's story.

Students will develop a board game that somehow illustrates the chronological development of civilization along rivers. They can choose to work in small groups or individually. The game must incorporate the different aspects of the topic studied . . . flood wipes out village, go back to start. Or enemy takes over fortress at opening of river and you lose your trading route, go back ten spaces.

Together the class will investigate the development of civilization along the Connecticut, perhaps focusing on one particular town. Again, area resources should be utilized: Jones Library, Amherst Historical Society, resident interviews, old newspaper clippings, museum visits. Perhaps the task could be broken up into smaller parts to be investigated by individual groups.

After the research is put together in the form of a report, perhaps each part presented orally or a class book combined, the class goes on a field trip to Old Deerfield Village, along the Deerfield River. This gives the students the opportunity to see an example of an early settlement, to compare what they see to what they determined in the report.

Individually, each child will choose a town on another river to research historically, reporting on topics similar to the whole class project, although resources may be limited to books due to proximity constraints. The student should gather information about how and why the town was settled, who settled there, how the town developed, what resources were used, the residents' way of life, climate, and so forth. The children will publish these as information books, with illustrations.

EXAMPLE 7.3. SUBUNIT TWO—SOUNDS OF POETRY (1½ WEEKS)

This is the second subunit, Sounds of Poetry, of a middle school unit on Reading and Writing Poetry.

Introduction

Poetry is intended to be read aloud and therefore the poet writes with attention to the way the poetry sounds. Sometimes words can function onomatopoeically, having meaning in the sound of the word itself. At other times the sound or cadence of words can express emotion or change the pace and mood of the poem. Alliteration and assonance are examples of this use of language. Poets also choose to use sound and the description of sound for the connotation of emotions, colors, and attitudes. All three uses of meaning conveyed through sound will be examined in this subunit. Students will be challenged to think of noises as words. They will read poems by a variety of authors, attending to the sounds of the language chosen. They will write poems describing the sounds of a scene and the images inspired by listening to music.

ILOs

1. Students will be able to respond to the question, "What is poetry?" They will realize that poetry expresses the voice of the poet in a way that differs from prose beyond the simple conventions of form.
2. Students will realize that people differ in their understandings of a poem, and know that poetry allows for more than a single interpretation.
3. Students will understand the importance of sound within a poem. They will recognize the use of and the significance of alliteration, onomatopoeia, and rhyme.
4. Students will be able to express their opinions and interpretations of a poem. They will be able to explain and give reasons for these interpretations.
5. Students will be able to use imagery in their poems.
6. Students will be able to write poetry using rhyme and free verse.

Instructional Foci

1. Poems include:
   "The Eagle" by Alfred Tennyson
   "Silver" by Walter de la Mare
   "The Peppery Man" by Arthur Macy
   "The Train" by David McCord
   "Poem to Mud" by Zilpha Keatley Snyder
2. Crumpling of paper / Clinking of glasses
3. Listening to music: the saxophone jazz of Kenny G
   Pachelbel's canon

Teaching Strategies

The first discussion will revolve around the use of alliteration, though this term need not be used. The teacher will read "The Eagle" by Tennyson aloud. Ensuing questions might include, What does the eagle look like? How do you know this? How would this poem be different if the poet had written "he held onto the rock with his sharp talons" instead of "he clasped the crag with crooked hands"? "Silver" by Walter de la Mare should also be read aloud with student attention drawn to the quick quietness alluded to in the repetition of sibilant sounds. Questions should demand progressively more introspection as students delve more deeply into poetic techniques.

Students will be asked to find adjectives to describe the sound of crumpling paper. Guidance should be provided with questions such as, What words did that crumpling sound like? If necessary the teacher can elaborate: Did it sound like "crumple" or more like "crackle," "crunch," "crinkle"? What other things can you think of that might sound like this? Again, examples can be given: crackers crunching under sneakers is the type of vivid image looked for here. Describing the clink of glasses will provide further practice in word choice. Students should be asked not only to think of descriptive adjectives but to think of words that evoke the sound but mean something different. An example given by the teacher as a starter might be "pink drink." In this way, using examples and demonstrations, the student will be encouraged to experiment with words that evoke noises and sounds in and of themselves.

The writing assignment following this lesson should be open ended, reading something like this:

1. The sounds in your kitchen when dinner is being made.
2. The sounds in your room as you are lying in the dark going to sleep.

Think about the scene, and how you feel in that place. You might write a poem in the midst of that activity!

The second section of this subunit will focus on expressing the mood of a piece of music through the art of poetry. Students will listen to one minute of upbeat jazz music. They will be asked to think about what mood the music conveys and what images it sparks in their minds. The second listening will be the basis for the next poem writing assignment; students will listen to Pachelbel's canon and then jot down ideas, feelings, colors, and scenes that come to mind. They will be encouraged to share these associative ideas. They will eventually illustrate these music poems, showing the interrelation possible between music, art, and writing.

Oral reading of "The Train" and "Poem to Mud," and the ensuing discussion, should serve as review for the techniques of alliteration and onomatopoeia. The poetic terms should not be used, instead letting students describe the techniques through their own observations.

EXAMPLE 7.4. SUBUNIT ONE—THE CAMERA

This is the introductory subunit, entitled The Camera, for a high school art unit on Black and White Photography.

Introduction

This subunit introduces the basic functions of a 35-mm, single lens reflex camera. Vocabulary and identification of the parts of a camera are introduced. The concept of a camera as a controller of light is accompanied by lessons on how to select appropriate shutter and aperture settings. The concept of depth of field is introduced here.

ILOs

1. The students will understand how the uses and technology of cameras have evolved over the past 150 years.
2. The students will understand the processes and techniques involved in photographing, developing, and printing black and white film with a 35-mm camera.

Instructional Foci

1. 35-mm camera
2. Textbook, Upton & Upton, *Photography,* pp. 37–85
3. Charts and posters in demonstration area
4. Many examples of shutter and aperture priority photographs
5. Vocabulary list on bulletin board as well as given in handout form to each student
6. Student folder
7. Current shows and exhibits on board
8. Photography journals, numerous books, and examples

Teaching Strategies

The teacher demonstrates with 35-mm camera while the students get hands-on practice using the controls and features of their own cameras. It is crucial at this point to mix in some aesthetic and creative elements with the technical aspects. The teacher should show quality examples of master artists' work and previous students' work highlighting the different features of the camera. The teacher initiates a discussion about how the camera features were manipulated to attain different images. The students are encouraged to comment on the images' visual impact, strengths, weaknesses, and if they feel they are effective. This is a great warm-up activity to introduce "critique" vocabulary while getting students familiar with this type of group discussion and evaluation process. Students are asked to keep an "eye" out for photographs from any source that would be good discussion material for the class in the technical and/or creative aspects. The teacher gives an assignment called "The Different Ways of Seeing: The Ten-Step Assignment."

This assignment is a great first photography exercise. You begin at one of the doors of your home. You stand in one place and look around until you find something that you frame (a slice of the world that looks interesting); you then take ten steps toward it to frame it (or part of it) at a closer perspective. You walk another ten steps and repeat this procedure. The rules of this assignment are that after each ten steps you must look up, down, left, right, straight ahead, and behind you, and try to explore every angle and perspective you can to frame something you believe to be interesting. This enables the photographer to experience a bird's-eye view or a worm's-eye view (squatting or lying down) and get a different "handle" on some familiar territory. Another important point is to try to remember to experiment with the vertical as well as horizontal orientation of your 35-mm camera.

INTRODUCTION AND TWO SUBUNITS FROM A HIGH SCHOOL ALGEBRA UNIT ON COORDINATE GEOMETRY

INTRODUCTION

The goal of the overall teaching strategy for this unit is to get students thinking in terms of practical application of newly learned mathematical concepts. This should be accomplished through class discussions and practice working with realistic examples both individually and in small groups. Any time group or individual practice is called for, the work should be submitted with written explanations of all operations. That is, any significant steps in the work should be fully explained in terms of what is being done and why. It is important that the groups be composed of different members each class period in order that each student's ideas, views, and skills be shared with all of the others. The primary instructional focus for the entire unit will be the application of newly learned concepts and skills to "real-world" data and examples provided by both the teacher and the students. The students should keep all of the distributed examples in a notebook, neatly organized and available for use in class each day. The two most critical intended learning outcomes to be emphasized in every subunit are the following:

1. Students will understand that real-world data can be represented graphically and quantified and idealized by mathematical formulations, which can be used to draw conclusions from a graph.
2. Students will be able to interpret mathematical relationships from graphs and make generalizations and predictions regarding their behavior both quantitatively and qualitatively.

EXAMPLE 7.5. SUBUNIT THREE—GRAPHING TWO-DIMENSIONAL LINEAR EQUATIONS

This is the third subunit from a high school algebra unit on Coordinate Geometry.

Central Concepts

- linearity
- slope of a line
- midpoint of a line
- forms of linear equations
- parallel lines and intersecting lines
- intercepts
- systems of equations .

Principal Intended Learning Outcomes

1. The students will understand the meaning of and uses of linear equations.
2. The students will recognize and be able to manipulate linear equations in order to find pertinent information regarding the graph of that equation.
3. The students will understand how performing operations on linear equations affects graphical representation and interpretation.
4. The students will understand the concepts of interpolation and extrapolation and how to use them for predictions.
5. The students will understand the structure of the Cartesian coordinate system and the use of ordered pairs for graphing linear and nonlinear equations.
6. The students will understand the mathematical relationships between parallel, intersecting, and perpendicular lines.
7. The students will understand the derivation and use of the distance and midpoint formulas.

Teaching Strategy

This subunit should begin with a class discussion on the topic of linearity. The students should be clear on the difference between linear and nonlinear relationships, and the examples should be reviewed and classified into linear and nonlinear categories in small work groups. This should be followed by the introduction of the concepts of slope, parallel lines, intersecting lines, and midpoint. Class discussion should focus on the relationship of the midpoint and midpoint formula to the concept of interpolation and the usefulness of slope for extrapolation. The groups can then practice finding and comparing the slopes of various lines in the examples and discuss the meaning of the differences.

At this point the students should have a fairly strong grasp of the structure of the Cartesian coordinate system. Working in small groups, the students should discuss ideas for relating and describing the points in a graph (i.e., a linear equation). Each group should present its ideas to the class, with the ensuing discussion centering around the merits of each. At this point, the concept of a linear equation may be formally presented to the class. Additionally, some attention should be given to the relationship of the roots of an equation to the intersection of a line with the axes on a graph (the intercepts). Variations on the equation of a line such as standard, point-slope, and slope-intercept form should be discussed with an emphasis on the benefits of using a particular form for a specific application. Students should then have an opportunity to practice finding and interpreting equations of lines from the examples, in groups and individually. Additionally, they should practice interpreting meaning from an equation describing some data.

Once the students are proficient and comfortable working with the equation of a line, the idea of graphing systems of equations can be introduced. The class should discuss the significance of graphing several lines simultaneously on one graph and the relationship to solving systems of equations. Special attention should be given to the meaning of the intersections of lines in a graph of simultaneous equations. The students should have group and individual practice with the examples to solve systems of equations using graphs.

EXAMPLE 7.6. SUBUNIT FOUR—OPERATIONS OF GRAPHS

Central Concepts

- translation and rotation of axes
- reflection
- symmetry and inverses
- angle of intersection

Principal Intented Learning Outcomes

1. Students will understand how performing operations on linear equations affects the graphical representation and interpolation.
2. Students will recognize and be able to manipulate linear equations in order to find pertinent information regarding the graph of that equation.

Teaching Strategy

At this point the students should be quite adept at working with and interpreting linear equations and graphs. The concepts of translation, rotation, and reflection should be introduced as methods of altering the visual presentation of data. Care should be taken during class discussions to ensure that the students understand that these operations change the way data is perceived but do not actually change the data itself. The discussions should also cover symmetry, inverses, and angles of intersection as additional tools for interpreting and evaluating graphs and equations. The students should work in groups, examining the examples to see if any of the graphs have been or should be altered for clarification and readability. They should also experiment with actually altering the graphs of the examples to see how it affects perception and interpretation.

COURSE PLANNING STEPS

Course Planning Step 7.1. Develop each of your selected instructional foci into a description of general teaching strategies. This description should be based on your ILOs and on the points and guidelines presented in this chapter. Pay particular attention to the high-priority unit ILOs. Avoid using the passive voice in your descriptions (for example, do not say: Terraria are constructed.) Instead, make it clear who is doing what in the strategy (for example, do say: Students construct terraria by following instructions the teacher hands out.)

Course Planning Step 7.2.   For each of your units write a brief (25–100 word) description, introduction, or rationale of the unit. Include what your unit contains, why it is important, how it builds on previous units (if it does), and how (if at all) succeeding units build on it. The introductions accompanying the River, Poetry, and Camera units are good examples.

Course Planning Step 7.3.   Reconsider your total instructional plan in the light of your rationale, checking for internal consistency and comprehensiveness. Add to the completed units any ILOs you had not thought of previously.

QUESTIONS FOR DISCUSSION: GENERAL TEACHING STRATEGIES

1. Did you add, change, or eliminate any of your ILOs in the process of specifying a general teaching strategy? Which ones, and why?
2. Which of your units at this point seem to be most complete, most appropriate, or simply best? Why?
3. Which of your units at this point seem to be least complete, appropriate, or perfected? Can you say why?
4. Compare your brief unit rationales with your course rationale. Do the units as described seem to support the course rationale fully? Does this comparison suggest that the course rationale be rewritten?
5. With your instructional plan in hand, could someone else now teach this course (assuming practical teaching experience and a knowledge of the subject matter)?
6. Of your ILOs, which two or three do you now feel most confident about accomplishing? Are there any you feel uneasy about? Why?

REFERENCES

Baron, J. B., & Sternberg, R. J. (Eds.). (1987). *Teaching thinking skills: Theory and practice.* New York: W. H. Freeman.

Bell-Gredler, M. E. (1986). *Learning and instruction: Theory into practice.* New York: Macmillan.

Bellon, J. J., Bellon, E. C., & Blank, M. A. (1992). *Teaching from a research knowledge base: A development and renewal process.* New York: Merrill.

Borich, G. D. (1992). *Effective teaching methods* (2nd ed.). New York: Merrill.

Borton, T. (1970). *Reach, touch, and teach.* New York: McGraw-Hill.

Bransford, J. D., & Stein, B. S. (1984). *The ideal problem solver: A guide for improving thinking, learning, and creativity.* New York: W. H. Freeman.

Brown, G. (1971). *Human teaching for human learning: An introduction for confluent education.* New York: Viking.

Charles, R. I., & Silver, E. A. (Eds.). (1988). *The teaching and assessing of mathematical problem solving.* Hillsdale, NJ: Lawrence Erlbaum Associates.

Doyle, W. (1983). Academic work. *Review of Educational Research, 53*(2), 159–199.

Educational Psychologist. (Spring 1987). *22*(2).

Gardner, M., Greeno, J. G., Reif, F., Schoenfeld, A. H., diSessa, A., & Stage, E. (Eds.). (1990). *Toward a scientific practice of science education.* Hillsdale, NJ: Lawrence Erlbaum Associates.

Gordon, W. J. J. (1966). *The metaphorical way of learning and knowing.* Cambridge, MA: Synectics Education Systems.

Greenwood, G. E., & Parkay, F. W. (1989). *Case studies for teacher decision making.* New York: Random House.

Halpern, D. F. (1989). *Thought and knowledge: An introduction to critical thinking* (2nd ed.). Hillsdale, NJ: Lawrence Erlbaum Associates.

Hawley, R. C., & Hawley, I. L. (1972). *A handbook of personal growth activities for classroom use.* Amherst, MA: Educational Research Associates.

Johnson, D. W., & Johnson, R. T. (1991). *Learning together and alone* (3rd ed.). Englewood Cliffs, NJ: Prentice Hall.

Jones, B. F., & Idol, L. (Eds.). (1990). *Dimensions of thinking and cognitive instruction.* Hillsdale, NJ: Lawrence Erlbaum Associates.

Liben, L. S. (Ed.). (1987). *Development and learning: Conflict or congruence?* Hillsdale, NJ: Lawrence Erlbaum Associates.

Morris, J. (1978). *Psychology and teaching: A humanistic view.* New York: Random House.

Raths, L. E., Harmin, M., & Simon, S. B. (1966). *Values and teaching.* Columbus, OH: Charles E. Merrill.

Resnick, L. B. (Ed.). (1989). *Knowing, learning, and instruction: Essays in honor of Robert Glaser.* Hillsdale, NJ: Lawrence Erlbaum Associates.

Resnick, L. B., & Klopfer, L. E. (Eds.). (1989). *Toward the thinking curriculum: Current cognitive research.* 1989 Yearbook of the Association for Supervision and Curriculum Development.

Rosenshine, B., & Stevens, R. (1986). Teaching functions. In M. C. Wittrock (Ed.), *Handbook on Research on Teaching* (3rd ed.). New York: Macmillan.

Schmuck, R. A., & Schmuck, P. A. (1974). *A humanistic psychology of education: Making the school everybody's house.* Palo Alto, CA: National Press Books.

Sizer, T. R. (1984). *Horace's compromise: The dilemma of the American high school.* Boston: Houghton Mifflin.

Stevens, J. P. (1971). *Awareness, exploring, experimenting, experiencing.* New York: Bantam Books.

Walker, D. (1990). *Fundamentals of curriculum.* New York: Harcourt Brace Jovanovich.

Weinberg, C. (Ed.). (1972). *Human foundations of education.* Englewood Cliffs, NJ: Prentice Hall.

West, C. K., Farmer, J. A., & Wolff, P. M. (1991). *Instructional design: Implications from cognitive science.* Englewood Cliffs, NJ: Prentice Hall.

Whitehead, A. N. (1916). *The aims of education.* Address to the British Mathematical Society, Manchester, England.

CHAPTER 8

Planning a Course Evaluation

After completing this chapter, you should be able to:

1. Comprehend the meaning of the terms *actual learning outcomes, main effects,* and *side effects.*
2. Specify appropriate behavioral evidence for any given ILO.
3. Specify likely side effects that may result from a course.
4. Gather and analyze behavioral evidence using a troubleshooting approach to course evaluation.

PERSPECTIVE ON EVALUATION

To this point, course planning has been concerned with setting up a focused, justifiable, interesting, feasible, and coherent course. But a course must also be effective, and as planners we need to know how effective it is. Typically we need information about the course's effectiveness in order to make decisions about the course. Such information gathering and subsequent decision making compose an evaluation aimed at course improvement.

The Uses of Evaluation

Evaluations can be used for many types of decisions. For instance, Cronbach (1963) identified three uses for evaluation: (a) course-improvement decisions, (b) decisions about individual students, and (c) administrative regulation. Evaluation for course improvement involves gathering information that will be useful in deciding which aspects of a course can and should be improved. Evaluation aimed at decisions about

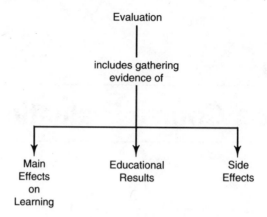

individual students consists in gathering information to be used in assessing student needs or in the grading, grouping, or selection of individual students. Evaluation for administrative regulation is directed toward assessing the merit of schools, curricula, materials, teachers, and so forth.

Cronbach (1963) argues that using evaluation for course improvement contributes more toward improving education than do the other uses of evaluation. This argument has been debated, most eloquently by Scriven (1967), who points out that decisions on the merit or worth of a course ("summative" decisions) are as important in improving education as decisions aimed at course improvement ("formative" decisions).

As mentioned, this chapter deals with course evaluation aimed at gathering and analyzing information that will be used for course-improvement decisions. That is, a formative evaluation is emphasized. This emphasis was not chosen because summative decisions are unimportant. But if the course is irremediably bad, this fact should become evident during the formative evaluation. The course can be abandoned on the basis of such data. On the other hand, courses can almost always be improved.

Range of Outcomes

Cronbach (1963), in discussing evaluation for course improvement, emphasizes the need for an evaluation to describe the broadest possible range of course outcomes. On this point Cronbach is in substantial agreement with others such as Scriven (1967), who also emphasize the description of course consequences.

Scriven (1967) elaborates further on the *range* of course outcomes to be examined. He distinguishes between two related but distinct enterprises, which he labels *evaluation* and *goal estimation.* Goal estimation (goal-based evaluation) focuses entirely on the extent to which a course has achieved its *stated goals or objectives.* Evaluation, on the other hand, requires gathering information on the *full range of course outcomes or consequences.* Goal estimation, as well as being more limited in focus, is viewed as less desirable than evaluation because goals are often unrealistic and thus an inadequate basis for information gathering.

Scriven's (1967) emphasis on evaluations that examine a full range of course outcomes has led him to propose *goal-free evaluation* as a radical alternative to goal estimation or goal-based evaluation. Goal-free evaluation views a course as an educational or instructional "treatment" and attempts to gather data on *likely consequences* of that treatment irrespective of stated goals and objectives. In contrast, a goal-based evaluation focuses only on stated goals and objectives.

This chapter combines goal-free and goal-based approaches in attempting to identify the important course consequences. ILOs are used to guide the collection of evidence that will determine whether or not intended learnings are actually achieved. The extent to which the course's ILOs are actualized constitute the *main effects* of the course. A second aspect of the evaluation is an examination of materials, methods, and other factors likely to result in consequences or effects that we did not intend or even consider. These unintended (and sometimes undesirable) outcomes are referred to as the *side effects* of the course. Once we collect information regarding both main and side effects, we can use it to make course-improvement decisions.

Using Information for Course Improvement

It may be helpful to think about course evaluation in the same way a TV repairer thinks about a broken TV. The repairer finds whether or not the set works by plugging it in, turning it on, and evaluating the quality of picture and sound. Assuming there is something wrong with the set, the repairer is faced with troubleshooting the problem. This process consists in setting up a series of probes that result in evidence pertaining to the operation of particular components of the set. The troubleshooting procedure allows the repairer to isolate that aspect of the system which is malfunctioning.

While troubleshooting a course is analogous to electronic troubleshooting, it is far more complex. The likelihood of identifying a single course component as *the* problem is slight. But if we want to be able to use the information gathered in an evaluation to improve the course, we have to relate particular kinds of information to particular course components.

The troubleshooting scheme presented in this chapter is largely based on the intended learning outcomes of the course. Guidelines for gathering evidence are presented first, followed by questions that facilitate the processing of this evidence.

To summarize, actual learning outcomes (ALOs) are those things learned by students during, or as a part of, the course. These ALOs consist of those learnings that were considered important and were thus stated as ILOs (that is, main effects) and those learnings that were not considered important or were thought to be undesirable and were thus not stated as ILOs (that is, side effects). These main and side effects together with an assessment of educational results form the basis of course evaluation presented in this chapter. The kinds of considerations important in this evaluation include the following:

Do all the intended learning outcomes turn out to be actual learning outcomes?

If not, which ILOs were and which were not achieved?

What ALOs were not planned for in the course?

Are the side effects desirable or undesirable?

To what extent were the educational goals achieved and were the ILOs relevant to the achievement of those goals?

The answers to these questions must then be applied in a troubleshooting approach in order to make course-improvement decisions. Applying the evidence for decision making involves thinking about the relationship between the evidence gathered and the various course components (for example, teacher behaviors, instructional foci, and the organization of units). To do this, evidence of learning must first be gathered.

GATHERING EVIDENCE ON MAIN EFFECTS

The course's ILOs refined in chapter 4 are of four types: cognitions, cognitive skills, affects, and psychomotor-perceptual skills. The task of evaluation planning for these ILOs is one of specifying what will constitute acceptable evidence, that is, evidence that will indicate whether or not an ILO has actually been learned. Evidence is defined as an outward sign; therefore, by definition, evidence of learning must be observable. Since the evidence will be gathered from students, we look for this evidence in observable student behaviors or observable products of student work.

In the ensuing discussions we will focus the evaluation on high-priority ILOs. We believe that a course evaluation should emphasize these ILOs over less important learnings. Typically, time and resources limit the scope of an evaluation; evidence of highest-priority ILOs may be all the evidence one can gather. These ILOs have been identified and asterisked in chapter 4 (Course Planning Step 4.6).

One way to conceptualize the differences between the types of ILOs from the standpoint of evaluation is to consider the extent to which the content or behavior is circumscribed or defined in a particular ILO. A useful rule of thumb is: whatever portion of the ILO was not circumscribed in chapter 4 now receives the greatest attention in specifying behavioral evidence. For a cognition, the content was highly circumscribed when stating the ILO; therefore, we now focus on the specification of sample behaviors that will serve as evidence. For a cognitive or psychomotor-perceptual skill, the behavior or performance was probably highly circumscribed when stating the ILO, and we must now specify sample contexts (that is, content) for those behaviors. Each type of ILO is treated separately in the following sections.

Cognitions

A cognition is an understanding and has no *directly* observable referent. Therefore, no *one* behavior constitutes acceptable evidence of understanding. The understanding of an idea has numerous and varied exemplifications. The evaluation task, therefore, is to specify a set of behaviors that together will constitute acceptable evidence of understanding. A useful question to ask is, "If someone demonstrates these specified behaviors, would I be willing to say that the person has achieved the intended understanding?"

When faced with the problem of gathering behavioral evidence on the extent of knowledge acquisition, caution is advised. The ability to verbalize an idea (for example, to give a definition or give a label for an object) does not mean that the learner has necessarily understood the idea. It is possible both to recite definitions of ideas that have never been understood and to be unable to formulate a definition of an idea that has indeed been understood.

Indicators that students have learned ideas that are classes or categories of objects or events (see p. 77) include the ability to identify an object by placing it into a category and the ability to recognize a nonexample (that is, an object that bears a "family resemblance" but is not a member of the set; for example, recognizing that a frog is not a reptile). Other behaviors such as defining, stating attributes, and describing relationships serve as evidence for these cognitions. The selection of behavioral indicators for cognitions depends, in part, on whether the cognition requires memory, comprehension, or justified belief:

1. The primary kinds of observable behavior that may indicate memory are stating (either wholly or partially) and recognizing the idea.
2. The primary kinds of behavior that may indicate comprehension include translating, paraphrasing, and explaining. Other behaviors that may be used include comparing, describing, and distinguishing.
3. Behaviors indicating justified belief include verbally justifying, defending, supplying evidence, arguing, and choosing an appropriate course of action based on specific information.

Knowing which properties relate to a particular cognition is a first step toward the specification of evidence. For each relevant property several behaviors should be specified.

Example 8.1.   *ILO:* The student should understand that regular medical check-ups are an essential aspect of good health. (This ILO involves the properties of memory, comprehension, and justified belief.)

Evidence of memory (recalls the assertion): When asked, "What is an essential aspect of good health?" the student responds, "Regular medical checkups."

Evidence of comprehension (comprehends the assertion): The student can explain in his or her own words some aspects of good health.

Evidence of justified belief (has evidence for the assertion): The student can argue the benefits of regular checkups. The student can explain the consequences of not having these checkups. The student can explain the reasons regular checkups are beneficial.

Example 8.2.   *ILO:* The student understands the idea of gravitational force.

Evidence of understanding the idea. The student defines "gravitational force." The student describes the relationship between gravitational force and other forces.

The student points out phenomena that cannot be explained by gravitational force. The student explains relevant phenomena using the idea of gravitational force.

Example 8.3.   *ILO:* The student understands the relationship between an organism and its environment.

Evidence of understanding the relationship: The student is able to create a map showing how the following terms are related. The student can label relationships where appropriate. (Note: There will be differences between your map and student maps as well as differences among student maps themselves. This evidence should be interpreted with an emphasis on the relationships depicted. A sample answer is shown in Figure 8.1.)

organism	decomposer
reproduction	food chain
niche	food
producer	environment
shelter	survival needs
adaptation	consumer

Course Planning Step 8.1.   If one or more of your high-priority ILOs are cognitions, write them down on a separate sheet of paper entitled "Evidence of Main Effects." Then, for each of these ILOs write down two or more observable behaviors that will count as evidence that the student has acquired these cognitions.

FIGURE 8.1 Student's conceptual map showing relationship between an organism and its environment.

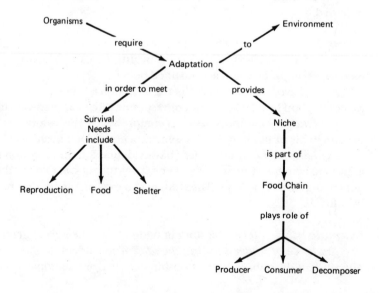

Affects

How an individual manifests an affective skill or understanding varies greatly from person to person and situation to situation. It may not always be reasonable to expect a person who has learned an affect to supply behavioral evidence of that affect on demand. Therefore, a useful strategy of course evaluation for affects is to keep your eyes open and observe behavior unobtrusively. The following guidelines should be helpful in using this strategy:

1. Describe what behaviors would evidence an individual's having a particular affective skill or understanding.
2. Consider the context or circumstance in which these behaviors would be likely to occur. That is, during what occasions, and in what places or situations, might a person behave in the desired manner?
3. Consider which of these circumstances arise in the educational setting and would thus permit you to observe a student demonstrating that affect-related behavior.

With these guidelines, you can become sensitive to the opportunities that arise where manifestations of these affects can be observed. The following examples illustrate how you might use these guidelines.

Example 8.4.   *ILO:* The student should act in a caring and sound manner toward the environment. (Affective skill)

Evidence of affect (behaviors, actions): The student doesn't willfully disturb any aspect of the environment. The student leaves natural conditions as they are found. The student instructs or reminds others of proper actions. The student states valid reasons for any intrusion he or she makes on a natural setting.

Circumstances: school grounds, field trips (nature hikes).

Example 8.5.   *ILO:* The student should recognize his or her tendency to either believe or disbelieve statements made by others. (Affective understanding)

Behaviors: The student can give an accurate description of his or her reaction to others.

Circumstances: When the student accepts outlandish arguments without questions, is being overly argumentative, and questions all statements made by others during class discussions and during interactions with peers outside of class.

Some affective skills and understandings can be evaluated more straightforwardly. That is, one can devise a means of gathering evidence that can be administered to students in a direct manner. The examples that follow illustrate this.

Example 8.6.   *ILO:* The student should understand how commercials and advertisements affect consumer behavior. (Affective understanding)

Evidence of affect: The student can explain how commercials try to appeal to individuals. The student can point out examples of consumer behavior where consumers pay more for an advertised product that is entirely equivalent to a less expensive unadvertised product. The student can given examples of how his or her own consumer habits are personally affected by commercials. The student can explain the difficulties in overcoming commercial "hype" surrounding certain types of consumer goods.

Example 8.7.   *ILO:* The student should be able to respond to another person's comments with empathy and without altering the content of the message. (Affective skill)

Evidence of affect: Given several transcripts of client comments, the student will write down responses. These can be judged for degree of empathy and how closely the client's meaning was understood.

Course Planning Step 8.2.   If one or more of your high-priority ILOs are affects, write them down on a sheet of paper entitled "Evidence of Main Effects." Then for each of these ILOs write down two or more observable behaviors that will count as evidence that the student has acquired the affect. Finally, write down a set of circumstances or contexts in which the behaviors are most likely to be observed.

Cognitive Skills

Cognitive skills are typically stated in terms of specific though not directly observable behaviors. Because the behavior is often circumscribed, which leaves less room for varied interpretations, the specification of behavioral evidence is generally more straightforward than for cognitions or affects. Two ideas that are helpful in thinking about the specification of appropriate content (or context) in which to demonstrate a skill are *difficulty* and *transfer*. Difficulty refers to the complexity of the content. For example, outlining a long and complex article is more difficult than outlining a shorter article; constructing a convincing argument is more difficult for a position with which you disagree rather than for one you agree with.

Transfer, while related to difficulty, refers to the degree of similarity between the content used for learning the skill and the content used for supplying evidence of the skill. For example, outlining a story or scientific article involves transfer if the learning tasks focused only on outlining newspaper items; having students use *Psychological Abstracts* to locate information when their learning tasks focused on the *Current Index to Journals in Education* also requires transfer. Whenever possible the kinds of evidence you gather for a cognitive skill should vary in terms of difficulty and transfer. This will provide more useful information for making decisions aimed at improving your teaching. The following examples illustrate the process of specifying evidence for cognitive skills.

Example 8.8.   *ILO:* The student should be able to plan a nutritionally balanced meal.

Evidence of cognitive skill: The student should be able to plan a nutritionally balanced meal for: a person with a large caloric requirement, a very hot and humid summer day, or a child on a cold winter morning.

Example 8.9.   *ILO:* The student should be able to propose ways to test a hypothesis.

Evidence of cognitive skill: The student should be able to explain, in writing, two different experiments to test a given causal hypothesis. The student should be able to state verbally the qualities of a testable hypothesis. The student should be able to describe empirical and nonempirical modes of hypothesis testing.

Course Planning Step 8.3.   If one or more of your high-priority ILOs are cognitive skills, write them down on a sheet of paper entitled "Evidence of Main Effects." Then write down two or more descriptions of behavioral evidence or indicators for each of these ILOs.

Psychomotor-Perceptual Skills

Psychomotor-perceptual skills are skills and abilities of a behavioral nature. The concern in specifying acceptable evidence is again in the *context* of the behavior. As with cognitive skills, students must be given sufficient opportunity to exhibit the behavior.

Example 8.10.   *ILO:* The student should be able to discern the sounds of orchestral instruments.

Evidence of psychomotor-perceptual skill (aural discrimination): The student should be able to match the names of fifteen different instruments to the sound of each instrument (assumes the student has previously memorized the names). The student should be able to name the instruments he or she hears used in a particular symphonic piece (specify the piece or criteria for selecting the piece).

Course Planning Step 8.4.   If one or more of your high-priority ILOs are psychomotor-perceptual skills, write them down on a sheet of paper entitled "Evidence of Main Effects." Then write down two or more descriptions of behavioral evidence or indicators for each of these ILOs.

GATHERING EVIDENCE OF EDUCATIONAL RESULTS

Educational results are overall course outcomes; they are due to the complex and cumulative effects of actual learning outcomes and other factors acting on students. Educational results are attributes, conceptions, or characteristics of the well-educated person. Anticipated or intended educational results are described by the course goals. Assessing and evaluating educational results are extremely difficult. Results may not be readily observable; or, being broad, they cannot be judged by a single behavior. Typically, results cannot be exhibited on demand. In fact, many results do not materialize until after the course is over. In spite of all these difficulties, if we are serious about our educational goals, we have an obligation to evaluate the educational results of our course.

Evaluating results for some courses means actually gathering evidence of these effects. The results of a driver education course can be assessed by looking at the driving records of students. A course aimed at helping teenage drug abusers can keep track of the students to see if they get and keep employment, succeed in school, and otherwise cope with life more successfully. Evidence of results for high school honors courses can be gathered by looking at what students take in college, what they major in, and how well they do. The results of many courses may be found in how well prepared students are for subsequent learning and by seeing how they fare in these courses.

Short of actually looking for course results, teachers should be receptive to the kinds of evidence that would indicate the effects a course has had. It is, after all, the anticipated results (that is, goals) that justify a course. We owe it to both our students and ourselves to try to determine how sound our justification is.

Although we have not included a course planning step concerned with gathering the evidence of educational results, we wish to alert you to the importance of this aspect of course evaluation. If evidence is available, it should be gathered.

There is a growing literature on nontraditional techniques for assessing student outcomes. This literature attempts to distinguish its approach from more traditional approaches that emphasize standardized testing, using terms like *authentic, performance,* or *alternative assessment.* An excellent example of this literature is Archbald and Newman (1988).

GATHERING EVIDENCE ON SIDE EFFECTS

Another important kind of evidence is that of side effects. To reiterate, side effects are those outcomes that were not intended and perhaps not even considered when planning the course. Gathering evidence on side effects is difficult because there are no statements that serve as guides for the evaluation. It is doubtful whether the full range of course side effects could ever be assessed. Even if it were possible, the effort necessary to accomplish such an assessment would be enormous. Therefore, only the most likely or probable side effects must be identified in order to guide the evaluation.

Moreover, since time and resource constraints are great, the side effects examined should be limited to those deemed undesirable. Given the goal of course improvement and the constraints typical of an evaluation, the probable undesirable outcomes are most in need of attention. If the situation permits, however, you may also want to assess desirable side effects in order to plan for and optimize their occurrence (in which case they may become intended learning outcomes).

Considering side effects is important when viewing your course because the discovery of potential side effects will probably change what you do in the course. It is particularly important to consider how likely the side effects are to occur and how undesirable they will be if they do occur. For example, a common side effect of an introductory psychology course is a sense of power on the part of the student. Some students may begin to "analyze" their friends and the social interactions in which they take part. Students might also decide that they can become "amateur therapists." If these side effects are likely and viewed as sufficiently undesirable, you might make changes in the course to head them off. For example, maybe all students should experience the discomfort of being "analyzed."

It is conceivable that some side effects are unavoidable and are so undesirable that the course should be abandoned. On the other hand, you might want to go through with the course but with an increased sensitivity toward the probable side effects. In the consideration of side effects you get a chance to "stand outside" your course and become your own critic.

The most effective method for identifying side effects is to examine the instructional plan carefully. The instructional plan is composed of planned interactions between learner and teacher, instructional foci, and the organization of course units in the context of various institutional factors. A few of these course components are examined in the following sections.

Learner interaction with teacher refers to what teachers do in the course, how they interact with, or behave toward, their students. There are many descriptors of teacher behavior; they include authoritarian, child-centered, and traditional. The important question is: What might students be learning as a result of the exhibited teacher behaviors? From a teacher who constantly emphasizes right and wrong answers, for example, students might learn that a particular subject is clearly defined with no gray areas or areas of debate, that knowledge is factual and either true or false.

There are almost always affective consequences of any prolonged type of interaction between teacher and students. Attitudes about self, school, and subject matter should be examined as possible side effects.

Instructional foci constitute the focal points of the learning experiences in the course. As focal points they can limit as well as enrich learning and can produce biased views of the content with which the course deals.

For example, learning entirely through the use of printed materials, a student might learn that a particular subject (or even learning in general) is a passive enterprise and that personal efforts of experimentation, discovery, or discussion do not lead to legitimate knowledge or learning. (This may apply to the exclusive use of any *one* kind of instructional focus.)

Instructional foci may also lead to undesirable learnings in that they are biased. Bias is evidenced by a particular treatment of certain societal groups (for example, minorities) or by stressing a particular ideology (for example, environmentalist views of the environment to the exclusion of other views).

Organization of course units may result in unintended learnings stemming from the relationships among the course's units. Considerations here focus on the sequence and grouping of units, that is, relationships implicit in the course organization.

For example, a history course organized on a chronological basis may lead the student to a cause-effect relationship. That is, a particular event occurred, which caused the following event, and so on. A chronological organization may hinder the student's learning of recurrent themes in history or important historical ideas (for example, nationalism). Or a botany course organized around plant parts in such a way that a student learns about the root, then the stem, seeds, leaves, and flowers in that order may result in the student's viewing a plant as a group of individual structures rather than as a single organism with specialized tissues forming its various parts.

Other factors bear on course outcomes. Such factors range from how students are seated (possibly the mere fact that they are seated) to the scheduling of units (for example, are interesting units lumped together or interspersed with other less interesting units?).

Examining the instructional plan in order to assess likely side effects is a complex task. The examples above should be helpful in pointing out the range of areas to investigate. Two general guidelines may be of further use in assessing side effects.

1. Examine the attitudes of students toward the subject, toward how it is being taught, and possibly toward school in general.
2. Examine the course for those features that are stable (that is, significant strategies, materials, or behaviors that the student experiences daily). These features should form the basis for answering the question: What might students be learning as a result of this?

Focusing the search for side effects on attitudes and other outcomes likely to result from the prominent aspects of the course places this search in a realistic perspective. The examples that follow may help prepare you to gather evidence of side effects.

Example 8.11.   Mr. Harris is teaching the senior honors section in world history for the first time. Mr. Harris values this opportunity highly and spends an entire summer preparing for the course, which will focus on "Revolutions of the World." His goal is to have students understand the historical forces that caused people to revolt and to relate these forces to current societal forces.

Rather than use available books, which Mr. Harris feels are inadequate, he bases the course on a carefully prepared series of lectures. Outside readings will be employed occasionally. The course focuses on the American, French, and Russian revolutions.

What effects might a lecture presentation have on students? How might students characterize revolution as a result of using the American, French, and Russian cases as examples? Are there other kinds of revolution that are not violent or not political? Do revolutions occur in non-Western countries? Do revolutions always result in stable political-social arrangements? Do the rebels always win? What role does ideology play?

Example 8.12.   Ms. Cole had taught junior English for several years. The course had always focused on a set of novels and plays read by the class in the same sequence. Ms. Cole had led discussions about the books and had found herself doing most, if not all, of the discussing. To remedy this she decided to take a nondirective role in the course. She provided a long list of readings to students on the first day of class. Students were free to read any six books they selected. During class, small groups were formed in which students discussed common readings. Often these groups were made up of only two or three students. One large group of students (about 17 pupils) always read the same book and were thus in the same group. Ms. Cole did not intervene and required only a written synthesis in which students described their reaction to the reading and group discussion.

By being nondirective, might Ms. Cole give students the impression that "expert opinion" has no place in discussions of literature? Is a student's choice of reading always a wise choice? Are aspects such as style and genre likely to be considered in these types of discussion? Can students distinguish good or great literature from lower-quality work?

These questions and those accompanying Example 8.11 illustrate a few side effects that seem likely as a result of these courses. These examples should point out the perspective needed when looking for side effects.

Course Planning Step 8.5.   Examine your course's planned interactions between the learner and (a) the teacher, (b) the instructional foci, (c) the organization of course units, and (d) the institutional setting of the course. On a sheet of paper entitled "Possible Side Effects," list unintended undesirable learnings that you as a teacher and course planner should be wary of as you teach the course.

TROUBLESHOOTING

Course planning has, at this point, ended. Troubleshooting, which consists of using the information gathered during evaluation for making course-improvement decisions, is done after the course has actually begun.

In evaluating a course, you should know whether the course's high-priority ILOs have been achieved. You should also be aware of any major undesirable consequences of the course. You may have some evidence that bears on the educational results of your course. The task now is to use this information to improve the course. Several authors discuss ways to use evaluation to improve teaching. Among these are Dick and Carey, 1990; Eby, 1992; Glatthorn, 1987; Hill, 1987; Kindsvatter, Wilen, and Ishler, 1988; and Kourilsky and Quarana, 1987.

Pinpointing the aspect of a course in need of improvement presents many problems. Assume, for example, that as a result of an evaluation you determine that one or two important ILOs have not been achieved. Does this mean that the instructional focus was inadequate? the teaching strategy faulty? the ILO unlearnable or unteachable? a prerequisite unprovided for? Any number of these factors could be involved. The following is a scheme for systematically trying to determine which course aspects need improvement:

1. *Gather all the evidence you can.* How many students failed to achieve a particular ILO? What students were they? What did these students do differently? Did anything else distinguish these students from those who did learn the ILO? How "close" did these students come to learning the ILO? *If you have evidence of an unachieved ILO, then*
2. *Examine the ILO.* Are prerequisites provided for? Does the ILO fit in with the other ILOs that were achieved? *If the ILO appears satisfactory, then*

3. *Examine the course organization.* Did the ILO receive proper emphasis in the unit? Was it preceded and followed by appropriate ILOs? Was the instrumental content appropriate for teaching the ILO? *If the course organization is satisfactory, then*

4. *Examine the general teaching strategies for the ILO.* Did the instructional focus provide the focus necessary for this ILO? Was the instructional focus interesting? Was the teaching strategy appropriate? Was enough time spent on this ILO? Was the ILO emphasized sufficiently? *If the instructional plan is satisfactory, then*

5. *Examine the instruction.* Was the instructional plan actually carried out? What details may have changed? Was the plan adequate to hold students' attention and interest? Did outside disturbances, unexpected events, scheduling changes, or other factors interfere with instruction?

If you have gathered evidence on your course's educational results, you will want to include this information in your troubleshooting. Since educational results are due to a variety of interacting factors (some of which are entirely outside the course), improvement decisions are difficult. However, depending on the importance of an unachieved goal or the undesirableness of an obtained result, course changes may be very necessary. Troubleshooting here will have to include external factors. Has something occurred in the school, city, or neighborhood that could affect course results? What other sorts of things are students involved in at this time? Much of the troubleshooting you have already done will apply here. Perhaps the problem is several unachieved ILOs or possibly discipline problems in the class caused you to employ unusual or harsh measures. If all your high-priority ILOs were achieved, and the course went smoothly, but yet the results were disappointing, you will have to ask some questions about whether your intended learnings are as appropriate for your goals as you had initially thought.

One further useful way to troubleshoot a course is to administer a questionnaire to the students. Questionnaires can ask students about a wide range of topics. The questions can be specific and detailed or they can require general and overall views. They can ask about the effectiveness of administrative and instructional procedures or about the students' reaction to personal characteristics of the teacher; they can inquire about ratings of current practices or they can ask for suggestions of new practices. Obviously, it is difficult to know what to ask and where to stop. A useful criterion in developing questionnaires is to limit them to questions that will help inform course-improvement decisions.

As you develop questions, center the questions on those areas in which you are willing and able to make changes. Then design your questions so that they solicit information useful in making those decisions. Don't waste your students' time with questions that do not or cannot lead to course improvements. For example, asking students to rate your overall performance as a teacher gives information too general to be useful and has the potential only to inflate or deflate egos. On the other hand, the students' reaction to the size of their within-class group may well be valuable information.

By carefully and systematically making changes and continuing to evaluate the course each time it is taught, the course should become more and more refined. As noted, troubleshooting cannot be carried out while a course evaluation is being planned. But when the course is actually taught, troubleshooting should be incorporated as a useful scheme that aids course improvement.

SUMMARY

This brings to a close the planning of your course. In a sense, course planning never stops but continues to evolve. Unless a course is scrapped or radically altered, however, further planning often takes the form of refinements based on the evidence gathered during evaluations as well as on "gut" reactions. To some extent we can know what we want to accomplish only as we try to implement preliminary plans. Thus, ILOs, educational goals, and other course components will be altered as you or others actually teach the course.

We hope that you have worked through, rather than around, the book to arrive at this summary. Much of what you have read and what you have been asked to do may have seemed highly technical. We recognize that a considerable amount of actual course planning also involves common sense and a great deal of creativity. What needs to accompany these two ingredients, however, is the talent for asking the right question at the right time and having the understandings and skills necessary to answer (and ask) these questions.

QUESTIONS FOR DISCUSSION: COURSE EVALUATION

1. Troubleshooting involves using evidence to think about course components. The links between various course components are often important to consider when deciding where to make course changes. In what ways are each of the following course components linked: (a) rationale–general teaching strategies, (b) ILOs–instructional foci, and (c) unit organization–ILOs?
2. Discuss any course you may have taken in which side effects or unintended learnings were of greater significance than the espoused aims of the course. What may have contributed to this?
3. In trying to improve a course, what is the benefit of making systematic improvements instead of "wholesale" course revisions?
4. What type of information would lead you to abandon a course?
5. What are the differences and similarities between course evaluation as presented in this chapter and pupil evaluation as you have experienced it?

REFERENCES

Archbald, D. A., & Newman, F. M. (1988). *Beyond standardized testing.* Reston, VA: National Association of Secondary School Principals.

Cronbach, L. J. (1963). Evaluation for course improvement. *Teachers College Record, 64,* 672–683.

Dick, W., & Carey, L. (1990). *The systematic design of instruction* (3rd ed.). Glenview, IL: Scott, Foresman.

Eby, J. W. (1992). *Reflective planning, teaching, and evaluation for the elementary school.* New York: Macmillan.

Glatthorn, A. A. (1987). *Curriculum leadership.* Glenview, IL: Scott, Foresman.

Hill, J. C. (1987). *Curriculum evaluation for school improvement.* Springfield, IL: Charles C. Thomas.

Kindsvatter, R., Wilen, W., & Ishler, M. (1988). *Dynamics of effective teaching.* New York: Longman. (teaching and evaluation and decision making)

Kourilsky, M., & Quarana, L. (1987). Effective teaching: Principles and practice. Glenview, IL: Scott, Foresman.

Scriven, M. (1967). The methodology of evaluation. In R. W. Tyler, R. M. Gagné, & M. Scriven (Eds.), AERA Monograph Series on Curriculum Evaluation. Volume 1: *Perspectives on curriculum evaluation.* Chicago: Rand McNally.

Epilogue

Our central message in this book has been that when we teach we should teach with a purpose. Further, our purposes should be made explicit in the form of educational goals and intended learning outcomes. There are no hard-and-fast rules for explicating our purposes; we must think for ourselves about our students, our subject matter, and our assumptions about education, and then express our purposes appropriately. We have to discipline ourselves to take our purposes seriously so as not to lie to ourselves. If we want students to learn to solve problems, mere content coverage just won't suffice. Our instructional planning must be appropriate for our purposes. These are the major lessons to be learned from this book.

Although the major purpose of designing a course has been to learn how to develop a curriculum, this was not our only concern. An unstated but nevertheless important benefit of working on this project was to learn what to look for in a curriculum, to begin the process of becoming a curricular "connoisseur" (Eisner, 1985). Developing a curriculum gives us a different perspective on curricula developed by others. This perspective enables us to look at curricula and talk about them more intelligently, precisely, and profoundly.

Often educators compare the educational enterprise to another activity, that of travel. In such an analogy the student does the traveling, teachers serve as travel guides, educational goals and intended learning outcomes are considered destinations, and instructional plans specify the means of transportation and the itinerary.

But there is a constant danger inherent in the planning of educational itineraries and the means of transportation; there is much more to a journey than arriving at the destination on time and unharmed. People also embark on journeys for the experience of traveling. A trip through France is not undertaken just to arrive in Paris. The French countryside, the French people, the French wine and food, and the enjoyment of a traveling companion are all as important for the "success" of the journey as the arrival in Paris. Nor should a kindergartner embark on an educational journey merely to receive a high school diploma or to learn the three R's. Thus, there are compelling reasons for expecting the educational process not only to help children become "well educated," but also to meet a set of criteria relating to the intrinsic, rather than instrumental, aspects of the process. The educational process should not only accomplish goals but also be humane, rational, engaging, enjoyable, and personally gratifying, to mention just a few such criteria. The most compelling reason for this requirement is not that such humane education is most efficient or effective (it may not be), but, instead, that schooling constitutes a substantial portion of people's lives and life should be lived in such a manner.

One final caveat in using this guide must be mentioned. In all our planning, research, and evaluation it is easy to forget that educational journeys are for the student-traveler, not for their teacher-guides, nor for the travel-agent administration. The educational travel industry is simply intended to help the student-traveler along on an educational journey; as much as we want to, we cannot make the journey for the student. We can only act as guides. It is in this spirit that this book is intended to be used.

REFERENCE

Eisner, E. (1985). *The educational imagination: On the design and evaluation of school programs* (2nd ed.). New York: Macmillan.

Colonial America: Social Studies Curriculum for Grade 5

Kerry Gaffney

The examples included in these appendixes represent courses or units that vary in subject matter and grade level. As has been the case for all the examples throughout Course Design, *these are not presented as models to emulate. Instead, each design reflects one teacher's way of addressing the requirements faced when planning for a particular age group and subject matter. Most importantly, each design reflects the individuality of the teacher-planner.*

COMMENTS

This is an excellent unit. While planned for fifth graders, the unit could easily be adapted for students in middle school by including more sophisticated readings and increasing the amount of student research that is expected. The unit's Introduction and Notes to Teachers emphasize the importance of understanding the nature of history as well as learning about colonial America. The general teaching strategies make extensive use of group and collaborative learning activities.

INTRODUCTION

Generally speaking, nine and ten year olds have reached a developmental stage at which they are ready to understand peoples and lands that are removed both by distance and time. In other words, they are ready to learn history. Up to this point, elementary social studies curricula usually focus on local or very familiar topics (Our School, Our Community) and may use those as background for study of modern cultures (Our Neighbors, Mexico and Canada). By fourth grade, students can transfer the structure of social "studies" to a historical perspective, particularly if the unit is constructed so as to take advantage of students' sense of and experience with history, even their own family's. For most of them, knights, Pilgrims, and pharaohs are already ideas they know, even without an understanding of the time periods in which they lived and the cultures from which they developed.

History is chronological by nature. There are commonalities by which eras and peoples can be studied. The Smith College Campus School social studies curriculum considers both of these factors in the sequencing of its units. The study of history begins in fourth grade with Ancient Rome. Fifth grade covers Medieval Europe and The Age of Exploration and Discovery. This unit, Colonial America, is designed to fit after these and to precede Industrialization in the United States. The unit could be isolated from this scheme, but it would have to be modified; understandings of medieval Europe are clearly necessary to learn it as is. Either fifth or sixth grade would be an appropriate level, but the expository texts suggested for the activities are sophisticated in several instances, making it difficult for grades lower than these.

In developing the unit, I have endeavored to make history real and exciting for students. Whenever possible, we simulate conditions and situations of the colonial period of the United States. Basal texts are used as only one of a variety of reading materials; in fact, as often as possible, students read about events and people from the primary sources available to "real" historians. These replicated authentic documents are more difficult to read, but they are far less "watered down" than social studies books. Another outstanding opportunity for students at the Campus School is a visit to Plymouth Plantation, where the Mayflower II is docked as its predecessor might have been in 1621 and the Plantation is as it was in 1627.

If no other goal is met, I would hope that students remain or become excited about the study of history and see it as a rich and relevant body of knowledge. Perhaps they will feel encouraged to discover the truths about their families' backgrounds. This is an age by which students have moved away from the egocentricity of young childhood; it is an age at which they can most appreciate the need for asserting one's independence and living out one's sense of adventure. What better people to study than the early colonists of America?

Notes to a Teacher

The order of the subunits in this unit is partly due to time schedules and may therefore need to be changed according to your schedule. A pivotal subunit seems to be the one focused on the field trip to Plymouth Plantation. If students go in the beginning of the unit, the benefit is high intrigue and interest. The downfall is lack of prior knowledge. Students with no formal instruction in the period who go to Plymouth tend not to ask good questions of the role characters, nor do they seem to remember much of the historical details. When they go with at least an introduction, and at least a spattering of reading (historical and biographical fiction, nonfiction, etc.), they remember names and events connected with characters, ask relevant questions about the period, and begin to know the historical figures more intimately. Ideally, the subunit should come early in the unit, though not first, and certainly with enough time left after the trip to take advantage of their new information, understandings, and excitement.

Subunit I is another that I considered inserting in other sequences for different purposes. I hope that when students study colonial America, they come to an understanding of what a colony is, not just colonial America but all colonies, past and present. To accomplish this goal, we must provide a structure for understanding "colony," including an accepted definition of the term, knowledge about a ruling country, reasons for and results of colonization, and aspects of typical colonial lifestyles. I chose to let the accumulated knowledge of colonial America stand as a basis for looking at the defining features of colonies and for comparison with other recognized colonies. It is just as reasonable, I think (though more boring for fifth graders, I suspect), to study "What is a colony?" first and then look at colonial America as an example.

One place where I am particularly unsure about the structure of the unit is in its lack of sequence. Historically, would it have been more sound to study the settlements in the order in which they occurred? I don't know, but I decided not to worry about order so much as a general sense of the period; in other words, I care less that students remember that Jamestown came 13 years before Plymouth than I do that they understand what made them colonies and the important aspects of colonial life.

A final word about materials: Wherever possible, I have indicated exact resources and even included some page references. This is because its function is as a working document by which teachers will instruct. A teacher of the unit should realize, though, that there are vast numbers of books, tapes, videos, filmstrips, and people with huge stores of information on the subject. I have picked and chosen, given my knowledge of this year's students and the general student population at S.C.C.S. However, while the resources may change, I would like to share with you my own "hidden agenda" for teaching history. I chose texts, often, because of (and not in spite of) the fact that accounts differed. I want students to know that a part of history, and part of a historian's job, is speculating. I want them to read in one book that 102 passengers came aboard the Mayflower, and from another that 101 came. I want them to be part of the process of looking at data, considering the source, checking in three places for more evidence, and still not knowing for sure what's right. In other words, I want them less impressed by the "correctness" of historical fact and more interested in the search for "the best that we can tell is. . . ."

Content Outline
    I. The Thirteen Colonies
        A. Why colonists came to America
            European conditions
            religious freedom
            immunity for prisoners
            adventure
            promise of riches
            missionaries
            expansion of trade
        B. Early settlements
            Roanoke, the "lost colony"
            Jamestown
            Plymouth Plantation

    C. Development of colonies

       land conditions

       villages and towns

       plantations in the south

    D. Relationships with Native Americans

       early assistance to colonists

       contributions to a mixed culture

       particular Native Americans

II. Society and Government

    A. Colonial society

       occupations

       religious influence

       family life; roles of men, women, and children

    B. Government

       Mayflower Compact

       Connecticut Chart

       Massachusetts Bay Charter

       voting requirement

       law enforcement

       famous leaders

III. The Home

    A. Houses

       materials

       shapes

       barn-raising parties

       Common houses

       furnishings

    B. Clothing

       woolens, linens, breeches, stockings, leggings

    C. Food

       staples

       regional differences

       growing

    D. Health

       the "starving time"

       diseases and malnutrition

    E. Recreation

       games played

       social gatherings

       taverns

IV. The Church and School

    A. The church

       prominent religions

       freedom or not

       blue laws

    B. School

availability of free, public schools
tutoring and apprenticeships
books used
V. Arts and Sciences
   A. Literature
   B. Painting
   C. Science
VI. Economy
   A. Farming
   tobacco farms
   need for labor, slavery
   B. Trade and industry
   whaling
   fur trapping
   C. Crafts
   pewter
   candle dipping

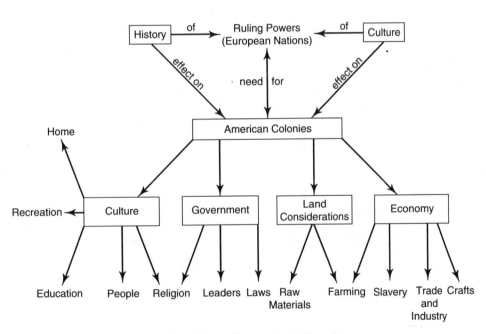

FIGURE A.1 Conceptual map for unit on colonial America.

STATEMENT TO ACCOMPANY CONCEPTUAL MAP

"American Colonies" is central on the page, and also in the unit. We begin the unit by exploring one of these as an example and then go on to look at how the history and culture of European nations affect its development.

The subsections of "American Colonies" (culture, government, land, economy) are focal points of instruction through which higher-level understandings of the concept of colonization are made.

"American Colonies" and "European Nations" ought to be the flexible factors— i.e., they're central to the unit, but only one of the two major cognitions* is contingent upon them; the other ** should be able to use a very similar map to study any colony.

Sequence of Subunits

    A. Coming to the New World
    B. Reasons for coming and reactions to life in the New World
    C. An early settlement: Plymouth Plantation
    D. Daily life in settlements and regional differences
    E. Government
    F. Religion in the colonies
    G. Relationships with Native Americans
    H. Indentured servants and slavery
    I. Why do we call them colonies?

SUBUNIT A: COMING TO THE NEW WORLD

Intended Learnings

Students will understand various reasons for coming to the New World as early colonists and the conditions that led to the immigration.

Students will understand what colonists found upon arrival in the New World and their reactions to the realities here.

Students will be able to describe conditions (particularly spatial) aboard the Mayflower.

Instructional Foci

"The Voyage of the Mayflower"; "The Adventure Begins"; "appraisement and valuation of the Mayflower's tackle" (replicas of documents); discussion; estimation and measurement of the main deck of the Mayflower.

General Teaching Strategy

Many students of this age and grade will already know that the Mayflower was the ship that carried Pilgrims to the New World. Some will know the year, or at least the era, and names of specific settlers or colonies. While encouraging these students to share

---

  * Students will understand how colonial America both reflected medieval and Renaissance Europe and created a culture of its own based on the conditions, lifestyles, individual colonists, and desire for a different kind of life.

  ** Students will understand what a colony is, the characteristics of most colonies and their ruling powers, some reasons for colonization and opposition to it, and benefits to both the ruling country and its colony.

their information, let it be clear to the class that students of history often begin study of an era without many specific facts; as fifth graders at the Smith College Campus School, they can be counted on to have solid understandings of the history preceding colonization of America; i.e., they've all studied medieval Europe. Prompt a discussion of the religious and political foundations set in medieval and Renaissance Europe, and development of the technology invented just after those "Dark Ages" they know so well. Give students the opportunity to summarize the general political and religious atmosphere present in Europe at that time. As discussions go on in this unit, look for ways in which connections to that knowledge can be made, or acknowledge the connections made by children.

In the beginning of this subunit (which also serves as the introductory lesson to the larger unit), help students understand the size of the Mayflower and the space available to its passengers and crew by having them (1) listen to a variety of historical accounts of the ship and her crossing, and (2) physically enclose themselves in an area akin to that of the Mayflower's main deck.

Any nonfiction reading that describes the above could be used for the first purpose. The two I've chosen are "The Voyage of the Mayflower" by Patricia M. Whalen, *Cobblestone*, 1989, and sections of "The Adventure Begins" from "The Mayflower and the Pilgrim Fathers" jackdaw packet. I particularly like these two as they contain the necessary information, but not quite exactly; I lead discussion into the discrepancies between the two sources.

For today's purposes, I ask students to listen for two things:

1. details about living conditions aboard the ship (things they saw, heard, brought . . .).
2. details about measurement that will help us reconstruct close approximations of the space aboard the main deck.

They listen with better intent to what is important and filter out what information is nonessential now if I give these directions before the reading.

The important data to glean from students before going on to the next activity is:

90' × 25' at the waist (Just what is the waist of a ship? Will we consider that?)

102 people aboard

"Space about the size of a modern day twin-size mattress"

five feet of head room

The idea of the activity is to mark off bow and stern points on a surface such as a blacktop. In a class of 20 students, each will have to represent about five. They may be able to use chalk to mark off "their" square footage, i.e., the space allocated, theoretically, to five people aboard the ship. Much cooperation is needed for the measuring and marking part. The result should help students visualize the space available and mentally place themselves back in their spots for later activities.

Independently, students begin composing a list of items they think colonists would have brought with them. It is helpful to discuss beforehand the time period and availability of resources, the knowledge Pilgrims had of the land to which they were traveling, and what was important to survival and culture. By doing this activity independently at first, students are more apt to think about, and be able to defend, their choice. Back in small groups, they may rethink their choices, combine their space for common provisions, or decide to fit it all in.

The class reconvenes to compare lists and consider space and needs. These lists can be reconsidered at other points in the unit, directly or indirectly, by students or the teacher.

Other Possible Activities

1. This would be an appropriate place to start the reading of Patricia Clapp's *Constance,* a historical novel depicting the life of a real Mayflower Pilgrim, and starting on the deck of the ship. Students will have immediate reactions to the comparison between fiction and nonfiction accounts of the story.
2. Scale models of a cutaway of the Mayflower may be drawn. Additional discussion about cross section and scale may be necessary.

SUBUNIT B: REASONS FOR COMING AND REACTIONS TO LIFE HERE

Intended Learnings

Students will understand various reasons for coming to the New World as colonists.

Students will understand what it was that different colonists found upon arrival in the New World.

Students will be able to differentiate between and define primary and secondary resources.

Instructional Foci

Expository texts, both primary and secondary, regarding reasons for coming to the New World, and colonists' reactions to conditions during early months; small group reading, discussing, listing; whole class discussions.

General Teaching Strategy

Have students name several resources one might go to in doing research on a topic or person. As they name them, list on the chalkboard under categories you recognize (but do not yet name) as primary and secondary. Note that some will fit under both, and others under one only. When the list seems quite complete, ask students to distinguish between the categories, and go on to discuss the differences between primary and secondary sources, their availability, and their validity.

Ask students which of them have had experience with keeping diaries or journals (if your class is like mine, it is already done in a variety of contexts); they should be able to name several purposes for keeping such records. Tell students that they will be getting the chance to investigate some of the diaries, journals, and early letters of colonists. Ask how this kind of reading might differ from reading a social studies book.

Before explaining the tasks for the next activities, read the introduction to Samuel Sewall's diary. This particular explanation tells of the religious reasons some colonists had for this kind of careful record keeping; that is, a record of occurrences that could later be examined for indications of having found favor or disfavor with God. This will be students' first direct experience with the Puritans' view of religion and its profound influence over their lives. Point out, too, the different purposes a ship's captain or colony governor might have for keeping a journal.

In random groups of four, have students read a sampling of primary and secondary resources. The task is to compile a list of reasons different settlers came to America, divided into the categories religious, political, economic, and social. Cite several examples that do not fall clearly into one or another, and explain that students should be able to justify whatever category they choose.

For this first part of the small group activities, students may struggle with the break-up of the task. Some will decide to split up the reading and do the list together, others to do all individually and compile at the end, still others to read each piece aloud with a recorder to keep track of ideas. The teacher may decide to have groups run all one way, or to continue to let them figure it out on their own. It is important, however, to have the whole class share their methods, so that groups have a chance to share from each other.

When the class reconvenes, the lists are shared aloud and recorded on class charts. Groups should appoint one spokesperson to do the sharing, but all must be involved in the listening. I ask all who are not speaking to do two things: (1) listen to the reasons being shared and mentally note whether or not their group got it, and (2) decide whether the reason could be paraphrased for better understanding. This keeps them accountable for the listening; I also can check the paraphrasing of their own or others' words to see if they've really understood.

This is also the appropriate time to make the distinction between primary and secondary sources vivid. Students can practice pointing out differences and also try to specify authors' purposes.

The second half of the subunit involves the same groups and similar types of readings. The groups are given a little background by the teacher in excerpts from William Bradford's journal and other letters. The groups are asked to read several other documents to find the positive and negative aspects of life in the New World. This is a chance for them to further practice group responsibility for understanding a text and for reading early American writings (which are characteristically full of invented spelling and much jargon of the day).

We meet back as a class again to share and discuss colonists' ideas about this new land they've settled.

Many of the issues that arise in this subunit are repeated within more specific subunits elsewhere. The context is broad, yet the experience with this method of inquiry and understanding of the general atmosphere of the colonies is critical. There has been no specific instruction of times, dates, or names, but when they appear in sources, we make note of them.

SUBUNIT C: AN EARLY SETTLEMENT: PLYMOUTH PLANTATION

Intended Learnings

Students will be able to describe conditions aboard the Mayflower.

Students will understand the roles of men and women in the colonial period.

Students will understand a typical lifestyle of colonists.

Students will understand how Plymouth Plantation arranged its houses, central buildings, protective structures, and farmland for safety and usefulness.

Instructional Foci

Books, pamphlets, brochures, maps, and photographs regarding Plymouth Plantation; field trip to Plymouth Plantation and the Mayflower II; letters, discussion, sense chart.

General Teaching Strategy

This subunit relies on scheduling to fit so perfectly into unit plans. If, in fact, it will not fit at this time, students may need different kinds of preparation or follow-up activities for the trip. The goal of the trip is to really "see" what it is we've been reading about, to make the information more understandable, and also to provoke further thoughts and questions about colonial life.

Before the trip, have students prepare in several ways:

1. Using the "street plan" in *Constance,* have students sketch their own maps with family names written next to their cottages.
2. Students should be fairly familiar with colonists' names by this time through reading the novel, but in any case, have each student choose one family or individual to be in charge of gathering specific information about during the trip. Have them prepare by researching as much as they can before meeting them, and preparing a list of questions they will ask. Students may have to rely on neighbors of the colonists as not all of them are represented at all times.
3. Have all students read the "interviews" with Sarah Morton and Mistress Fuller found in *Cobblestone,* November, 1989. Several students who are comfortable with the reading could volunteer to play the parts of Sarah, Mistress Fuller, or the interviewer.
4. Read aloud to students other nonfiction accounts of the plantation.
5. Tell students some of the general categories under which the rest of the unit will be studied: government, religion, relationships with Native Americans. . . . They will have a better sense of the kinds of questions to ask with a structure for study already set in their minds.

During the course of the trip, remind students about these points of interest; help them ask questions that will get specific information as well as a general sense of the life of these Pilgrims. Students who have a clear purpose, enthusiasm and motivation about a subject, and a willing adult can usually lead themselves to where they want and ought to be. Life on the Plantation is full of chance occurrences of daily life; it is impossible to prepare students for these, but help them get the most out of them. For instance, one year a lamb was born moments before we arrived. We returned to its yard several times over the course of the day, watching the afterbirth, the mother feeding, and attempts at first steps.

Upon returning, all of the preparations must be accounted for, their purposes fulfilled. Students need the chance to talk about everything. A "sense chart" hung on a bulletin board is one way to share. Sections can be divided into "I tasted . . .", "I smelled . . .", "I saw . . .", and so on. During the subsequent days, give students the opportunity to add to this board.

Our class makes it a habit to write letters of appreciation to people who share things with us or teach us. For these letters, students have someone specific to write to: the person about whom they were gathering information. Encourage students not only to thank them but to share learnings and ask questions; students need every opportunity to see learning as ongoing.

SUBUNIT D: DAILY LIFE AND REGIONAL DIFFERENCES

Intended Learnings

Students will understand how colonial America both reflected medieval and Renaissance Europe and created a culture of its own based on the conditions, lifestyles, individual colonists, and the desire for a different kind of life.

Students will understand the differences among colonies of the northern, southern, and middle Atlantic regions.

Students will understand the roles of men and women in the colonial period.

Students will understand a typical lifestyle of colonists.

Students will understand the religious influence on many colonists and on the culture of the early colonies.

Students will be able to name some of the religious laws of the colonies.

Instructional Foci

Nonfiction books, magazines, texts, filmstrips, historical fiction, simulated journals

General Teaching Strategy

This subunit is the most research oriented of the subunits. It has been placed in this sequence because the activities involved in Subunit C serve as models for the product (a simulated journal such as a book read aloud, *Sarah Morton's Day*), but it could be used at this or any later point.

Before beginning independent research, have all students read the text section on different regions. Distinctions must be made among land conditions, weather, industry, and commerce.

Following this introduction, tell students they will be creating a simulated journal such as the above example. They will be assigned a gender and region but must make choices for other topics. Some of the information they must include is time of year, fictional name, occupation, and colony/town. They must also include information regarding religion, some laws and leaders guiding them, activities of their daily lives, and some of their personal hope and dreams. Illustrations should accompany the text.

Assign roles randomly, posting lists so students can use each other as resources, especially among same-region characters. Set aside a sharing time once journals are complete, and save for evaluation purposes.

SUBUNIT E: GOVERNMENT

Intended Learnings

Students will understand how governments and the ideals of governing grow from one another.

Students will name several laws that governed early colonists.

Instructional Foci

Magna Charta, Mayflower Compact; nonfiction resources; discussion.

General Teaching Strategy

To begin the whole class discussion, the teacher will either read aloud or have students preread "Mutiny on the Mayflower." The focus of interest for this part of the lesson is twofold: events and atmosphere leading up to the writing and signing of the Mayflower Compact and actual provisions of the document. Students will be questioned as to how they understand conflict to have been the predecessor to that document, and how its development was, in effect, conflict resolution between two factions of people and a multitude of opinions. In a similar way, the Magna Charta will be reexamined by the class (all of whom have previously studied the Middle Ages) for similarities. It is the "spirit of the law" students should be asked to respond to, as well as the dissatisfaction with situations that led to each.

In smaller groups of three to four, students will look for evidence of the laws of the colonial period being carried out in everyday life. They will post the examples found in a variety of nonfiction resources so that the class can use them as examples.

Some recognition should be made at this point of the heavy weight religion was given during this period, even in civil laws. Through an evaluation piece associated with the above Intended Learnings, this will become even clearer.

SUBUNIT F: RELIGION IN THE COLONIES

Intended Learnings

Students will understand the influence of religion on many colonists and on the culture of the early colonies.

Students will understand the irony of the persecuted becoming the persecutors, most especially in this subunit, as illustrated by the hypocrisy of those who came seeking religious freedom and denied others the freedom to worship or not as they chose.

Students will be able to name some of the religious laws of the colonies.

Students will be able to explain the history of witchcraft and its significance during the witch crazes of the colonial period.

Instructional Foci

Chart of laws from Subunit E; books; magazines; video movie; social studies textbook.

General Teaching Strategy

In the first part of this subunit, many connections are made to the understandings of religion in Europe during the Middle Ages and after. Students will need a chance to remember, or even reconstruct, these understandings throughout the subunit.

The class together should reconsider the list of laws that groups found and displayed on chart paper in the last subunit. A student or teacher can color code or underline those which the class decides are religiously based. Independently, have students read the text sections about religion, keeping track on a prepared note chart of differences among the colonies' religious states. The teacher should choose excerpts that differentiate among the 13 colonies and how religion often determined founding.

In the discussion to follow, have students recognize where and when church and state acted as one, asking for instances in which that is no longer true. Students may be on the lookout for current news events that illustrate the separation taken for granted or challenged even today.

The second part of this subunit focuses on the much-publicized witchcraft of the colonial period. The teacher should give students a historical background of witchcraft, from ancient Greece and Rome, noting societal attitudes toward it and commonly accepted uses of it.

After a preliminary discussion of conceptions of witches from their historical fiction reading and other exposure to the ideas of witches, show students the movie *Three Sovereigns for Sarah.* Excerpts may be sufficient to give students the idea of cultural pressures, greed, and ignorance as partly responsible for the crazes. Have students read several fictional pieces as well as several nonfiction pieces about witches and witchcraft. The class will then be able to distinguish, orally and in writing, between the images presented.

Many students are intrigued by the subject and opt to do additional reading. Provide a variety of accounts of witchcraft in the American colonies; some are in script form that students can present to the rest of the class.

SUBUNIT G: RELATIONSHIPS WITH NATIVE AMERICANS

Intended Learnings

Students will understand the contributions of Native Americans to the survival of European settlers.

Students will understand the speculative nature of history, and the role of historians and readers of history in making inferences.

Instructional Foci

The Double Life of Pocahontas by Jean Fritz; textbook; charts.

General Teaching Strategy

This novel was chosen specifically because of the style in which it was written; Fritz makes it very clear to the reader that she had to make guesses about history given what information she had available to her.

The activity is structured to be understood in its totality; all groups provide pieces of a story told in sequence to the class. Groups of four students will be asked to read one chapter of the book. Probably most effective use of time would be for individuals to read ahead of class time and then collaborate in the classroom. Groups are to record main events and characters in the chapter they read so that, retold to the class, all will get a comprehensive and chronological story of Pocahontas's life. The groups should chose a storyteller, with all to add details before the next group begins.

The other focus of the activity is to look for evidence that Jean Fritz, historian, had to make guesses. Direct quotes from each of the chapters will be posted for the class to see.

The same groups will have a second chance to work together after the story of Pocahontas has been told and discussed. Using the history texts, students will read about early life in the colonies, noting contributions made by Native Americans. Postreading discussion should center around those contributions as well as the ultimate "thanks" these groups of people received. This will give students a chance to make connections to their fourth grade study of Native Americans.

SUBUNIT H: INDENTURED SERVANTS AND SLAVERY

Intended Learnings

Students will understand how the different land conditions of the colonies of the North and South meant the South had a greater need for laborers.

Students will understand the irony of the persecuted becoming the persecutors, specifically in this subunit, the landowners' use of humans as things.

Students will be able to explain the roles of indentured servants and slaves during the colonial period.

Students will be able to trace and explain the slave triangle between Africa and the Americas.

Instructional Foci

Various books, stories, articles, and a play; broadsheet of slave notices; role playing.

General Teaching Strategy

Many people do not connect slavery with early colonial America. Students will have many opportunities to read about, act out, and discuss the common situations during this period throughout the subunit. Their most recent common experience with indentured servants is in hearing about two examples of such servants through the read aloud *Constance*. Discussion could begin with the conditions recognized through this historical fiction piece and go on to a nonfiction account of indentured servants from the earliest colonies. *Meet the Real Pilgrims* is one such example, but there are several. Also share with students copies of a real indenture and have the class interpret it together.

Small groups of students will then read together a mock trial of an indentured servant, each presenting an excerpt of that script to the rest of the group. All through this first half of the subunit, emphases should be placed on the attitudes and conditions of life of indentured servants. This will ultimately serve as a contrast to the same for slaves.

Tell students they will be participating in some role playing for which there are no scripts. Ask them to identify some information they would think important if they were to play the part of another person. Share the broadsheet of slaves being auctioned off with the whole class. A teacher-led discussion should again come back to living conditions and the attitude that it was acceptable to own, buy, and sell people. The teacher prepares realistic scenarios for small groups of children to read, discuss briefly, and then improvise the action of in front of the class. For example, a slave couple celebrating the birth of another child is interrupted by the arrival of their master. He has come to congratulate them, and at the same time inform them that their oldest child, a strong teenage boy, has been sold.

The students will then read a complete account of a slave's travels from Africa to slavery in America. They will keep a simulated journal of the important events of his life, his fears, hopes, and dreams, and the travels he takes. Where possible, actual maps will be included. These rather real life accounts will be compared to other nonfiction resources' information on early slavery.

The teacher should lead students to an understanding of the extent of slavery in the South, greatly due to the large plantations that needed to be worked. The group as a whole should discuss major differences between indentured servants and slaves. Primarily, that indentured servants chose their lot, were of many races, and had realistic hopes for the future were the factors that separated them from African slaves taken by force and kept for a lifetime against their will.

SUBUNIT I: WHY DO WE CALL THEM COLONIES?

Intended Learnings

Students will understand what a colony is.

Students will understand the characteristics of most colonies and their ruling power.

Students will understand some reasons for colonization and opposition to it.

Students will understand benefits to both the ruling power and the colony.

Instructional Foci

Discussion, record of comments; encyclopedia; group notes.

General Teaching Strategy

So what will students think of colonies after many weeks of concentrated study? The teacher is now in a position to ask. This is no longer prior knowledge, but very current knowledge. It is, however, unlikely that it has been synthesized in quite this way.

For the whole class, the teacher leads a discussion with some of the following questions:

So, we've studied Plymouth and Jamestown, and . . . what are we calling them?

What, then, do we want to say a colony is? (It will take some time and argument to decide on some defining features of colonies.)

What would make a country like England want to pour all that money into a colony? Or any powerful country for example? Let's make a list of some viable reasons for colonizing.

Why would anyone go? What are their responsibilities to England (or whatever ruling country)?

In this way, all the major defining points of colonization are discussed prior to giving any formal definition. The students have American colonies as a common background, and their arguments will demonstrate some of the discrepancies that are, in fact, not clear in considering American colonies.

The students, though, will want and deserve some answers. Give groups the encyclopedia entry for colonization. Have groups decide what makes a colony a colony. Their second task is to make a two-sided argument giving evidence that we were, indeed, colonies . . . and that we were not, alas, really colonies.

Back as a class, read through all groups' arguments, discussing once again the uncertainty in the final analysis. Students should reach a level of comfort in understanding of colonization to acknowledge both sides. They will need this reinforced in looking back through the various subunits, as it is one of the most important cognitions of the unit. If, in fact, the "American colonies" and "European nations" aspects of the unit's conceptual map are flexible, this is the understanding that should be the strongest, the one most able to stand when memory of 102 passengers has faded.

EVALUATION

The evaluation piece of the unit here addresses only the two main cognitions. Other understandings as well as cognitive skills do need to be evaluated to gain a sense of students' progress through the subunits and at the conclusion of all subunits.

1. Students will understand what a colony is, the characteristics of most colonies and their ruling power, some reasons for colonization and opposition to it, and benefits to both the ruling power and the colony.
   a. Given a description of a modern so-named colony, students will write an essay explaining how it truly is a colony (as we understand the term) and how it is not. Their skills in brainstorming, organizing ideas, developing arguments, and other essay-writing steps will be crucial. To eliminate the disparity between what students know and what they can express in writing, an oral interview on this same topic would work, but it would be very time consuming.
   b. Students will write two letters to government officials, one urging colonization by the United States and the other protesting it. The letter should include comments on our history as colonies, reasons for/against, possible benefits/drawbacks, and ethical considerations.
2. Students will understand how colonial America both reflected medieval and Renaissance Europe and created a culture of its own based on the conditions, lifestyles, individual colonists, and the desire for a different kind of life.
   a. Besides a formal evaluation, the teacher should make note of individuals' understandings of the connections between medieval Europe and colonial America. It is clearly stated in the Introduction that this is a crucial connection for students at the Campus School, given their previous studies.
   b. Given a list of general topics related to culture, living conditions, and so on, students will fill out a chart showing similarities and differences in these areas between medieval life and colonial life. In addition, they will be asked to give examples to support their ideas.

APPENDIX B

A Survey of Western Art

Margaret Timmerman

COMMENTS

This is a very well conceived design for a yearlong art history course aimed at high school juniors and seniors. Students would have to have some background in the history of Western civilization. The course could serve nicely as an elective in humanities or history. The use of flowcharts to explain the complex skills of analysis and research in art history is very helpful. The course, while designed as yearlong, does not contain exhaustive lists of ILOs or overly detailed general teaching strategies. Individual teachers are given clear direction and guidance but also have considerable freedom to select the artworks that will serve as examples and the specific learning activities that will achieve the desired learnings. These features are strengths for teachers who know this material. At the same time, anyone without a solid background in art history would find teaching this unit difficult.

RATIONALE

Historians often point out that during times of upheaval the arts are usually on the front line of change. Because art is produced by individuals, rather than by institutions, art can react more quickly to the social climate and is thus seen as heralding future conditions. Change itself is one of the predominant aspects of life today, and it is important for society that its citizens be able to keep up with the rapid fluctuations in culture and technology. Citizens who have knowledge in a variety of fields, including art, will be better able to cope in such a rapidly changing society.

Art history is an important means of understanding our cultural heritage, and the diverse societies that produced that heritage. It can serve as a balance to the increasing importance of technology in our society. And it is a way of training people to see beauty, in a world that is growing increasingly ugly. With such training people may be aroused to fight against the aesthetic decay that surrounds them.

For the learner, art can be an interesting introduction or adjunct to the study of history. It can inform one about our cultural heritage, and provide a means of understanding past societies, from which our modern society is derived. It provides the learner with both the sensitivity and the vocabulary to be aware of and describe his or her own feelings and reactions to pieces of art. It also can provide the student with a chance to refine the use of language. By both reading and writing about art and aesthetics the student will be able to understand and communicate subtle differences in expression. He or she will also be able to apply the vocabulary of art to the world.

Usually, the study of art history is not begun until the student has reached the college level. However, the benefits that derive from this field are such that I think it is important to offer it at the high school level. For those students who then go on to study it further in college, it will provide them with a head start and allow them to do more advanced work in the field. For those who do not go on to college, or choose not to study it in college, this course will at least offer them a basic understanding of the concepts and methods used in the discipline. Thus they will at least accrue the benefits outlined above, whatever their opportunities for further study.

INTRODUCTION

This course is designed as a survey of Western art for eleventh and twelfth graders. It is a full year course, and although it could be shortened somewhat this is not recommended due to the amount of material covered. The course assumes that the students are not familiar with the study of art history, and thus there are no required prerequisites. However, students will find it useful to have had at least one basic studio art course.

The material in the course is sequenced chronologically. This sequence was chosen deliberately, for two reasons: (1) an understanding of the art of ancient Greece and Rome is necessary for the study of all subsequent Western art, and (2) any artistic style is usually related to the artistic events that preceded it, thus necessitating a chronological approach. The units employed cover fairly large time spans, in the hope that this will make it easier for the student to relate the various eras and grasp the overall flow of history. In order to achieve this it is also necessary for the teacher to deal with the material in a cumulative manner, whenever possible making comparisons with the art of earlier periods.

This course attempts to answer three central questions:

1. How is an artwork related to the culture in which it is produced?
2. Are there any artistic traditions evident in the history of art, and if so, when and how are they manifested?
3. How does the viewer objectively evaluate a work of art? This final question is part of a larger, more general goal of making the students sensitive to their own likes and dislikes in art. If students are aware of

how they react to an artwork, and are also aware of the criteria generally used to designate a good piece of art, then it is hoped that they will be able to appreciate many kinds of art. Appreciation and enjoyment do not always go hand in hand.

The intended learning outcomes (ILOs) are derived from these central questions. The ILOs for this course are pertinent for every unit, and the teacher should feel free to emphasize different ones at different times.

ILOS

Primary ILOs

1. Students will understand the relationship of major styles to the cultures in which they were produced and will know what thoughts and events influenced the development of these styles.
2. Students will be able to identify major pieces in the history of art, giving the artist, style, and approximate date, and will be able to give a justification for their identification.
3. Students will know about the recurrence of certain traditions in the history of art and will be able to point out when and why these recurrences appeared.
4. Students will be able to use the vocabulary of art to clearly analyze the formal elements in an artwork.

Secondary ILOs

5. Students will know something about individual artists and what makes them important in the history of art.
6. Students will be able to conduct basic art historical research.

In order for the teacher to have a clear idea of what he or she wants the students to learn, it is also helpful to group the ILOs according to the type of learning outcome, i.e., into cognitions, corresponding cognitive skills, psychoperceptual skills, and affective understandings.

COGNITIONS

1. Students will be able to identify major pieces in the history of art and give a justification for their identification. Corresponding cognitive skill: Students will be able to recognize some of the masterpieces in the history of art. "Recognition" here implies a kind of memorization of visual stimuli and does not necessarily mean the student would be able to give reasons for the identification.

2. Students will understand the relationship of major styles to the cultures in which they were produced. "Understand" here implies that the student will be able to point out some cause/effect relationships.
3. Students will know many of the vocabulary words used when discussing art. "Know" here implies that the student will be able to give a definition of the words. Corresponding cognitive skill: Students will be able to use the vocabulary of art to analyze formal elements. "Use" here implies that the student will be able to apply specific vocabulary to any number of different examples.
4. Students will have an understanding of artistic traditions. "Understanding" means that the student will be able to give examples of works from different periods and discuss how they are similar.

PSYCHOPERCEPTUAL SKILLS

Students will be able to do basic art historical research. This implies that they know the steps involved and will be able to carry them out in a logical sequence.

AFFECTIVE UNDERSTANDINGS

Students will have an appreciation for many kinds of art. Appreciation indicates that they know why the artwork is significant, regardless of whether or not they like it.

Figure B.1 is a conceptual map that shows the major ideas that the course will cover and the relationships between these ideas. In this course it is possible to make a more specific map for each of the periods covered, as the example for Prehistoric Art shows. These specific maps, while time consuming to make, would be useful for the students to have, as they would serve as a concise synopsis of the course. The flowcharts in Figures B.2, B.3, and B.4 outline the steps involved in skill ILOs 2, 4, and 6 listed above.

INTRODUCTION TO THE COURSE

One Period

The introduction to the course as a whole is designed to give students an idea of what art history is. This is important, because at this age few have been exposed to a systematic study of art. For those students who are unsure of what the course is about, the introduction should let them know if they are really interested in this subject.

Teaching Strategies

During this period the teacher should outline the content to be covered, the materials and techniques that will be used, and what is expected of the students. It would be useful to give each student a copy of the course conceptual map and discuss it with

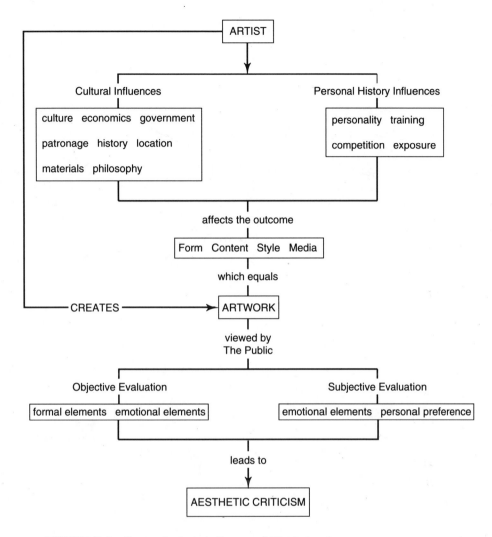

FIGURE B.1 Conceptual map: Survey of Western art.

them. The teacher should then go through a series of slides representing the major periods that will be covered. During this presentation the teacher should introduce some of the basic vocabulary, the major historical periods, and the concepts outlined on the map. Then the teacher should tell the students what instructional devices will be used in the class, including slide lectures, class discussions, worksheets on the readings, quizzes, museum trips, art projects, and a short research paper. This list is flexible, and the students should know that if they come up with good suggestions these can be incorporated into the class structure.

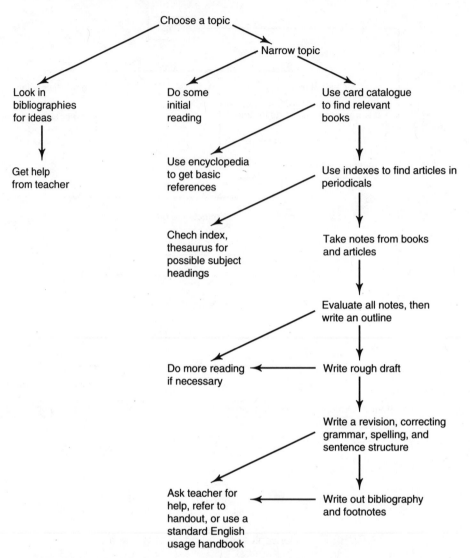

FIGURE B.2 Flowchart for cognitive skill one: Doing basic art historical research.

UNIT ONE: THE ANCIENT WORLD

This unit covers a very large time span and a variety of countries and styles. These can be broken down into three groups: prehistoric, Egyptian, and the ancient Near East; the Aegean, and ancient Greece and Rome; and early Christian art. The unit will concentrate primarily on painting, sculpture, and architecture but will also introduce students to mosaics and pottery. The emphasis will be placed on the Greek, Roman, and early Christian works, and how these influenced all subsequent Western artists until the twentieth century.

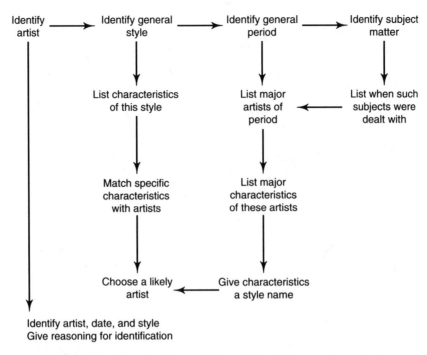

FIGURE B.3   Flowchart for cognitive skill two: Recognition of major masterpieces.

ILOs

Numbers 1–4

Instructional Foci

Slide lectures, class discussions, quizzes, worksheets on the readings, a museum visit

Teaching Strategies

For the primitive period the teacher should concentrate on the transition from a nomadic society to an agricultural one. Concepts should include nomadic living, hunting and gathering, communal living, domestication of plants and animals, and what we mean by civilization.

Another major area should be religion and the effect it had on the arts. Students should understand such ideas as ritual, monarchy, divine rule, monotheism, and polytheism. They should also know when religions became organized for large groups of people.

During the Greek and Roman periods the emphasis should be on the flourishing of civilization, the rise of large cities, and the development of various forms of government: democracy, republic, and empire. The students should understand the

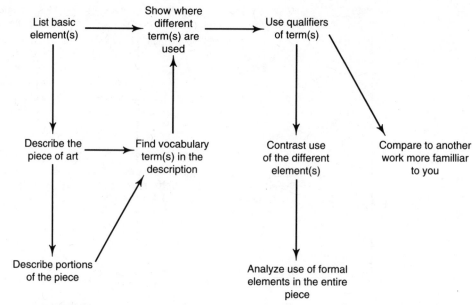

FIGURE B.4   Flowchart for cognitive skill three: Analyze the formal elements in an artwork.

impact of trade in diversifying the economy and acquainting the people with other cultures. Once again religion is very important, and the students should know the major gods and some of the stories associated with them. (Readings outside of the text, such as Edith Hamilton's *Mythology*, should be utilized.) Another important consideration is that of the philosophic systems developed during this period: rationalism, Epicureanism, Stoicism, individualism, and empiricism should all be outlined. Finally, students should be aware of the development of mathematics and geometry, and of the reemergence of writing and the importance of literature and drama as art forms in these societies.

The early Christian period is included in this unit because these new art forms emerged in Imperial Rome. Students should be shown the similarities to pagan art, but should understand the new synthesis of symbolism that was achieved in biblical representations. They should also understand the basic differences between the Christian religion and the Greek and Roman religions that preceded it. Students should know of the conversion of the emperor Constantine in the early fourth century, and the significance for art of Christianity becoming the official religion. Emphasis should be placed on catacomb paintings, funerary sculpture, and the development of a Christian architecture.

Special Notes

1. In first introducing students to art history it is very important to stress the flexibility of stylistic names. We use names such as archaic or hellenistic in order to make it easier to discuss various general

characteristics. However, seldom is a work solidly of one style; usually it will have attributes of several periods. Such stylistic names are convenient handles but should not be regarded as rigid. This is an important point to make at the very beginning, because these names become even more nebulous in the nineteenth and twentieth centuries.

2. If the students seem to have a good grasp of the formal characteristics of Greek art, it would be good to try to discuss the archaic-classic-baroque sequence that is evident. This is a pattern that recurs in the history of Western art, always reflecting the original qualities in these three Greek periods.

UNIT TWO: THE MIDDLE AGES, 5–6 WEEKS

This unit can be broken down into four parts: Byzantine, Carolingian and Ottonian, Romanesque, and Gothic. The works studied will concentrate on the spread of Catholicism and its influence on art. Forms included will be panel paintings, manuscripts, architecture, and architectural decoration (sculpture and mosaics). Special care should be taken to show students that this art, in general, was based on entirely different ideas than the art of Greece and Rome. However, they should also be shown where the classical influence appears during this period.

ILOs

Numbers 1–4

Instructional Foci

Slide lectures, readings, class discussions, quizzes, short opinion papers, a field trip to a museum or to look at local architecture, if applicable

Teaching Strategies

For the Byzantine period the teacher should make clear the similarities and differences between this and early Christian art. The students should have a clear understanding of the Byzantine Empire: where it was, how long it lasted, why it was important, what brought about its collapse. They should understand the importance of official church patronage and the effects of the Iconclastic Controversy, including the split between Roman Catholicism and the Greek Orthodox church. They should be aware of how church architecture was synthesized to fit the liturgical needs of the religion.

In dealing with Carolingian and Ottonian art forms, students should learn about the emergence of the monastery as a self-contained community. They should know the basic facts about Charlemagne's empire and its successors, and its attempts to restore the Holy Roman Empire. Students should be able to identify the major manuscripts of the period and understand how illumination became an art form. They should be aware of the importance of writing and literature within the hierarchy of the nobility and the church. They will be able to relate the invasions that periodically swept across the European continent, and the gradual shift of power from southern parts of Europe to those further north. Especially important is the concept of revivalism.

In studying the Romanesque period, students should be aware of the triumph of Christianity throughout and beyond Europe and the growing sense of religious enthusiasm. They should understand that Romanesque refers to many regionally distinct yet related styles that sprang up across Europe. It did not have a central source and thus differs greatly from the two court styles that preceded it. Other important concepts include the revival of Mediterranean trade routes, a regrowth of commerce and manufacturing, and the subsequent flourishing of city life. At this time a middle class composed of merchants and craftsmen also appeared and had a large impact on medieval society. Students should be able to distinguish between the many regional variations in the style and also note their similarities. In sculpture and painting they should be able to point out Byzantine influences.

When introducing students to Gothic art, the teacher should make clear that the style originated in the area around Paris, gradually spread and mutated until it became international, and then waned in importance. Students should also understand that the characteristics of the style first appeared in architecture and only later took hold of sculpture and painting. Another art form that should be introduced at this time is stained glass. In church philosophy, the students should be able to distinguish the basic differences between the patristic theology of the early church and the scholastic doctrines of the Gothic age. They should also understand the structure of feudalism and why it was important economically and politically.

Special Notes

1. At this point in the course it is important to make sure the students are thinking about the material in a cumulative fashion. Lectures and quizzes should include slides from the ancient world for the purpose of comparison. It is necessary for the teacher to point out the reappearances of older styles, for this link will otherwise often be missed by students. Only if they get in the habit of thinking about works they already know will they be able to view the history of art as a somewhat coherent series of developments.

2. If field trips are being planned it is good if the teacher knows what pieces will be on display. Then he or she can assign short oral reports in which each student discusses a particular work. These reports could cover such things as history of ownership, iconography, identification or forgery problems, media used, or special innovations or techniques. This will give the field trip more focus, make it more interesting, and take the burden of explaining off the teacher.

UNIT THREE: THE RENAISSANCE, 5–6 WEEKS

This unit covers a somewhat shorter time span, but a vast number of major artists and artworks. It can be broken down into three phases: the early Renaissance, the High Renaissance, and mannerism. Emphasis is primarily on painting, sculpture, and architecture, although if possible it would be good to expose the students to some drawings and graphics at this time. Once again the art is based on that of classical antiquity, although the premise of the Renaissance artists was quite different than those who tried to revive antiquity during the Middle Ages. During this period the artists tried to compete with the classical ideal. This is an important distinction. Finally, students should know that during this period the north and south of Europe followed two essentially different stylistic paths.

ILOs

Numbers 1–4

Instructional Foci

Slide lectures, readings, class discussions, quizzes, and an art project. (If possible, have the students briefly explore the development of painting techniques, including tempra, fresco, and oils.)

Teaching Strategies

The early Renaissance was marked by a specific aim, that of understanding the visible world. This desire produced very different effects in the north and the south, which should be understood by the students. In the north, the period is usually called "Late Gothic," and is characterized by extreme detail, disguised religious symbolism, the device of atmospheric perspective, and the development of a new relationship between the picture space and real space. Students should be aware of the impact of the development of the oil painting medium on the art of this period. They should also know about the evolution of printing and its effects on both books and pictures. Students should have an understanding of the processes involved in woodcut, engraving, and drypoint. In the south, the important ideas were individualism and humanism, which lead to a new acceptance of art as the work of the creative mind rather than mere handicraft. This lead to an increase in portrait painting and the signing of artworks. The Italians also invented linear perspective, just one example of their rational, scientific approach to the world around them. Another important concept is that of the rise of the vernacular and the decline of Latin. Finally, the students should know the basics about Neo-Platonism, the philosophy developed to fuse the Christian faith with ancient mythology.

The High Renaissance applies only to Italy, and only to the work of six men. Students should be aware of how this art was a culmination of early Renaissance ideals but also how it differs from those ideals. Especially important are the concepts of genius, divine inspiration, and visual effectiveness. Students should understand why this "period" was so short lived, and yet why it had such a powerful impact on following artists.

What is called the northern Renaissance occurred because of a sudden influx of Italian influence. This influence varied from area to area, producing a diversity of styles that have primarily a period of time in common. Important concepts include the Reformation and the attitudes of Protestant leaders toward art, the desire to assimilate Italian art, and the development of new subject matter that was not religious.

Mannerism is a recently coined term that covers the art produced in the second two-thirds of the sixteenth century. It appeared in both the north and south and was based on two conditions. First, it was an artistic reaction to the instability produced in Europe by the Reformation. Second, it was a reaction against the ideals of the High Renaissance. Artists knew they could not hope to imitate that style and thus chose to concentrate on other aims. Most expressed an inner vision that was not dependent on nature or the classics. Students should be aware of the formal elements that make this art so "unclassical."

Special Notes

1. If they are not already, students should be made aware of the origins of the style names that are used. If they understand what the name refers to it should help them remember the characteristics of the style, and also make clearer why such names are inexact.
2. From the Renaissance on we become aware of the names of individual artists, including those who were women. It is important to try to include slides and reproductions of the work of female artists, so that the students get a sense of their contribution to our artistic tradition. It is also important to discuss why there were, historically, fewer women than men engaged in this pursuit.

UNIT FOUR: THE BAROQUE AND ROCOCO

This unit covers what are designated as the dominant styles during the seventeenth and eighteenth centuries. These styles were prevelant throughout Europe and England, with variations between north and south. Emphasis will be placed on painting, sculpture, and architecture, but attention should be paid to the use of "mixed media," which reached a new height. The baroque is a problematic period in terms of its sources, and students should try to decide if the style was a culmination of Renaissance ideals (like the archaic-classic-baroque sequence in ancient Greek art), or whether it was unrelated to the art that came before it.

ILOs

Numbers 1–4

Instructional Foci

Slide lectures, readings, class discussions, quizzes, field trip to a museum

Teaching Strategies

The baroque in all of Europe was influenced by three things: the renewal of the Catholic faith, the absolutist state, and new discoveries in science.

In the southern parts of Europe the baroque style was based on the Counter-Reformation. It was an attempt by the Church to lure people back to it, by making the concepts of the religion easier to understand. The main idea was that of bringing the divine down to earth, in order to make God comprehensible to the common man. Students should know about the rise of Spanish power and should understand the causes and effects of the Sack of Rome. They should be aware of the Council of Trent, the Universal Inquisition, and the foundation of new Catholic religious orders, all aspects of the reform of the church.

Central Europe was dominated by the rise of France and the development of art forms suited to the aristocracy. Art became a weapon of propaganda for the state and helped glorify national power. Students should understand the effects of a lack of competition among patrons of the arts and how dependence on government commissions lead to a standardization of art. They should also know about the growth of academies, in literature and music as well as in painting and sculpture.

In the northern parts of Europe the middle class was the dominant force in government and economics. The impact of Protestantism forced artists to find patrons, and subject matter, that were not church related. Students should understand the effect of this free market system on painting and sculpture and should be aware of the kinds of buildings that were needed by the middle class. They should also understand the emphasis on the home during this period.

All these aspects of the baroque found a sort of synthesis in England. Here the opposing views of tradition and of modernism managed to coexist. The important concepts are: an earth-centered versus a sun-centered universe; theoretical political unity versus practical political diversity and balance of power; philosophy of the supernatural versus that of naturalism; reliance on religious faith versus reliance on scientific experimentation; and the unity of Christianity versus the rise of many religious sects.

The rococo was essentially an extension of the aristocratic baroque style, tempered so as to be suitable for domestic buildings as well as palaces. The most important idea to emerge during this period was that of rationalism, which led to this being called the "Age of Enlightenment." Students should understand the spread of this philosophy to the middle classes and its effect on the arts. Students should also see how this relatively calm era led to the revolutionary nineteenth century.

Special Notes

The baroque style is usually considered an acquired taste. Thus, this unit should pay special attention to the general goal of helping students define what they like, and why. It is important for them to see the baroque in its wider context, which may help them appreciate it even if they do not particularly like it.

UNIT FIVE: THE REVOLUTIONARY AGE, 5–6 WEEKS

This unit covers all of the nineteenth century and can be broken down into four major styles: neoclassicism, romanticism, realism, and impressionism. Students should be aware of the diversity of revolutions that occurred during this period—industrial, social, technological, political, scientific, and cultural—and should know how these affected the arts. Emphasis will again be on painting, sculpture, and architecture, including what was happening in America.

ILOs

Numbers 1–4

Instructional Foci

Slide lectures, quizzes, readings, class discussions, a field trip, and an art project (if possible)

Teaching Strategies

The neoclassicists based their art on that of republican Rome. Rome itself thus became a symbol for revolutionary protest, and neoclassicism became a way of life rather than just an artistic style. The ancient classics and histories were widely read. This revival was different from any previous classical revival, however. Students should understand the ideas of archeological accuracy, heroism, simplicity, and self-sacrifice.

By contrast, romanticism was eclectic; it embraced a number of past styles, including the classics, the Middle Ages, and the East. These artists were interested in emotion for its own sake. This art was based on close observation of nature, as opposed to the conventions of neoclassicism. An especially important concept was that of the sublime, that is, awe in the face of the unknown and the unknowable. This notion had a large impact on the early landscape painters in America.

The realists based their art on the Dutch and Flemish naturalists of the seventeenth century. Most of these artists were for a new social order based on the needs of the middle class; many of them were thrown in jail for their participation in social movements. Students should understand why this unpretentious art was not immediately accepted by the critics, and also how it led to the work of the impressionists.

Impressionism was the first complete artistic revolution since the start of the Renaissance in Italy. These artists were interested in capturing a fleeting moment, and based their attempts on the effects of light. The students should learn the basics of color theory and understand the idea of optical mixing. It is important to discuss the subject matter that the impressionists chose to portray and the reasons for their great popularity.

The postimpressionists were a loosely formed group who agreed with the impressionists' desire to capture a fleeting moment, but not with the means they used to achieve this. The postimpressionists were divided into two camps, those interested in achieving permanence of form and those who gave primacy to emotional expression. Students should understand the change in the structure of the art world, from one of many artists working in a similar style with similar ideas, to one in which artists became increasingly individualistic and difficult to classify.

Special Notes

1. During the study of impressionism it would be interesting to have each student produce a small painting, using what they have learned of color theory and optical mixing. This project could take two to three class periods and would give the students firsthand experience with the effects these artists were trying to capture.

2. At the beginning of this unit the teacher should assign a research paper, which the students will have six to eight weeks to complete. The teacher should set up a timetable and check each student's work every week, to make sure they are learning the processes involved. The timetable could include such things as choosing a topic, narrowing the topic, researching in books, researching in periodicals, writing an outline, writing a rough draft, and doing a revision. This will familiarize the students with the processes and formats used in research. It is also an exercise that will force them to study several points of view and then come to their own conclusions. (This project can be modified in scope according to the library facilities available to the students.)

UNIT SIX: THE TWENTIETH CENTURY, 5–6 WEEKS

The twentieth century must be viewed differently than the preceeding artistic periods, due to the rapid nature of change in society and the arts. Three ideas are especially important: local artistic traditions gave way to international trends; the artistic capital shifted from Europe to America; and the process of creating became at least as important as the actual final product. The unit should focus on architecture (especially the impact of new building materials), sculpture, and painting, but should also expose the students to some more minor forms: photography, drawing, stained glass, graphic arts, "found objects," and "happenings." Special attention should be paid to gaining an understanding of the philosophies behind the various art movements and to understanding if, when, and how these forms are related to previous styles.

ILOs

Numbers 1–4

Instructional Foci

Slide lectures, class discussions, quizzes, readings, a visit to a contemporary art gallery, and a lecture by a visiting local artist (if possible)

Teaching Strategies

This unit does not break down into convenient time periods, so it is probably easiest to deal with the material in one of two ways. The first would be to break it down according to medium, so that painting, sculpture, and architecture are dealt with separately. The second would be to break it down according to artistic movement. I would recommend the first treatment, keeping in mind that it is necessary for the teacher to point out parallels between the media. If the teacher does not do this it will be difficult for the students to see the relationships between the various art forms.

Students should also be reminded that these movements are not at all clear-cut. Some artists did not belong to any organized movement, while others belonged to several. Some movements were spontaneous, while others were planned. The various styles often overlapped and borrowed from each other, and the dates of none of them can be pinpointed with exactitude. Such characteristics should be related to the rapidly changing, increasingly complex world in which we live.

Like the baroque, many modern styles are an acquired taste. Students should at least be able to appreciate the incredible vitality and ingenuity that characterizes the art of our age, even if they do not personally enjoy it.

This leads to the idea that much modern art is ugly or inane looking. This would be a good time for pupils to reassess their notions of what art is. They should be asked to explain their ideas on aesthetics, beauty, and the purpose of art.

Special Notes

1. One way to make this unit more interesting to students is to include some study of the contemporary art scene in their town or city. This could include a trip to a local gallery, a lecture (and/or demonstration) by a local artist, a visit to an artist's studio, or a trip to a museum that has a modern art exhibition.

2. This unit also lends itself to two possible group art projects: having the class make a piece of art out of "found objects" (each could bring one thing), or having the class create a "happening." (The rest of the school could be invited to this, if it were properly planned.) Both these activities could lead to significant discussion among the students about the nature of art and how it is created.

3. If a final is planned for the end of the year, three or four days should be set aside for in-class review and questions.

COURSE EVALUATION

Evidence of Main Effects—High-Priority Learning Outcomes

1. Students will understand the relationship of major styles to the cultures in which they were produced.

   a. The student can state, in oral or written form, how a work reflects the philosophy of the culture in which it was produced.

   b. The student can outline the basics of the form of government and the economic system of a period and show how these affected the arts.

   c. The student will know the major religions of various places and periods, and how these affected the arts.

    d. The student can state broad general differences between the art of two places and/or periods.

2. Students will be able to identify major masterpieces in the history of Western art and will be able to give a justification for their identification.

    a. The student can look at an artwork (which he or she may or may not have seen before) and state who did it, when it was done, and what style it is.

    b. The student can justify that identification by comparing the piece to other works by the same artist and noting similarities.

    c. If the student does not recognize the specific artist, he or she can state the style of the work and justify the choice by comparing it to other works of the same period.

3. Students will have an understanding of artistic traditions, and when and how these are manifested in the history of art.

    a. When shown an artwork, the student can state past influences that are visible in the piece.

    b. When shown an artwork, the student can state how it influenced subsequent artists or styles and can give two or three examples.

    c. The student can write a short essay tracing the development of a specific style over a large period of time. Once again, he or she should be able to refer to specific examples.

4. Students will be able to use the vocabulary of art to analyze the formal elements of a piece.

    a. When shown an artwork, the student can point out the use of specific elements (e.g., color, line) when asked to do so.

    b. The student can compare and contrast two works of similar or different styles and state how they are the same or different in their use of specific elements.

    c. When presented with a style name, the student can state the formal characteristics that are used to define that style.

        The evidence of all the above learnings will show up in class discussions, on quizzes and worksheets, and during museum trips.

Evidence of Main Effects—Secondary Learning Outcomes

1. Students will be able to say what they like in an artwork, and why it appeals to them.

    a. The student will understand and be able to explain the emotive elements in a work.

    b. The student will be able to explain why a particular piece, style, or subject appeals to him or her, in both its formal and emotive elements.

    c. The student will know that different kinds of artworks appeal to different people.

2. Students will develop an appreciation for many kinds of art.

    a. The student will be able to state why a certain work or style was important in the history of art.

    b. The student will be able to say why some works are classified as masterpieces and others are not.

    c. The student will be aware of the changing concepts of beauty and aesthetics throughout the history of art.

3. Students will be able to do basic art historical research.

    a. The student can write down or state the major steps one takes in doing research.

    b. The student can present the results of each step as he or she completes it (e.g., show an outline or a rough draft).

    c. The student should be able to present a properly documented paper five to ten pages in length, using standard research format.

    d. The student will be able to present diverse points of view and then reach his or her own conclusion about the issue.

Possible Undesirable Learning Outcomes

1. Those that result from interaction with the teacher:

    a. The student may get the feeling that all essay and identification questions have a right or wrong answer, rather than realizing that the justification is the important point.

    b. The student may notice the teacher's own bias for or against certain artistic periods and may feel that these biases are correct.

2. Those that result from the choices of instructional foci:

    a. The student may feel that all great artists are male.

    b. The student may decide that only those pieces that are considered masterpieces are worth studying.

    c. The student may become dependent on reproductions and not know how to react to an actual work (especially true of architecture).

    d. The student may develop a passive attitude toward art and not be able to understand the actual act of creation.

3. Those that result from the organization of the course:

    a. The student may get locked into the chronology and not be able to make comparisons that cover large time gaps.

    b. The student may not be able to see broad relationships through long periods of time.

    c. The student may come to believe that stylistic names are absolute.

    d. The student may remember the different forms of government in the various periods but not the religions, the philosophic systems, and the cultural aspects of the different eras.

4. Those that result from the institutional setting:

    a. The student may have trouble developing a concept of beauty if the room is messy or run down.

    b. If there are not a lot of visual stimuli around (posters, books, slide viewers), the student may have trouble learning to memorize visual elements.

    c. The student will not be able to develop a true appreciation for art if he or she does not have some chances to see actual pieces rather than just reproductions.

A NOTE ON TEXTS

Several textbooks that are available would be suitable for use in this course. The four best are listed alphabetically below, along with their advantages and disadvantages.

Art: A History of Painting, Sculpture, and Architecture. Frederick Hartt. New York: Harry N. Abrams, 1976. Vol. 1, 433 pages, Vol. 2, 491 pages. Contains a glossary, bibliography, index, time lines, and maps. Beautiful reproductions. Very similar to Janson (see below), although slightly more simplified.

Arts and Ideas. William Fleming. New York: Holt, Reinhart, & Winston, 1980. 482 pages. A very good text for this age group. Gives a good overview of all the artistic forms, including music. Also includes a complete account of the philosophic ideas of each age, which would be a very good introduction to philosophy for most high schoolers. Includes a glossary, index, maps, and timetables. Fair reproductions.

Discovering Art History. Gerald F. Brommer. Worchester, MA: Davis Publications, 1982. This book is still unavailable in most libraries, and thus I don't have specific information about it. However, it is designed specifically as a high school art history text.

History of Art. H. W. Janson. New York: Harry N. Abrams, 1977. 730 pages. This is the definitive art history text used in college survey courses. It assumes a bit more historical knowledge on the part of the reader than the other three books. It includes a glossary, index, time lines, maps, and suggestions for further reading. It has superb reproductions, which make it somewhat expensive for this level. Since students who go on in art history are likely to encounter this text in college, I feel it is better if they use some other text during high school. Whatever text the teacher chooses to use, it is recommended that supplementary readings be used whenever time permits. Particularly useful are pieces of literature that represent a specific period, as it is often possible to notice similarities between the literature and the visual arts of each period. Examples could include portions of Dante during the late Gothic, Petrarch during the early Renaissance, Wordsworth during romanticism, and Tom Wolfe during the twentieth century.

A NOTE ON COGNITION

This course requires that students study, learn, and memorize a lot of visual information. For some this comes fairly naturally, for others it is very difficult. There are three things the teacher can do to improve the students' visual cognitive capacity. These are:

1. Expose students to many, many pieces of artwork. The more they see, the more likely they are to remember broad characteristics or even small details. Every time they look at a work they are getting practice at sharpening their visual skills.

2. Expose students to actual pieces, not just reproductions. Being face to face with a painting, sculpture, or building is a different experience from looking at a slide, and the students are likely to remember more from it. They will also be able to recall it more easily.

3. Make the students talk about what they see: the elements used, what they like or dislike, what is successful and what isn't. Talking or writing about art often helps students remember the pieces they have seen.

Immigration: A Social Studies Unit for Sixth Graders

Michelle Chang

COMMENTS

This is an ambitious unit that attempts to convey an understanding and appreciation of our country's cultural diversity by examining immigration. It has been said over and over that the United States is a country of immigrants; this unit attempts to bring this understanding to upper elementary students. The unit could be easily adapted to a middle school or junior high school audience. Among the unit's strengths are its coverage of immigration over a rather long historical span, the personal connection of exploring one's own heritage, and the explicit consideration of culture and the interplay of one's native culture in the process of assimilation.

INTRODUCTION

Coming to America has been a dream for generations of people around the world. The English began small settlements in the New World in the 1600s and were followed by people from all over Europe. Many immigrants left their families and friends behind and endured great hardship coming to America. They believed America was the "promised land" where you were granted the freedoms of life, liberty, and the pursuit of happiness, and money grew on trees. Many immigrants came to the United States expecting to stay only for a brief time and then return to their homeland with something to show for their hard work in the States. More often than not, these immigrants never returned to their native land. In the latter part of the twentieth century the United States has been the destination for an increasing number of people from Asia and Latin America who have left their homelands for many of the same reasons as earlier immigrants.

Immigration has long played an important part in the settling and development of this country. Successive generations of immigrants have climbed the socioeconomic ladder. As money seems to be a major requirement for acceptance or approval by established Americans, those immigrants who have experienced financial success are more quickly accepted by previous immigrant groups. New groups of immigrants have been feared and ostracized by those people already settled because they are different. However, it is those differences brought to the United States by immigrants that make this a unique country. The United States is a nation of immigrants.

Today, of the many problems our nation faces, several can be traced back to ethnic differences. Courts across the country must grapple with cases involving racism every day. Affirmative action hiring policies have been debated by employers and employees. Segregation in schools and housing patterns have plagued politicians and concerned citizens for decades. Though many steps were taken by the government in the 1960s to address the injustices of inequality in this country, there is still a great distance to go before these problems will be adequately resolved.

Currently, most elementary school social studies curricula focus on the local community, the state, and the history of the United States. The theory is to start with what is familiar, the local community, and expand the sphere of study as the child progresses through the grades. Some schools incorporate a unit on the history of black Americans or study famous black Americans in the month of February, which has been named Black History Month. Many schools also study Native Americans. However, few social studies curricula examine the variety of ethnic groups that have immigrated to the United States and more importantly, the experiences of these groups of people. Thus one must search for appropriate materials, as few can be found in prepackaged social studies curricula. Many hope that future generations will be able to ease ethnic tensions in our country, but this task seems absolutely impossible unless children learn about the different groups that make up this ethnically diverse country. Studying immigration provides a vehicle for gaining knowledge about ethnic groups and helps students understand the conflicts and tensions between various groups in the country and in the world. This knowledge will perhaps provide students with the insight needed to resolve some of the aforementioned problems in this country.

This nine- to ten-week unit on immigration is designed for sixth graders but could certainly be adapted for other grade levels. Forty-five minutes to an hour a day is the recommended instruction time for this unit, with more time being spent when needed for field trips or guest speakers. Although the concepts surrounding the subject of immigration are complex, I believe this unit can be taught effectively to sixth graders. Eleven and twelve year olds are relatively idealistic and thus it may be hard for them to see different sides of issues. Nevertheless I think the subject of immigration will fascinate sixth graders. Immigration also provides a vehicle to study one aspect of social studies in the United States that is currently underplayed in most social studies curricula. The students must have relatively strong reading skills, as a fair amount of information will be gained by reading. Students must also be able to put themselves in someone else's position, not an easy task for an egocentric child. Students must be able to work together. They must also be able to articulate their ideas orally and in writing. This unit promotes the use of problem-solving skills, which sixth graders are developing. It would be helpful if students had some understanding of the history of the United States (U.S. social studies is currently taught in the fifth grade in a great number of schools), but it is not essential, as this unit could be expanded. Immigration could be taught as one part of a yearlong study of the United States. Students knowledgeable in the history of the United States will have a context for the study of immigration and thus will better understand factors affecting immigration.

As students study U.S. immigration it is hoped that they will gain an appreciation for individual immigrants', refugees, and various ethnic groups' contributions to American society and culture. It is also hoped that by putting themselves in an immigrant's or refugee's shoes students will gain an appreciation for their struggle between assimilation and maintaining their own culture. Ours is a nation of immigrants, and it is important that students understand and appreciate the important roles immigrants have played and continue to play in American history.

CONCEPTUAL MAP

Figure C.1 details the major learnings of this unit. It does not include all the details surrounding these main concepts; rather it is designed to be read in conjunction with the entire unit plan. For details refer to the content outline. The map is meant to be read from top to bottom. Students will study the factors that pull immigrants to the United States and push refugees out of their homelands. Students will also study the laws and regulations of the sending countries and the United States that pertain to immigrants and refugees. Once in the United States there are several factors that affect the success and failure of immigrants and refugees. At this point some people may return to their homeland. If they choose to stay, immigrants and refugees must struggle to find a balance between assimilation and maintaining their own culture. This conceptual map is designed to accommodate the study of any of the many immigrant and refugee groups that have come to the United States throughout the history of this country.

INTENDED LEARNING OUTCOMES

Cognitions

1. Students will know characteristics of different immigrant and refugee groups from Northern Europe and Scandinavia; Central and Eastern Europe; Asia; and Latin America.
*2. Students will understand factors that pull immigrants to the United States and push refugees out of their homelands.
*3. Students will understand factors affecting immigrants' and refugees' success and failure in the United States.
4. Students will understand the concept of assimilation.

---

* Learning outcomes of greatest importance

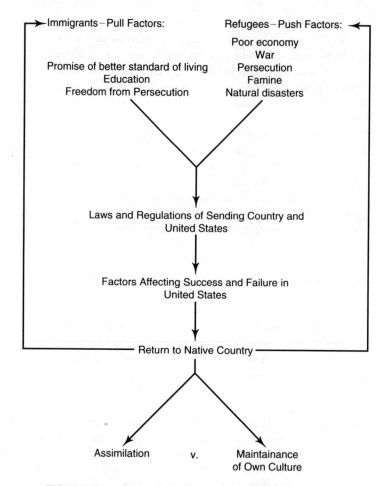

FIGURE C.1 Immigration unit conceptual map.

5. Students will understand the process of immigration.
   a. Students will understand the relationship between immigration patterns and the laws and regulations that pertain to immigration.
   b. Students will understand the relationship between U.S. foreign policy and U.S. immigration laws and regulations.
6. Students will understand the "average" experience of an immigrant.
7. Students will understand their own family history of immigration.

Cognitive Skills

*1. Students will compare and contrast characteristics of different immigrant groups.

---

* Cognitive skill of greatest importance.

2. Students will be able to distinguish between push and pull factors and how these affect immigration.
3. Students will identify the contributions immigrants have made to American society.
4. Students will compare and contrast the characteristics and experiences of "old" and "new" immigrants.
5. Students will be able to distinguish differences and similarities between first, second, and third generation immigrants.
6. Students will compare and contrast general experiences of immigrants and refugees.
7. Students will learn how to take notes from fiction and nonfiction sources.
8. Students will write a research paper utilizing the notes taken previously and present their findings orally to the class.

COMPLEX SKILL: WRITING A RESEARCH PAPER

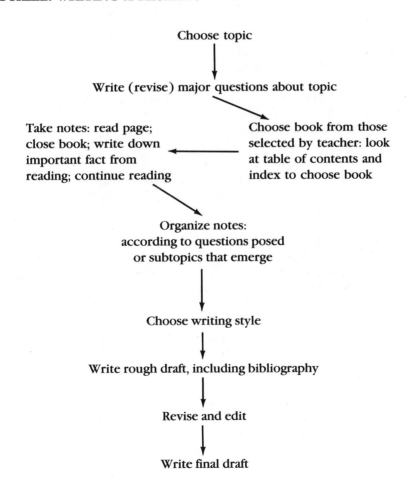

Choose topic

Write (revise) major questions about topic

Take notes: read page; close book; write down important fact from reading; continue reading

Choose book from those selected by teacher: look at table of contents and index to choose book

Organize notes: according to questions posed or subtopics that emerge

Choose writing style

Write rough draft, including bibliography

Revise and edit

Write final draft

Content Outline

I. **Why Come to the United States?**
   A. Immigrants and pull factors
      1. promise of better standard of living
      2. education
      3. freedom from persecution
   B. Refugees and push factors
      1. persecution
      2. poor economy
      3. war
      4. famine
      5. natural disasters
   C. Examine own heritage
   D. Patterns of immigration
      1. Northern Europe, Scandinavia
      2. South and Eastern Europe
      3. Latin America
      4. Asia

II. **U.S. Laws and Regulations Pertaining to Immigration**
   A. Period of open immigration
      1. immigrants by choice
      2. picture brides
   B. National Origins Quota System—1920s
   C. War brides—1945, McCarran-Walter Act—1952
   D. 1965 legislation
   E. 1980 Refugee Act
   F. Present policy

III. **Factors for Success and Failure of Immigrants**
   A. How immigrants came—boat, plane, walking
   B. What they came with
      1. money
      2. skills
      3. education
      4. language
      5. friends and family v. alone
   C. Where they settled
      1. community's attitude toward immigrants
      2. number of immigrants from similar background in community
      3. economy of community
      4. presence of friends and family in community
   D. Customs and traditions
      1. familiarity with U.S. customs and traditions
      2. similarities and differences between native country and United States
   E. First, second, and third generation immigrants and refugees

IV. Immigrants' Contributions to U.S. Society and Culture
   A. Arts
      1. fine art
      2. music
      3. dance
      4. theater
   B. Food
   C. Religion
   D. Customs and traditions
   E. Language
   F. Technology, skills, methods of accomplishing tasks
   G. Architecture
V. Current Events
   A. Current immigration policy
   B. Alien farm workers
   C. Sanctuary movement
   D. Implications of new Eastern Europe on U.S. immigration
   E. Racism
      1. segregated neighborhoods, schools
      2. discrimination
      3. reverse discrimination
   F. Bilingual education

SEQUENCE

Basically there are two obvious sequence choices: begin with the past and work forward, or begin with the present and work backward. I have chosen the sequence outlined above because it allows students to role-play immigrants' and refugees' lives in a natural sequence of events. In other words, students will study topics as they would come up in an immigrant's life, excluding the final subunit. However, other sequences are possible. In any of the possible sequences one could first explore U.S. laws and regulations pertaining to immigration and then study why come to the United States, or vice versa.

An alternative to the above sequence would be:

   I. Current Events
   II. Immigrants' Contributions to U.S. Society and Culture
   III. Why Come to the United States?
   IV. U.S. Laws and Regulations Pertaining to Immigration
   V. Factors for Success and Failure of Immigrants

This sequence begins with current events related to immigration. Studying current events would motivate students to explore present issues more deeply and the history behind these issues. One could also begin with immigrants' contributions to U.S. society and culture. This would motivate students to examine the backgrounds of individuals and groups of people who have affected American society and culture. However, I have chosen the sequence outlined in detail above because of the instructional foci I have selected to pursue and the fact that this sequence most closely follows an immigrant's own experience.

INSTRUCTION

SUBUNIT ONE: WHY COME TO THE UNITED STATES?

Introduction

This subunit is three weeks long and is designed to familiarize students with the history of immigration and the experiences of immigrants. Students may begin this unit with a variety of background information about immigration, all of which will enrich class discussions. One must be prepared for students to bring misconceptions and misunderstandings about immigration to this unit. These can be discussed by the entire class as they come up. The topics studied in this subunit will be referred to continuously and reexamined throughout the unit. This subunit can be expanded to a more in-depth study of U.S. history as well as the study of immigration.

Instructional Foci

1. Brainstorm
2. "American Immigrants: Part I," *Cobblestone,* December 1982, pp. 4–5
3. Interview family member to construct family tree showing where family members came from and where they settled
4. Keep journal of imagined experiences as if you are an immigrant
5. Guest speaker on experiences of immigrants, refugees, aliens
6. Research on immigrant group

ILOs

Cognitions: 1, 2, 6, 7

Cognitive Skills: 1, 2, 4, 6, 7, 8

General Teaching Strategies

The introduction of this unit will begin with a whole class brainstorm on the topic of "Who is an Immigrant?" and "Why Did Immigrants Come to the United States?" The teacher can expect students to identify several immigrant groups: English, Irish, Mexicans, and so on, as well as some of the reasons immigrants came to the United States: religious freedom, money, land, and so forth. Students will then read the article in *Cobblestone,* which gives a brief overview of immigration and introduces students to some key terms relevant to the study of immigration: *native, emigrate, immigrate, promised land,* and *melting pot.* A discussion about the terms introduced may follow the reading.

Over the course of the next few days, students will examine their own family heritage. Students will interview a family member or members to determine their own family heritage. With this information students will make a family tree, indicating where their ancestors came from and where they settled in the United States. Students will share their family trees with the class so students can get an idea of the diversity of backgrounds present in their classroom community. If many students have very similar family backgrounds, the teacher might challenge some students to create a family tree for another family with a heritage unlike their own. Students would have to interview a person from another family to gain information to make an accurate family tree. If this challenge is pursued, the family trees will then represent the diversity of the community in which the students live.

Having an understanding of their own ethnic heritage, students will choose an immigrant or refugee, real or fictitious, to impersonate or role-play for the next several days. To accurately impersonate an immigrant, students will need to conduct research on that particular immigrant group. Again, students may conduct research on an immigrant group of a different ethnic heritage than their own family. This research will be put together in the form of a research paper (the process is explained under "complex skill" on the preceding pages). The research project will extend for several weeks and, after a few days, will mainly be conducted during writing process time, not social studies. The research project is designed to enrich students' learning about immigration as well as give students experience in conducting research and writing a major research paper. Students will share information from their research project with other students throughout the unit.

As a part of the role-playing, students will keep a journal of the experiences and/or thoughts and feelings they might have as an immigrant. The teacher may guide some of these journal entries. For example, the teacher might ask students to close their eyes and imagine their journey to the United States and then have the students write about that experience. Throughout this subunit students will keep this immigrant journal, which will be collected periodically by the teacher, who may maintain a running dialogue with students in the journal.

Initially students will focus their research on the push and pull factors affecting the immigration of their chosen group of immigrants. In the second week, after students have conducted adequate research, the class will spend a few days making a chart listing the push and pull factors and discussing each of these and how they are relevant to particular immigrant groups.

In the third week students will work in cooperative groups. Students will be grouped according to the region of the world from which their group of immigrants came: Northern and Western Europe and Scandinavia; Southern and Eastern Europe; Latin America; Asia. These cooperative groups will develop a presentation for the class in which they will give the class a sketch of the experiences of immigrants from that region of the world. The presentation will include characteristics and experiences of immigrants from the same region; what these people had in common, and how they were unique. The teacher or individual groups may require students to read background material prior to presentations. The information presented by the groups will be displayed on a bulletin board in the classroom for future reference.

Guest speakers presenting material on any of the topics covered in subunit one on the "content outline" would be a welcome addition. Students would benefit a great deal from hearing the personal experiences of an immigrant or refugee.

It is suggested that the teacher hold students accountable for the information presented throughout this subunit by giving students some form of test or quiz or making assignments based on the information presented by other students, the teacher, and guest speakers. This will be discussed further in the "evaluation" segment of this unit plan.

SUBUNIT TWO: U.S. LAWS AND REGULATIONS PERTAINING TO IMMIGRATION

Introduction

In this subunit students will learn about the laws and regulations that affect immigration. The length of this subunit is one week. U.S. immigration laws have largely been reactionary. After an issue or problem has developed, the Congress has passed legislation to regulate immigration. Until the turn of the century, immigration was largely unregulated because of the need for workers and the abundance of resources in the United States. However, in the 1920s legislation was passed to restrict immigration. The laws regulated immigration according to the national origin of the immigrant and were primarily aimed at keeping Southern and Eastern Europeans and Asians from coming to the United States in large numbers. Throughout the late 1800s and early 1900s, picture brides from Asia were common, particularly on the West Coast where there were more Asian immigrants. As a result of World War II, in 1945 legislation was passed allowing brides of U.S. citizens entry into the United States. In 1952 the McCarran-Walter Act barred the entry of communists and gave preference to those who had special skills that would benefit the United States. This law was passed at a time when the fear of communism swept the United States. It was not until 1965 that the United States dramatically changed its immigration policy. This legislation abolished the national origins quota system, gave preference to family members of U.S. citizens, and limited the number of immigrants from the Eastern and Western hemispheres. In 1980 the Refugee Act addressed the problem of people seeking freedom from persecution in their native country. Students will be introduced to these laws that affect immigration, but the goal will not be to memorize the laws. The main objectives are for students to understand the relationship between immigration patterns and U.S. laws and to understand how immigration laws are connected to U.S. foreign policy.

Instructional Foci

1. Time line
2. Readings on periods of U.S. history relevant to major waves of

immigration, such as "The Picture Brides of San Francisco," *Cobblestone,* January 1983, pp. 22–23

3. Role-play concept of "anchor"

ILOs

Cognitions: 1, 2, 5

Cognitive skills: 1, 2, 4, 6

General Teaching Strategies

To facilitate studying the history of immigration laws students will construct a large time line. The teacher may give students the information, the students may gain some information from readings, or a combination of the two. The time line should include important dates relevant to immigration and a brief description of the laws and regulations. This time line should be posted around the walls of the classroom so it is visible to all students. Students will discuss the importance of these laws and how they affected immigration and immigrants' experiences in the United States. Discussions may be held in small groups or with the entire class.

An expansion of this unit could be to study the legislative process of how a bill becomes a law. Students could follow an immigration bill through the legislative process.

Since the 1965 legislation that placed a preference on relatives of U.S. citizens, the concept of an "anchor" in the United States has become very important. To illustrate the importance of an "anchor," several students could role-play an extended family trying to immigrate to the United States. One student would play the "anchor," or the family member who is a U.S. citizen whose status would allow other family members to legally immigrate. By acting out the process of immigration for that one family, students would physically see how this policy affects immigration.

SUBUNIT THREE: FACTORS FOR SUCCESS AND FAILURE OF IMMIGRANTS

Introduction

Though there are many different groups of peoples who have come to the United States, over the years many of the factors that affect the success and failure of immigrants have remained constant. In this subunit students will identify several factors that affect how immigrants "make it" in the United States. Students will also have the opportunity to study how immigrants struggle to maintain their own culture and assimilate. The length of this subunit is two weeks.

Instructional Foci

1. Debate

2. Brainstorm

3. Research customs and traditions of two countries that have sent a number of immigrants to the United States
4. Interview family members

ILOs

Cognitions: 1, 3, 4, 6, 7
Cognitive skills: 1, 4, 5, 6

General Teaching Strategies

This subunit will begin with a debate on "What is success and failure?" The point of this debate is for students to examine their own concept of success and failure and compare it to that of an immigrant. This debate will help students understand the immigrants' dilemma of maintaining their native culture and assimilating.

The class will then brainstorm what they think immigrants need to be successful as defined by the debate. After a list is compiled, students will select five to ten factors and spend the next few days writing why they think these are important. If the teacher feels that the brainstorm did not adequately cover the factors presented in the "content outline," the teacher may make additions to the brainstormed list. Students will share what they have written and discuss the factors in small groups.

The second week students will examine the similarities and differences between customs and traditions in the United States and two other countries of each student's choice. Students will pick five customs or traditions for two countries and briefly research them. Students will then compare and contrast these ten customs and traditions with U.S. customs and traditions. The class will create a list of foreign customs and their American equivalents and customs not practiced by most Americans. This list will be the focus of a class discussion about how immigrants' familiarity with U.S. customs and traditions and similarities between customs can affect the success or failure of immigrants. Students will also discuss the positives and negatives of both assimilation and the maintenance of native culture.

In the latter part of the second week students will go back to their family trees and identify first, second, and third generation family members. Students will then take a chart showing, for each generation, customs and traditions, characteristics (language, education, field of employment, etc.), and experiences. Information for the chart may be gained by interviewing family members. Students will compare their charts in small groups. Each group will create a set of generalizations that can be made about each successive generation of immigrants. These generalizations will be discussed by the entire class.

It is hoped that this subunit will give students an appreciation for immigrants' struggle between maintaining their own culture and assimilating. Students should also have an understanding of how and why characteristics of immigrant groups change and remain the same over the course of time.

SUBUNIT FOUR: IMMIGRANTS' CONTRIBUTIONS TO U.S. SOCIETY AND CULTURE

Introduction

The purpose of this two-week subunit is to familiarize students with immigrants' contributions to American society and culture. Many students may already know some ways immigrants have influenced American society. This knowledge will enrich class discussions.

Instructional Foci

1. Analyze immigrants' contributions to local community
2. Guest speaker from local ethnic group
3. Study famous immigrant or refugee who made contribution to U.S. society and culture
4. Cultural fair

ILOs

Cognitions: 1

Cognitive skills: 1, 3, 4

General Teaching Strategies

Students will begin this two-week subunit by examining the ethnic makeup of their own community. This information can be gathered using publications from the local government. An informal way to ascertain this information is to note the names of local businesses. For instance, in Northampton there are a number of businesses with Polish names. This reflects the number of people of Polish descent who live in Northampton. Students will then determine what cultural contributions various ethnic groups have made to the community. A guest speaker from a local ethnic organization will give students the opportunity to hear firsthand about an ethnic group's contributions to the community.

In the second week, students will study a famous immigrant and his or her contributions to American society. Students will choose an immigrant from a list compiled by the classroom teacher. Students will write of the famous immigrant's contributions in the first person, as if they were that person. These will be shared with the class. The goal of this activity is that students will gain an appreciation of the wide variety and scope of immigrants' contributions to American society.

This subunit will culminate with a cultural fair complete with food, music, and dance from a variety of ethnic groups.

Throughout this unit the teacher should expose students to the variety of contributions ethnic groups have made to American culture. This can be done by displaying various ethnic groups' fine art, playing music, teaching dances, watching theater (possibly on video), looking at architectural influences, and teaching commonly used words that come from other cultures.

SUBUNIT FIVE: CURRENT EVENTS

Introduction

This one-week to ten-day subunit is designed to bring students up to date with current issues in immigration. It is assumed that throughout the unit students will be bringing in articles relevant to the study of immigration and that daily class discussions will be held around these articles. This subunit allows students to focus on current events. After studying immigration for eight weeks, students will be better prepared to learn about and discuss related current events.

Instructional Foci

1. Recent newspaper and magazine articles
2. Debate on alien farm workers
3. Debate on current immigration policy (liberal vs. conservative)
4. Create a scrapbook or publication of current events

ILOs

Cognitions: 1, 5, 6

Cognitive skills: 1, 4, 6

General Teaching Strategies

Students will begin this subunit by browsing through current events articles and categorizing the articles according to issues. These articles will serve as important sources of information for other activities. Class discussions may come up surrounding these articles. The teacher may select a few particularly interesting articles and structure a class discussion around those specific articles.

The next day students will prepare for their debates. Students will be involved in one of two debates: alien farm workers or current immigration policy. The teacher will assign roles for the students to play and give students the necessary background information. The teacher will also outline the rules of the debates. Students are free to collect additional information that will help them in the debate. For each debate the students who are not involved in the debate will serve as the judges. Discussions will follow the debates.

For the final project on immigration students will create a scrapbook or newspaper around the theme of current events in immigration; the students or teacher may decide which is more appropriate. Individuals or small groups of students would be responsible for gathering information on different immigration issues: the sanctuary movement, emigration from Eastern Europe, racism, and bilingual education, to name a few. Students would be encouraged to use current events articles previously collected. Students would present material on that issue in writing and the written work would be compiled into a class newspaper or scrapbook. The finished product would then be shared with the entire class.

UNINTENDED LEARNING OUTCOMES

The most obvious outcome of this unit is that students will become disinterested in the subject of immigration. This disinterest can be combated by teaching stimulating lessons. For individuals who show a lack of interest, the teacher might find an area of immigration in which the individual is interested and allow that student to pursue study in that area.

It is possible that students will not understand or appreciate the complexities of immigration. If this proves to be the case, the teacher can make adjustments in the curriculum to simplify materials and assignments. Simplification will allow students to get a firmer grasp of concepts that can then be enriched with more complex materials and assignments.

Students who need a greater challenge can work on projects related to concepts currently being taught to the entire class.

Students who have poorer reading or writing skills may need to have assignments and readings adjusted to their abilities. This must be done on an individual basis.

Although highly unlikely, it is possible that students will not gain an appreciation for ethnic differences in this country and will see only their own experiences as acceptable. Students must understand the human element of immigration. It is not an "us" and "them" world; we are all people who share dreams and goals and have similar frustrations. If a tinge of racism enters the classroom, the teacher must address it promptly. It may help to have guests come to the classroom and speak about their own experiences as immigrants. This will bring some of the issues in immigration to a human level.

EVALUATION

Throughout the unit the teacher will collect and evaluate students' written work. There are several places in this unit where the teacher might assign students written work. For example, the teacher might create an assignment to focus students' reading of an article. The teacher will also note individuals' contributions to class discussions. Evaluation should be based on students demonstrating comprehension of materials and concepts.

I am including a test covering material from subunit one through three as an example of the type of evaluation that can be done. This test is designed to evaluate students' knowledge in regard to the following three basic learnings:

Cognitions

Students will understand factors that pull immigrants to the United States and push refugees from their homelands.

Students will understand factors affecting immigrants' and refugees' success and failure in the United States.

Cognitive Skills

Students will compare and contrast characteristics of different immigrant groups.

Thorough, well-written answers will be evidence that students have moved toward accomplishing the desired learning outcomes. Other assignments throughout the unit will also provide the teacher with evidence of students' achievement of the above mentioned ILOs. The test is to be done at school and completed at home. Students are free to use any material to help them answer the questions. Teachers should not feel that a test or quiz is required at the end of every subunit. Some of the projects completed during the subunits will provide the teacher with a more accurate picture of students' understanding.

TEST

You have two days to complete this test. You will work on it in school as well as at home. You may use any materials to help you answer the questions. This test should be worked on alone. You may ask *only* your teacher for help.

I. Your answers for the following questions should be written in complete sentences in paragraph form. You should provide evidence or details to support your statements. In both of your answers you should consider push and pull factors affecting immigration.

1. How did immigrants from Northern Europe differ from immigrants from Eastern and Southern Europe?
2. What do Asian and Latin American immigrants have in common? How are they unique?

II. You are an immigrant, fleeing famine in your homeland, and coming to the United States in 1990. You are coming from a country very different from the United States, with different customs and traditions, as well as language and food. Though you do not speak English, you have gone to college in your homeland. You worked as an elementary school teacher in the small farming town where you lived. You have very little money and have brought just a small suitcase of personal belongings. You are not married. Your entire family has stayed behind, but you do have a friend with whom you went to school in your native country who now lives in Northampton. Your friend has told you that Northampton is a friendly town filled with people from all over the world. Your friend has already found you a job washing dishes at a local restaurant.

Describe what you think your experiences will be like in the United States. Consider how you will both assimilate and maintain some of your own cultural traditions. Define success and how you will achieve that success. Remember, you are an immigrant!

POSSIBLE SOURCES

Cobblestone, December 1982, "American Immigrants: Part 1."

Cobblestone, January 1983, "American Immigrants: Part 2."

Cohen, Barbara, illustrated by Michael J. Deraney. (1983). *Molly's Pilgrim.* New York: Lothrop, Lee, & Shepard Books.

Freedman, Russell. (1980). *Immigrant Kids.* New York: E. P. Dutton.

Shippen, Katherine B. (1950). *Passage to America: The Story of the Great Migrations.* New York: Harper & Brothers.

Stein, R. Conrad, illustrated by Tom Dunnington. (1979). Cornerstones of Freedom, *The Story of Ellis Island.* Chicago: Children's Press.

Tripp, Eleanor B. (1969). *To America.* New York: Harcourt, Brace, & World.

A Metric Measurement Unit for Grades One and Two

Susan M. Etheredge

COMMENTS

This excellent example of a unit plan for young children has some features worth noting. The author includes an introduction in addition to a rationale. This was an excellent opportunity for her to express her thoughts on the unit immediately after planning it. ILOs are stated in order of priority and not by type of learning category. This has advantages and disadvantages. While readers get a good picture of the overall course emphasis, they do not ever get "talked through" the conceptual map or see the skill development sequence.

If the work is to be used by others, stating the ILOs by priority and by type of learning outcome is probably worthwhile.

The introductions to subunits and the description of general teaching strategies are easy to read and address themselves to sequence, emphasis, and children's thinking, although the use of the passive voice tends to obscure who is doing what in the classroom.

These are matters of central concern; they convey a sense of enthusiasm and they show evidence of thoughtfulness, of having grappled with difficult issues and decisions. They are characteristic of a plan that will be truly useful to teachers. A good plan captures something of the planner, something intangible but clearly recognizable in course designs such as this one.

RATIONALE

At one time junior and senior high school students learned metrics to aid them in their study of chemistry. It now seems imperative that the study of metrics should begin in elementary school classrooms to prepare students for the swing toward metrics that is reaching into every facet of American life. Metric conversion is seen in the goods we buy, the material we read (textbooks, newspapers, cookbooks, road maps, and signs), and the leisure activities we pursue.

Complete transition to the metric standard may or may not happen in the United States, but the influence that metric conversion has on our daily life provides sufficient reason for metric education in the elementary classroom. This unit plan, designed for first and second graders, introduces children to the concept of measurement in general and then, more specifically, to metric measurement.

Children at this age, although still somewhat egocentric, are beginning to show interest in the world around them and are ready to learn new things not directly related to themselves. The egocentricity still evident at this age can be appealed to in a study of measurement by using familiar topics, for example, height, weight, and body measurements or the weights and volumes of food and liquid children consume.

Six- and seven-year-olds just beginning to learn about measurement should acquire some basic knowledge about the need for standard units of measurement. They should know that they are learning a form of communication that enables people to understand one another. Above all, the children should have many practical experiences with linear, weight, volume, and temperature measurement. These experiences should combine actual measurement with estimation.

This metrics unit is designed to be taught separately from any teaching of our measurement system as it now exists. It is not to be taught as a comparative unit with the American system. Conversion from one system to the other is not at all important in this unit. I have found that there is less confusion and better understanding when metric measurement is taught separately from our present measurement system.

Throughout this unit the children should become aware of the presence of metrics around them. They should begin to understand that they are learning a special language important to universal communication. Their study of metrics from unit to unit and year to year will become increasingly meaningful and valuable as they begin to relate it to their world outside of school.

CENTRAL QUESTIONS

1. What is measurement?
2. What do we measure?
3. How do we measure?
4. What are units of measurement?

INTRODUCTION

This metrics unit is designed for first and second graders. The unit can be adapted for any number of children, but the primary consideration would be the availability of measuring equipment. It is suggested that there be a centimeter ruler, a tape measure, and a meter stick for each child; a metric balance or scale for every two children; and a set of liquid measuring equipment for every two children. The suggested time block per day is about forty minutes for actual teaching and practice. More time should be allowed on days when the children are expected to set up and put away their own measuring materials.

The prerequisites are few in number, but important: (1) The children should have a facility with numbers. They should be able to read and write numbers from 1 to 100 satisfactorily. For this reason, it is best, especially with a mixed first- and second-grade group, to plan this unit for the end of the year. They should also be able to compute simple addition and subtraction problems. (2) The children should have a clear understanding of the meanings of greater than, more than, less than, bigger than, larger than, smaller than, higher than, and lower than. (3) The children should have had some previous experiences and instruction in nonstandard measurement and informal measuring. This unit is designed on the assumption that the children have had experiences measuring with rods, books, clips, cards, balances, and so on (nonstandard forms).

This metrics unit is outlined into subunits. There are four subunits: Linear Measurement, Weight Measurement, Volume (Liquid) Measurement, and Temperature. There is also a "get ready" day outline to review briefly nonstandard measurement and to prepare the children for the first day's discussion.

The sequence of the subunits is intentional and serves a purpose. The child begins with a form of measurement that is the easiest to measure and read—linear measurement. Next come weight and liquid measurements which are somewhat more difficult and abstract for young children just beginning a study of precise measurement. Finally, there is temperature, a form of measurement that the children do not really interact with in the same way they do with the other forms. The understandings in this subunit are the most abstract.

This sequence might be described as going from the concrete to the abstract. The understandings and the skills grow more complex and sophisticated as the unit progresses.

The closing statement in this introduction is a personal one. So often measurement units are taught with a pure skill emphasis. Children may become precise measurers, but they don't understand why they measure or even what can be measured. In designing this unit, the cognitive-psychomotor skills seemed to reoccur continually as high-priority learning outcomes. I was at first disturbed about this, thinking that some of the cognitions should receive first priority, but through the unit planning I came to the realization that for those final learning outcomes to happen the children would first have to understand many of the cognitions.

INTENDED LEARNING OUTCOMES FOR THE UNIT IN ORDER OF PRIORITY

1. *Cognitive-psychomotor skill.* The child should be able to measure in the metric units:
   a. measure and record length, width, height, and perimeter in metric units and state measure as whole units or combination of units—for example, 1 meter and 6 centimeters
   b. measure, record, and compare weights of two or more objects and order up to three objects by weight

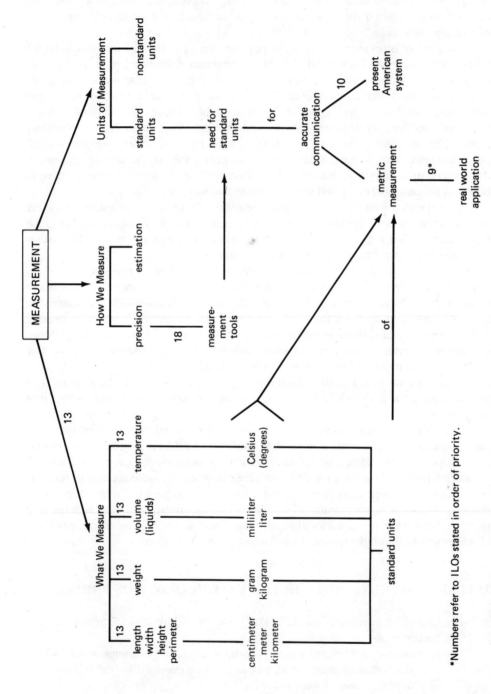

FIGURE D.1 Conceptual map for "A Metric Measurement Unit for Grades One and Two."

*Numbers refer to ILOs stated in order of priority.

    c. measure and record volume of a container using liter and milliliter, compare volume of two or more containers, and order up to three containers by volume

    d. measure and record daily temperature, compare temperature of two or more days, and order up to three recordings by temperature

2. *Affect.* The child should have confidence in his or her ability to measure in the various metric units.

3. *Cognition.* The child should understand the concept of measurement.

4. *Cognition.* The child should know what a standard unit of measurement is.

5. *Cognition.* The child should understand the need for and importance of standard units of measurement.

6. *Cognitive skill.* The child should be able to explain what a standard unit of measurement is and why it is important.

7. *Cognition.* The child should be aware of the present uses of metric measurement in all areas of daily life: shopping, cooking, traveling, weather, work, recreation, and so on.

8. *Affect.* The child should appreciate the practical application of metrics in everyday life.

9. *Cognition.* The child should understand that the metric system is the system of measurement used by most countries in the world.

10. *Cognition.* The child should understand that we in the United States are presently using another form of measurement, but need to know (and possibly practice) the metric system since it is being used in the United States.

11. *Cognitive skill.* The child should be able to explain why he or she is learning metric measurement.

12. *Psychomotor-perceptual skill.* The child should be able to:

    a. measure accurately with a centimeter ruler, a tape measure, a meter stick, and a trundle wheel to the nearest whole number

    b. measure accurately with a balance scale using gram and kilogram weights to the nearest whole number

    c. operate a metric scale, using the sliding weight, to the nearest gram or kilogram

    d. read a metric scale

    e. measure the volume of liquid, using metric spoons and flasks, always to the nearest milliliter or liter

    f. read the thermometer in degrees Celsius, to the nearest whole degree

13. *Cognition.* The child should understand that we measure the following things:

    a. length, width, height, perimeter

    b. weight

    c. volume (liquids)

    d. temperature

14. *Cognition.* The child should understand the meanings of;

    a. length, width, height, perimeter (linear measurement)

   b. weight

   c. volume

   d. temperature

15. *Cognitive skill.* The child should be able to discuss what things are measured and define each term:

   a. length, width, height, perimeter

   b. weight

   c. volume

   d. temperature

16. *Cognition.* The child should know the basic units for the different measurement forms:

   a. centimeter, meter, and kilometer are all units for linear measurement

   b. gram and kilogram are units for weight measurement

   c. milliliter and liter are units for liquid volume measurement

   d. degrees Celsius are units for temperature measurement

17. *Cognitive skill.* The child should be able to name the basic units of measurement for each type of measurement:

   a. centimeter, meter, and kilometer for linear

   b. gram and kilogram for weight

   c. milliliter and liter for volume

   d. degrees Celsius for temperature

18. *Cognition.* The child should understand what the word *precision* means and what tools are needed to measure precisely in metrics:

   a. centimeter ruler, meter stick, tape measure, and trundle wheel are used to measure the length, width, height, and perimeter of something

   b. scale and balance are used to measure weight

   c. measuring spoons, cups, and graduated flasks are used to measure liquid volume

   d. Celsius thermometer is used to measure temperature

19. *Cognitive skill.* The child should be able to identify which measurement tools are used to measure precisely a specific thing:

   a. centimeter ruler, meter stick, tape measure, and trundle wheel for linear measurement

   b. scale and balance for weight

   c. measuring spoons, cups, and graduated flasks for liquid volumes

   d. Celsius thermometer for temperature

20. *Cognition.* The child should know the approximate amounts the following units represent:

   a. centimeter, meter, kilometer

   b. gram, kilogram

   c. milliliter, liter

   d. 0°C, 30°C, 100°C

21. *Cognitive skill.* The child should be able to represent the approximate value of these units either with "real world" examples or physical demonstration:

    a. centimeter, meter, kilometer
    b. gram, kilogram
    c. milliliter, liter
    d. 0°C, 30°C, 100°C

22. *Cognition.* The child should understand what the word *estimation* means and what it means to estimate in measurement.
23. *Cognitive skill.* The child should be able to estimate measurement in the various metric units, within a reasonable scale for each unit.
24. *Cognition.* The child should understand what it means to compare, more specifically, to compare the results of an estimate and a precise measurement.
25. *Cognitive skill.* The child should be able to compare his or her estimations with precise measurements.

"GET READY" LESSONS AND DISCUSSION

This is a brief review of nonstandard units. As stated in the Introduction, the children should already have had measurement experiences of the type described in the Teaching Strategy below. It is hoped that the children have acquired some knowledge from their earlier study of measurement. The purpose of the "get ready" lesson and discussion is to reactivate that knowledge and to prepare the children for the new information to follow.

Intended Learning Outcomes

Numbers 3, 4, 5, 6, 9, 10, 11.

Instructional Foci

Books, Cuisenaire rods, paper clips, pieces of string of various lengths, beans, pencils, straws, tiles, pieces of paper, file cards—any items you can use to measure something. Paper and pencil for each child.

Teaching Strategy

Each child will be given one item with which to measure. Most of the items are different. The teacher will tell them to use their item to measure the following things: the length of a chalkboard, a doorway, the top of a desk, and so on. They will record their measurement of each object.

A discussion will then follow. The ideas to be highlighted and emphasized are as follows: everyone got different answers—their measuring devices are called nonstandard units of measurement—everybody needs to use the same unit of measurement—otherwise we will have a confused group of people—won't understand each other—need for standard units—what are some standard units of measurement—why do we need these standard units—what is accurate communication—why is it important—awareness that there are two types of standard measurement units for accurate communication—metrics and the system we use now—we're going to study metrics—most of the world is using the metric system of measurement—we don't, but it is being used more and more in our country and we should understand it. This "get ready" activity should close with a discussion of "What Are We Doing When We Measure?"

SUBUNITS

The intended learning outcomes that will appear under each subunit are those particular to that subunit. At this time the ILOs that are common to all *four* subunits are 2, 3, 4, 5, 6, 7, 8, 9, 10, 11, 22, 23, 24, and 25.

The reader is asked to remember that the ILOs listed above are included in every subunit. The wording of these ILOs is of a general nature. It is up to the teacher to see that these learnings are reinforced and understood in the context of each subunit's topic or theme.

Subunit I: Linear Measurement

The concepts of length, width, height, and perimeter will be explored and defined in this unit. We will talk about length as the longest side of an object, width as the shortest side of an object, height as the distance from the bottom to the top of an upright object (often synonymous with length), and perimeter as the distance around an object. The metric units centimeter, meter, and kilometer will be introduced and used throughout the unit. The measuring tools presented will include the centimeter ruler, the centimeter tape measure, the meter stick, and the trundle wheel. Both estimation and precision will be discussed and stressed in this unit.

Intended Learning Outcomes: Numbers 1a, 12a, 13a, 14a, 15a, 16a, 17a, 18a, 19a, 20a, and 21a.

Instructional Foci: Centimeter rulers, centimeter tape measures, meter sticks, trundle wheels; teacher-made posters with linear units and abbreviations written out; series of worksheets; classroom objects to measure (pencils, pens, books, paper clips, staplers, paper, file cards, blocks, crayons, and so on); Metric Measuring License (see p. 250).

Teaching Strategy: The terms *length, width,* and *height* will be introduced and discussed. The children and teacher will spend time identifying the lengths, widths, and/or heights of various objects.

Then the standard metric units of linear measurement—centimeter, meter, and kilometer—should be presented. These units should be presented one at a time, not as a group. The organization and sequence is important here. First the centimeter should be introduced and discussed. Then the measuring tools to measure a centimeter should be presented. The estimation and measurement of items under 100 centimeters is necessary before presenting the meter. It is essential to perform the same sequence with the meter before discussing the kilometer.

The children should be given a frame of reference for each linear unit. For instance, a centimeter is about the width of your baby finger, the thickness of a slice of bread, or the width of a popsicle stick. A meter might be the distance from the floor to a six-year-old's chin (use a meter stick to determine this), the width of a standard-size door, or the width of a newspaper opened up. A kilometer might be the distance from the school to the local movie theater or the Y.M.C.A.—use a locality with which the children are familiar. These estimates will provide the children with some concrete, familiar ground before their actual measuring experiences begin. Teacher-made posters accompanied by pictures illustrating these metric units would be useful here.

The word *estimation* is to be defined and discussed. What does it mean to estimate? Why do we estimate? When might we make estimations? How do we estimate? Motivating questions at this stage might include: About how many centimeters long do you think this pencil is? About how many meters wide do you think this chalkboard is? Let the children actually use their pinkies and other visual or physical aids for rough estimates.

This will lead into the presentation of the linear measurement tools: the centimeter ruler, the tape measure, the meter stick, and the trundle wheel. The word *precision* should be introduced here. What does it mean to measure precisely? Why and when would we need precise measurements? Provide the children with hypothetical situations and ask, "Would it be better to estimate or measure precisely in this situation?"

Instruct the children in the use of each tool. Allow for many measuring experiences using classroom objects and any personal belongings the children may want to measure.

Worksheets should include both estimation and precise measurement and a comparison of results. How close was I? Did I estimate too much or too little? Actual problem solving using simple addition and subtraction could be integrated here. How many centimeters (meters) off was I? How much longer (wider) is the book than the paper? Perimeter should be introduced once the children have successfully estimated and measured lengths, widths, and heights.

Accurate measurement should be stressed. Estimation is of secondary importance. Accurate measurement, the ease with which it's done, and the written recording of measurements are of primary importance. An understanding of which measurement tool is best to measure various dimensions is also of high priority (use a centimeter ruler for a smaller length, a centimeter tape measure for distances around an object, a meter stick for a longer length, and a trundle wheel for very long distances). The children should also be able to measure and record distances as a combination of units, for example, 2 meters and 4 centimeters.

The Metric Measuring License is an activity that can be included in the complete Metrics Unit. (See the example on page 250.) It can act as a thread that runs through each subunit, unifying the Metric Measurement theme. It reflects the learnings of each subunit. The children work in pairs, helping each other with the measuring and recording of their personal data.

Metric Measuring License

for centimeter, meter, gram, kilogram, milliliter, liter,
and degrees Celsius

cm = centimeter   m = meter   g = gram
kg = kilogram   ml = milliliter   l = liter

This license entitles _____ , upon completion of the form below, to be an OFFICIAL METRIC MEASURER, authorized to measure, at any time, using OFFICIAL METRIC UNITS, anything than can be measured either with

OFFICIAL MEASURING TOOLS or by ESTIMATION: height _____ arm

spread _____ nose to fingertip _____ hand span _____ palm _____

thumb _____ index finger _____ middle finger _____ ring finger _____

pinkie _____ knee to floor _____ foot length _____ foot width _____

shoe length _____ shoe width _____ plain step _____ giant step _____

around head _____ around neck _____ around chest _____ around

wrist _____ around waist _____ around thigh _____ around ankle _____

weight _____ weight of shoe _____ weight of relaxed hand _____

weight of favorite book _____ volume of lunch milk or juice _____ your

body temperature _____ outside temperature today _____

age _____ years _____ signature _____ date _____

All of the measurements will change—Keep your Metric Measuring License up-to-date!

The centimeter and meter are worked with more often than the kilometer in this subunit. The kilometer is discussed in more abstract terms. The children and teacher may take a "Kilometer Walk" someday, but it is introduced as the unit used to measure very long distances, like a distance you may walk, run, drive, or fly. It can be used in the problem-solving sense—How many kilometers did Pat run if she ran 1 kilometer on Monday and 2 kilometers on Wednesday? Or, Would you use meters or kilometers to tell someone how far it is to Amherst? The kilometer is to be taught in a more abstract way—there are no actual measurement experiences with the kilometer at this level.

The teacher should provide time for discussions of practical, real-life applications of linear measurement. Children should have ideas about possible situations when precise measurement would be essential and when estimation would be sufficient. They should understand clearly how precision is different from estimation.

The final lesson(s) should combine the three linear units: centimeter, meter, and kilometer. The children are to understand what unit and what tool is used to measure what linear dimension. The teacher is expected to check this understanding with observations of their interactions with the measuring equipment and their daily written and oral work.

Suggested time to spend on this subunit: 5 days, 30 to 40 minutes each day.

Subunit II: Weight Measurement

What is weight and the way it's measured in the metric system is the topic of this subunit. We will talk about weight as the amount of heaviness something has. This type of measurement is to be contrasted with linear measurement. How is it different? How are they alike? The gram and kilogram are the measurement units introduced. Precision and estimation are important elements again in the subunit.

Intended Learning Outcomes: Numbers 1b, 12b, 12c, 12d, 13b, 14b, 15b, 16b, 17b, 18b, 19b, 20b, and 21b.

Instructional Foci: Balances, sliding weight scales, metric scales, weights of assorted sizes (grams and kilograms), dollar bill, nickle, piece of chalk, magic marker, golf ball, tennis ball, stick of butter, softball, loaf of bread, two-pound box of sugar cubes, pencils, paper, series of worksheets.

Teaching Strategy: This subunit will begin with a discussion of weight. What is weight? Does anyone know how we measure it? How is weight measurement different from linear measurement? How are they similar?

The gram is introduced as the basic unit of measurement of weight. Items that weigh various amounts are passed around for the children to hold: dollar bill (1g), nickel (5g), new piece of chalk (10g), large magic marker (25g), tennis ball (50g), stick of butter (100g), softball (200g), and a load of bread (500g). A chart is made with the children to record these amounts.

The children then estimate the weights of various objects under 500g using the above items to compare. They record their estimations.

The next lesson will be devoted to precision measurement. Gram weights are introduced and explained. The children are taught how to use a balance and sliding weight scale. They work in pairs or alone, depending on the number of scales and children. They weigh the objects they had previously estimated, record the precise weights, and compare their estimates with final results.

The kilogram is then introduced as the unit used for weights larger than a thousand grams. A two-pound box of sugar cubes, a kilogram weight, and any other items weighing about a kilogram are given to the children to handle. Estimation of items and precision measurement are again done, this time with the kilogram. Each child is weighed on a metric scale at this time.

The children will be asked to measure, record, and compare the weights of at least two or more objects and then order those objects by weight. They will also graph *or* order (heaviest to lightest) the weights of all the children in the group, providing that it does not cause any child undue embarrassment. They will also need to complete the sections of their Metric Measuring Licenses that apply to weight.

In order to relate metric weight measurement to the real world, the children will be asked to make a list of at least five packaged goods they can find in their homes that have a designated gram or kilogram weight. Together, the teacher and children can make a composite list. Discussion of weight application to other daily experiences is also important.

Suggested time to spend on this subunit: 5 days, 30 to 40 minutes each day.

Subunit III: Volume (Liquid) Measurement

Volume is the key word in this subunit. Volume will be presented as the amount of liquid that is needed to fill a particular amount of space. Amounts of water will be estimated, measured, and compared. The distinction between weight and volume will be an important point of discussion. Once again, estimation and precision will be emphasized. The milliliter and the liter will be introduced as the basic units of liquid measurement.

Intended Learning Outcomes: Numbers 1c, 12c, 13c, 14c, 15c, 16c, 17c, 18c, 19c, 20c, and 21c.

Instructional Foci: Measuring spoons, liter flasks, milliliter eye droppers, containers of various shapes and sizes, water table if possible, pencils, paper, series of worksheets.

Teaching Strategy: The first lesson will begin with a discussion of liquids the children drink. Containers (bottles, glasses) will be available for illustrative purposes. Do you usually drink this much orange juice? How many glasses of juice would we need to fill this bottle? Do you know how we measure liquids?

The distinction between solid weight measurement should be clarified in the children's minds. It should be demonstrated that we are not trying to find out how much the liquid *weighs*, but how much *space* it takes up in the container.

A milliliter will be introduced as a very small unit of liquid measurement. Together, with milliliter eye droppers, we will find out how many milliliters of water it takes to fill up various sizes of small containers. They will see that a common size cup is 250 milliliters. Precision measurement is stressed here.

The liter is introduced as the next unit of liquid measurement after the milliliter. The children will be told that it takes 1000 of those milliliter drops to fill the one-liter container. The children will be asked to estimate the amount of liters needed to fill various large-size containers, to precisely measure the amounts of liquids, and then to compare the volume of two or more containers, ordering up to three containers by volume. They will record their findings.

The children will look at home to see if they can find liquids packaged or bottled in milliliter and liter containers. A class list will be made. They will also complete the liquid volume section of their Metric Measuring Licenses.

Before starting the temperature subunit, the teacher and children will bake a sweet. They will follow a very simple recipe using both weight and liquid measurements. (See page 258 for cookbooks with metric recipes.)

Suggested time to spend on this subunit: 4 days, 30 to 40 minutes each—1 day for the cooking activity.

Subunit IV: Temperature

Temperature—what is it? We will talk about temperature as the amount of hotness or coldness as measured on a definite scale. Degrees Celsius will be presented as the metric unit for measuring this amount. The Celsius thermometer will be introduced as the instrument, or scale, used to measure these degrees of hotness or coldness. Reference points on a Celsius thermometer will be established to help the children see the comparative nature of understanding temperature.

Intended Learning Outcomes: Numbers 1d, 12f, 13d, 14d, 15d, 16d, 17d, 18d, 19d, 20d, and 21d.

Instructional Foci: Indoor Celsius thermometer, outdoor Celsius thermometer, numerous Celsius thermometers—at least one to measure human body temperature—pencils, paper, series of worksheets, one large-scale model of a Celsius thermometer with "movable" parts.

Teaching Strategy: The topic of temperature will be introduced with a discussion of everything the children already know about it. What is temperature? How do we measure temperature? Why do we need to know temperatures?

The children will learn how to read a Celsius thermometer by using a large-scale model with movable parts that can be changed to many different temperature readings. We will talk about the different places thermometers can be used and the different types of thermometers (outdoor, indoor, freezer, refrigerator, meat, body, and so on).

Working in pairs or small groups, the children will take readings of various temperatures: outside, inside the classroom, a bucket of ice, a pot of boiling water, tap water (hot and cold), a refrigerator, a freezer, and body temperature. They will record their readings. Together the group will discuss their findings and will make a chart of the various readings. We will order them from coldest to hottest. We will talk about the degrees that represent very cold things, lukewarm things, and hot things. The following chart will then be presented.

$-20°C$	very cold
0	freezing
10	cool spring day
20	nice spring day
25	good room temperature
30	nice summer day
35	swimming weather
37	heat wave

40	normal body temperature
100	boiling water

A daily temperature reading will be taken. At the end of this subunit the children will order the readings from hottest to coldest and will answer questions pertaining to them. On what day was it the hottest? the coldest? How much hotter was it on Tuesday than on Wednesday? They should work with five readings. The teacher will need to supply two of them since this is a three-day subunit.

As a final lesson, the children will need to give approximate temperatures in degrees Celsius for various situations. Here are a few examples. It's a hot summer day. How many degrees Celsius do you think it is? I want to make a cup of tea, but I need boiling water. How many degrees Celsius will the water need to be? If it's winter and there's ice on the ground, it's probably _____°C. What would you wear outside if the thermometer read 10°C? −20°C? What would you do outside if it was 25°C? Where would you be if your mom or dad took your temperature and it read 40°C? Those children who need to use the chart may do so.

The children should complete their Metric Measuring Licenses at the end of this subunit.

Suggested time to spend on this subunit: 3 days, 30 to 40 minutes each day.

Note: A final activity that might be interesting to try at the end of this subunit would be to construct a conceptual map with the children. Give them the headings What We Measure, How We Measure, and Need for Standard Units of Measurement. See what ideas they can come up with to fit under each heading.

It may illustrate the structure of their thinking, the "chunks" of learning they've acquired from the unit, and the connections they have made among the "chunks."

UNINTENDED LEARNING OUTCOMES

1. The child who has already had some experiences with metric measurement or learns the material quickly may become bored and uninterested in the unit.

   Possible solution: Enrichment! The child could learn more of the basic units in each measurement area: millimeter, decimeter, dekameter, milligram, and kiloliter. The child could begin doing some simple conversions within metrics. For example, 20 centimeters = _____ decimeters; _____ milliliters = 4 liters; 3000 grams = _____ kilograms. The child could be exposed to a number of application problems that involve more advanced computational skills or reasoning, for example, How many meters of fencing are needed for a rectangular playground that measures 11 meters wide by 22 meters long? The height of a ceiling is 300 centimeters. How many meters is that?
   The concept of area could be introduced and explored with square centimeters, square meters, and square kilometers.

2. A younger child in the group or a child who is not grasping the concepts may become frustrated and self-conscious because of unsuccessful attempts.

   Possible solution: Remedial attention! Don't expect the child to learn all the measurement units presented. Allow the child to work only with the meter, gram, and liter. Stress measurement over estimation if that's the child's strength. Simplify the material. Pair the child with another slower learner so they may work together at their own pace rather than feel the pressure from a faster worker.

3. If a child has a good understanding of our present measuring system, he may want constantly to "talk conversion." This may confuse the child who is unable to understand that this is a measurement system unrelated to the one he or she already knows. The child may become frustrated with the teacher's unwillingness to compare centimeters with inches, for instance.

   Possible solution: The teacher does not have to ignore the child's desire to know comparable amounts in our system. It can be done on an individual basis, so that the other children will not be confused with the information. The teacher should make it clear to the child that they are studying metrics as a measurement system by itself and are trying not to compare it with our system.

4. A child who consistently estimates poorly may feel as though he or she is not doing well or succeeding. Even though accurate estimation is not of the highest priority, it is included in many lessons. The child may feel like a failure if he or she is a poor estimator.

   Possible solution: As stated in the remedial ideas section, deemphasize estimation with this child. Give the child more experiences with precision measurement. Have the child estimate more spacious dimensions that allow for "physical" aids—hands or feet, for example. Or allow them to have examples (liter flask, kilogram weight) by their side for constant comparison. Allow the child to estimate with the help of concrete aids, rather than with mental-visual pictures.

EVALUATION OF HIGH-PRIORITY INTENDED LEARNING OUTCOMES

EVIDENCE OF MAIN EFFECTS OF THE FIVE HIGH-PRIORITY ILOS

1A–D. Cognitive-Psychomoter Skill

Evidence of cognitive skill/psychomotor skill: The child is given hypothetical situations and asked to solve them. Here are some examples:

Situation 1: There's a wall in my living room that is 2 meters long. I want you to measure that desk to see if it will fit against that wall. The child will have to figure out what measurement tool to use, measure the length of the desk, record the length, and then explain whether it will fit or not. (The desk should be straight edged and easily measurable.)

Situation 2: I have three objects: an apple, a mug, and a golf ball. (Try to have items that weigh about the same as the gram weights.) I want you to measure them, write down the measurements, and then tell me which one is heaviest, next heaviest, and then lightest. The child will have to decide what measurement tool to use to find out how heavy or light an object is, weigh it, record, and then order the objects by weight.

Situation 3: I have three containers: A, B, and C. They're all filled with different amounts of water. (The containers should all be different sizes, but not obvious as to how much liquid they hold.) I want you to measure each one, record the measurements, and then order them to show which container has the smallest amount to the largest amount. The child will have to choose the correct measuring instrument, measure the amount of water in each container, record, and then order them by volume.

Situation 4: I have three containers. One is filled with ice, one is filled with water that's been sitting here for awhile, and the last one is filled with very hot water. I want to know the exact temperature of each container and then I want you to order the temperatures from highest to lowest. The child will need to take a temperature reading of each container, record them, and then order the readings.

2. Affect

Evidence of affect (behaviors actions): The child attacks the problems stated above in a confident, comfortable manner. The child doesn't hesitate when given measurement tasks; he or she doesn't need constant direction while measuring. The child is able to decide quickly what measurement tool is necessary to solve a problem. The child offers to help other children who are having difficulty with precision measurement or estimation. The child exhibits little difficulty in the recording of measurement results.

Circumstances: group activities in the classroom, written work, testing situation.

3. Cognition

Evidence of understanding: The child describes what sorts of things we measure, why we might want to measure these things, and how we measure each particular thing. The child is able to contrast the various types of measurement: linear, weight, volume, and temperature. The child is able to compare precision measurement with estimation.

4. Cognition

Evidence of understanding: The child is able to give examples of standard and nonstandard units of measurement. The child is able to categorize a list of words into standard units of measurement and nonstandard units of measurement.

5. Cognition

Evidence of understanding: The child should be able to explain, in his or her own words, why we need to have standard units of measurement. The child should be able to give examples of confusing situations when nonstandard units are used.

The daily written work and a final worksheet that would combine the four subunit topics of metric measurement would also be useful evaluative tools. Daily observation of the children interacting with the materials and the measuring equipment is the best way to assess the psychomotor-perceptual ILOs.

A final worksheet that combines linear, weight, volume, and temperature measurement would serve as a means to evaluate once again the children's learnings of some of the cognitions and cognitive skills. The worksheet could look something like this:

I would need to find	Unit I'd choose	Measuring tool I'd choose
length of this room		
outside temperature		
width of a book		
body weight		

The following are some ideas for questions. Directions would be to choose the best estimate. They could be done orally for nonreaders or beginning readers.

1. The height of a ceiling in a home is:
  a) 3 meters
  b) 1 centimeter
  c) 4 grams
2. The length of an ant is:
  a) 5 meters
  b) 1 centimeter
  c) 2 liters
3. The weight of a newborn baby is about:
  a) 3 kilograms
  b) 30°C
  c) 500 milliliters
4. Your thermos might hold:
  a) 5 liters
  b) 30°C
  c) 500 milliliters

BOOKS THAT MAY BE USEFUL IN PLANNING A
METRICS MEASUREMENT UNIT

Mathlab Metric Editions, Grades 1–2, Action Math Associates, Inc. *Series of activities— editions for grades 1 through 6.*

Metric Can Be Fun!, Munro Leaf, Scholastic Book Services, 1976.

Steve Morgenstern (1978). *Metric Puzzles, Tricks, and Games.* Sterling Publishing Co.

Desserts and *Cakes and Cookies,* cookbooks printed by Playmore, Inc., New York, 1978. Many easy recipes given in metric measurement—good for classroom use.

Glossary

Actual learning outcome. A change in a person's capability or state of mind that results from interaction with people, ideas, or objects. Changes such as physical injuries, physiological maturation, and those that are drug induced are excluded from this concept.

Affect. An umbrella term for two types of intended learning outcomes: affective understandings and affective skills.

Affective skill. A type of intended learning outcome dealing with the ability to behave in ways that reflect certain attitudes.

Affective understanding. A type of intended learning outcome dealing with self-knowledge or knowledge about the interaction of self with others.

Assertion. An idea that can be stated as a proposition, that is, asserting something to be true—facts, principles, generalizations. Assertions constitute one set of ideas for students to learn.

Central question. One of the fundamental questions with which a course deals and which identifies the focus of the course.

Clustering ILOs. The grouping of ILOs into unit-sized chunks.

Cognition. An idea that is intended to be learned.

Cognitive skill. The ability to use or apply cognitions.

Conception. A type of cognitive intended learning outcome. Conceptions entail a way of looking at the world; that is, a person's theory or belief system regarding some set of phenomena.

Conceptual map. A chart depicting the relationship among the important ideas with which a course deals. The map describes the organization of understandings in the course.

Curriculum. An organized set of intended learning outcomes presumed to lead to the achievement of educational goals.

Curriculum development. The process by which intended learning outcomes are selected and organized.

Educational goal. A desirable attribute of a person (for example, literate, tolerant, or creative) that is expected to result from the educational process. These goals are "educational" (rather than societal or institutional) if they are achievable through learning.

Educational result. A description of the kind of person that develops as a consequence of the complex interactive and cumulative effects of formal and informal education, as well as maturation. These may or may not correspond with the intended educational results, that is, the "educational goals."

Evaluation. The collection and analysis of data for the purpose of making a judgment or rendering a decision.

Flowchart. A diagram depicting the components of a complex skill in terms of subskills and understandings.

General teaching strategy. The instructional events that are planned around an instructional focus for the accomplishment of ILOs. These strategies are described at a level more general than daily lesson plans but more specific than a list of materials to be used.

Goal setting. The process by which goals are formulated.

Instruction. Providing experiences for learners with the intention of bringing about particular learnings.

Instructional focus. A theme, problem, activity, stimulus, or vehicle for communicating ideas designed to facilitate the learning of a set of ILOs. They are termed "foci" because they serve as focal points for learning and lend coherence to a set of ILOs.

Instructional plan. An outline for a course specifying its units and the means for teaching each unit. For each unit in the plan, intended learning outcomes for the unit, the unit rationale, and general teaching strategies should be described.

Instructional planning. The process of forming and organizing unit-sized chunks of a course, specifying an instructional focus for each unit, and designing a set of instructional events around each focus.

Intended learning outcome (ILO). Something that the student is expected to learn. A course's ILOs may consist of cognitions, cognitive skills, psychomotor-perceptual skills, or affects.

Main effect. An actual learning outcome corresponding to a course's ILOs.

Psychomotor-perceptual skills. Physical or perceptual competencies and abilities intended to be learned.

Rationale. There are two kinds of rationales: (a) *Course Rationale,* a statement justifying a course in terms of the course's educational goals. These goals are discussed in the context of the planner's conception of the learner, the society, and the subject matter. (b) *Unit Rationale,* a statement describing what a particular unit is about, how it builds on previous units, and how subsequent units build on it.

Sequencing principle. The reason behind, or the basis for, ordering course units in a particular manner.

Side effect. An unintended and often undesirable learning outcome resulting from a course's methods, materials, or organization, as well as other factors.

Skill. A gross category of intended learned outcomes comprising the things a teacher wants students to be able to do as a consequence of instruction.

Understandings. A gross category of intended learning outcomes including ideas a teacher wants students to acquire as a consequence of instruction.

Unit. A coherent chunk of a course.

Value. An ideal or a state of affairs toward which one or more persons has a high affective regard, for example, equality of educational opportunity.

Selected Bibliography

Bellon, J. J., Bellon, E. C., & Blank, M. A. (1992). *Teaching from a research knowledge base: A development and renewal process.* New York: Merrill.

This book synthesizes important resaerch in a variety of areas such as classroom management, motivation, direct instruction, feedback, and small group instruction. The authors also include, with each synthesis, a section entitled "Development and Renewal Activities." This section provides an excellent start for teachers interested in action research, that is, generating answers to their questions about specific teaching practices they use or wish to try out.

Bransford, J. D., & Stein, B. S. (1984). *The ideal problem solver.* New York: W. H. Freeman.

Describes a problem-solving model. Problem solving is broadly conceived and includes learning through understanding, intelligent criticism, generating new ideas, and effective communication. Very useful for designing instruction for these and other high-level cognitive outcomes.

Doyle, W. E. Academic work. *Review of Educational Research, 53*(2) (Summer 1983), 159–199.

A perspective of classroom life that focuses on academic tasks, that is, the intellectual work in which students are actually engaged. The relationship between academic tasks, learner processing, and learning outcomes is explicated. This should prove useful in instructional design. The article also includes a description of the social context of classrooms and how this influences academic endeavors.

Gagné, R. M., & Briggs, L. J. (1979). *Principles of instructional design* (2nd ed). New York: Holt, Rinehart, & Winston.

A detailed account of one school of design theory.

Gall, M. D. (1981). *Handbook for evaluating and selecting curriculum materials.* Boston: Allyn & Bacon.

The only comprehensive guide to curriculum materials. Contains useful checklists of criteria, lists of catalogues, bibliographies, and suggested procedures.

Goodlad, J. (1984). *A place called school.* New York: McGraw-Hill.

A descriptive study of schools intended to be used in efforts to improve schools. The study is inspired, in part, by the fact that while we know about certain specific features of schools, we know little about schools in a holistic sense. Useful information about what is covered in the school curriculum as well as a set of comprehensive goal statements for schools is included.

Johnson, M. (1977). *Intentionality in education: A conceptual model of curricular and instructional planning and evaluation.* Center for Curriculum Research and Services, 63 Northgate Drive, Albany, NY.

A highly detailed presentation of the "Johnson Model" (see our chapter 1). Although this book is usually considered difficult reading by students, it is highly recommended for its careful specification of terminology, invention of a symbol system, and identification of logical relations among concepts.

Novak, J. D., & Gowin, D. B., (1984). *Learning how to learn.* New York: Cambridge University Press.

An extensive treatment of concept mapping, among other useful techniques. Contains many examples.

Popham, W. J., & Baker, E. L. (1970). *Systematic instruction.* Englewood Cliffs, NJ: Prentice-Hall.

A simplified presentation of design theory as represented in the work of Tyler, Popham, Bloom, and Gagné.

Posner, G. J. (1992). *Analyzing the curriculum.* New York: McGraw-Hill.

A new text intended to introduce students of curriculum to the understanding and interpretation of curriculum documents. It presents five basic theoretical orientations or "perspectives" on curriculum development and relates these views to mainstream curriculum topics. Case studies of significant curricula in all four core school subjects at both elementary and secondary levels make the discussion more concrete. In addition, the reader is guided through an individual project consisting of the analysis of the assumptions underlying a curriculum of the reader's own choice.

Schaffarzick, J., & Hampson, D. H. (Eds). (1975). *Strategies for curriculum development.* Berkeley, CA: McCutchan.

A collection of essays by directors of curriculum projects describing the procedures of each project.

Schubert, W. H. (1986). *Curriculum: Perspective, paradigm, and possibility.* New York: Macmillan.

An engaging, basic text on curriculum that emphasizes the philosophical assumptions underlying curriculum decisions. This text can be used to support the rather limited discussion of philosophy we present in chapter 3.

Senesh, L. (1973). *Our working world: New paths in social science curriculum design.* Chicago: Science Research Associates.

An excellent example of the relationships among conceptual maps, major assertions, intended learning outcomes, unit organization (scope and sequence), and activities for a K–6 social studies program.

Walker, D. (1990). *Fundamentals of curriculum.* New York: Harcourt Brace Jovanovich.

A comprehensive and especially well written text on curriculum that departs from other texts in its emphasis on the practical, deliberative dimensions of curriculum development. The treatment of curriculum policy making and curriculum change serves as a complement to our more technical aspects of curriculum development.

Wigginton, E. (1985). *Sometimes a shining moment: The Foxfire experience.* Garden City, NY: Anchor Press/Doubleday.

Includes a complete description of a course in English composition taught using the Foxfire approach. More importantly, the book contains a stimulating discussion on how to design and redesign courses to serve "double duty," that is, to accomplish state or district goals and also to help students understand their roots and their responsibilities.

Zais, R. S. (1976). *Curriculum: Principles and foundations.* New York: Harper & Row.

An excellent general text on curriculum. It includes very readable and comprehensive discussions of curriculum history and curriculum foundations (that is, philosophy, social issues, human nature, and learning theory), as well as extensive treatment of topics contained in *Course Design*.

Index

Note: Page numbers followed by *n* indicate material in footnotes. *Italicized* page numbers indicate material in tables or figures.

Abstractions, in knowledge acquisition, 77–78
Academic tasks, 145–146
Accountability, 145–146
Actual learning outcomes (ALOs), 8, 169, 259. *See also* Main effects
Adaptation, of curriculum, 13–16
Affective skills, 73, 259
Affective understandings, 72, 73–74, 259
Affects, 72, 76
  defined, 73, 259
  evaluation of, 173–174
  examples of, 82
  expressing, 81–82
  teaching strategies for, 148–149
Alexander, W. M., 126
Ambert, A., 56
Analyzing the Curriculum (Posner), 264
Anderson, T. H., 32
Appreciation-oriented courses, formulating central questions for, 29
Archbald, D. A., 176
Assertions
  defined, 259
  ideas as, 78, 79
Assumptions, as basis of course rationale, 52–54
Atkin, J. M., 122
Attitudes, side effects and, 177, 178–179
Attributes, intended learning outcomes vs., 73–74
Atwell, Nancie, 46
Audience, for course. *See also* Students
  in course planning and design, 5
  course rationale and, 55–56
Austin, G. A., 77, 122
Ausubel, D. P., 122, 124

Baker, E. L., 264

Baker, R. L., 68
Banks, J. A., 56
Barell, J., 46
Baron, J. B., 150–151
Beach, K. M., 125, 127
Behavioral objectives, 69
  intended learning outcomes vs., 70–71
Bell-Gredler, M. E., 146
Bellon, E. C., 146, 263
Bellon, J. J., 146, 263
Berger, Margaret, 102*n*
Blank, M. A., 146, 263
Bloom, A., 55
Bloom, B. S., 72*n*, 83, 125–126
Borich, G. D., 143
Borton, T., 150
Bransford, J. D., 147, 263
Briggs, L. J., 68, 263
Brown, G., 150
Bruner, J. S., 77, 122–124

Cahn, A. D., *40*
Carey, L., 108, 179
Central questions. *See also* Instructional focus
  characteristics of, 31
  defined, 259
  formulation of, for specific course types, 28–31
Champagne, A. B., *40*
Chang, Michelle, 223–239
Charles, R. I., 151
Chase, J. B., 55
Clark, C., 16
Clustering ILOs, 121–137
  defined, 259
  sequencing principles for, 121–137

267